ECHOES FROM THE BLUFFS

VOLUME I

BY

THE GREEN RIVER HISTORIC PRESERVATION COMMISSION
GREEN RIVER, WYOMING

Echoes From the Bluffs: Volume I

Cover design by Brigida R. Blasi

Originally published in 1998

2018 Reprint by

The Sweetwater County Museum Foundation

Green River, Wyoming

ISBN-13: 978-1725811904

ISBN-10: 1725811901

In memory of James William June
who, as a council member for the
City of Green River, Wyoming,
was instrumental in the formation of the
GREEN RIVER HISTORIC PRESERVATION COMMISSION
established by ordinance on the 19th day of June, 1990.
He was an enthusiastic member of the Commission
until his death in 1996.

ECHOES FROM THE BLUFFS
VOLUME I
BY

THE GREEN RIVER HISTORIC PRESERVATION COMMISSION
GREEN RIVER, WYOMING

One of the objectives of the Green River Historic Preservation Commission is to capture the fascinating history of the Green River area and to preserve it for the enjoyment of generations to come. In November of 1991 the Commission began composing and publishing historical articles periodically in the *Green River Star* weekly newspaper under the heading *Echoes from the Bluffs*.

This Volume One gathers together the articles published in *Echoes from the Bluffs* from 1991 into 1998 and provides a variety of historical subjects for your reading pleasure.

Green River Historic Preservation Commission members at publication in 1998 were:

Ruth Lauritzen

Marna Grubb

Bill Duncan

Bill Thompson

ECHOES FROM THE BLUFFS
VOLUME I

As originally published in the *Green River Star* 1991-1998

CONTENTS

Page number

1998

Riding the Iron Horse

by Ruth Lauritzen

In May of 1869 the tapping of a golden spike into a polished laurel tie reduced a grueling, hazardous journey of up to several months to a mere week of travel. Just five days after the historic joining of the rails at Promontory Point passenger service began on the new Union Pacific transcontinental railroad, giving westward voyagers a shorter and less dangerous alternative to wagon train and stagecoach travel.

One passenger train left daily from both Omaha, the eastern terminus of the line, and Sacramento, the western terminus. Fares ranged from $40 to over $100 and were based on the level of comfort and service one received on the journey. Emigrant class was the cheapest and most uncomfortable way to travel. There was no provision made for comfort with the plain wooden benches and, cramped seating. These coaches were also, more often than not, attached to freight trains instead of the much faster passenger express lines.

Second class passengers traveled in day coaches which were considerably more comfortable, but still made no provision for night accommodations. First class passengers traveled in plush cars with seats that could be made into berths for sleeping. Both of these coaches traveled on express trains and the transcontinental fare was $80 and $100 respectively. A weekly Pacific Hotel Express was available for an additional $30 or so in which guests enjoyed extremely elegant and comfortable surroundings, and most remarkable, meal service on the train.

A prominent publisher, Frank Leslie went on an extended rail excursion west in 1877 on one of the hotel cars. He was accompanied by, among others, his wife Florence and her dog. Mrs. Leslie described railroad dining in glowing terms.

At six the tables are laid for two each, with
dainty linen and the finest of glass and china, and
we presently sit down to dinner. Our repast is
Delmonican [Delmonico's was a famous New
York restaurant] in nature and style, consisting of
soup, fish, entree, roast meat and vegetables, followed by the conventional dessert and the
essential spoonful of black coffee.

Food for the general travelling public was less gourmet and
certainly more difficult to procure. Unless one chose to carry food
on the train, meals were to be had only at certain stops where eating houses were located. The stopping time at these stations was
only twenty minutes, thus getting a meal was always a mad rush.
Frequently payment was requested upon ordering and it was not
unheard of for unscrupulous eating house proprietors to bribe con-
ductors to cut the stop short, forcing hungry passengers to leave
their bought and paid for meal to be sold again to the next unfortunate traveler.

Meals at the eating houses were in general considered good,
but plain. A 1873 traveller, Susan Coolidge claimed that "it was
necessary to look at one's watch to tell whether it was breakfast,
dinner or supper, these meals presenting invariably the same
salient features of beefsteak, fried eggs, fried potato."

Green River was a meal stop and the earliest eating house was
the Desert House, located in a building near the tracks. In the late
1800s the Union Pacific Hotel was built to feed and house both
travelers and workers on the railroad. The building had rooms for
overnight guests as well as eating facilities. It was initially built
near the railroad tracks about where the present depot stands, but
was moved across the street to the corner of North Second East
and Railroad Avenue when the depot was built in 1910. The
building was torn down in the 1950s.

If one had a few spare moments after dining, there was much
to see in Green River. In 1877 Frank Leslie commented on "...a
choice assortment of Rocky Mountain Curiosities..." advertised at
the Green River station. *The Pacific Tourist,* an 1884 travelers
guide, noted that, "At Green River you will find the dining-room
entrance fairly surrounded with curiosities, and the office filled
with oddities very amusing." Leslie also noted the presence of
"California lions" or mountain lions in a cage near the depot.

The completion of the transcontinental railroad ushered in a
new era of travel. For most passengers travel remained somewhat

difficult and uncomfortable, but when compared to the long and dangerous journeys made by wagon train and stage coach, a ride on the train was unbelievably rapid and trouble-free. More and more people began to travel the west not just as intrepid explorers or settlers, but also as tourists. The American West seemed to be slowly yet surely opening its arms to civilization.

❖

Green River:
"Nature's Art Shop"

by Marna Grubb

The title of this column - *Echoes from the Bluffs* - reminds me of an article by my uncle, Otto Jessen. Otto was born in Green River on January 2, 1901 and died December 27, 1934 - a short 33 years. He spent the greater part of his life in Green River, with the exception of a short period when he served Wyoming as Deputy State Insurance Commissioner under Governor Ross. He served as Deputy County Clerk for Sweetwater County under William Lewis and William Yates, and was serving in that capacity under Helen Y. Hamm when death came so unexpectedly - just ten hours after his wife had presented him with a son at Wyoming General Hospital in Rock Springs.

Otto's article (which appeared in the *Green River Star* January 18, 1924) still holds true for Green River today. His description of "nature's most wonderful masterpiece" follows:

WHEN GREEN RIVER IS FAST ASLEEP
(by O.W. Jessen)

Thousands of tourists pass through Green River, each season, and stop for but a moment to obtain gas or water and are gone again, while a few stop overnight at the camp ground and they are gone again in the morning reminding one of that verse written of the sea: "Ships that pass in the night and greet each other in passing; only a voice and a sound and darkness again and the silence:" and so it is with Green River. The average tourist waves his hand as he passes through, remarking that it seems to be a pretty little place but can not have any interesting sights as he had heard nothing of it and his road map shows or says nothing in particular about

The Sunbonnet Girl sits on a bluff to the left as one travels east of Green River. (Photo courtesy Sweetwater County Historical Museum)

it, so he goes on and leaves Green River in its darkness and silence, blissfully sleeping and dreaming of being great someday.

Dreams come true if made to come true and so Green River's dreams for greatness can come true if just a little effort is put forth to let the people know what we have here.

There is no doubt that of all the wonderful scenery that is promised a tourist when he leaves his home in the east for the wonders of the west, that certain part which in my opinion is as unique and interesting as any in this country, and which the tourist hears the least about, are the works of nature on the Lincoln Highway and surrounding our own fair city.

The thousands of tourists who pass through here every year see little or any of this beauty as they know nothing of it and see only piles of rocks, sand and sage brush, hoping that soon they will be away from it and saying that they will never return to this Godforsaken country; where if the beauty of nature as it appears here was but called to their attention, they would delight in the sight and smell of the sage, gasp with awe and wonder at the marvels of nature's most wonderful masterpieces, which are the work of ages of wind and storm.

These same tourists who curse this part of the country now would soon love it and instead of spending a few minutes in Green River, would spend weeks examining, exploring and enjoying

The Kneeling Camel rests along the Palisades west of Green River. (Photo courtesy Sweetwater County Historical Museum)

nature's works; and once here they would always come back; for he who once tastes the beauty of this country will always want more.

Castle Rock, which stands a sentinel, guarding the city through the ages, is by far a more imposing picture than any grand old castle on the Rhine, and is built by nature on the original American plan, being a perfect figure of an Indian head when seen from the west.

The Sphinx of Egypt, built ages ago by the toil of man and taking years in the making, can in no way be compared to our own man's face, which in the past centuries has watched the steady stream of humanity from the east, passing westward to a new home. What a story he could tell, if he would just but speak.

No sculptor has ever duplicated the work of nature in the Lion and Mouse, which is easily seen from town, and which in itself is as delicate a work of art as could be molded from clay or chiseled from stone, and, of the thousands of tourists who yearly pass within a few feet of this masterpiece, none have ever seen it.

Not far from the Lion and Mouse can be seen three bears ambling along one behind the other, while further west is that monarch of the plains, the Bison, looking over his old feeding grounds.

On the new road west of town, one must pass by Toll Gate Rock, massive and splendid, which afforded a good chance for freebooters to collect toll from the early pioneers, as the old

Overland Trail.

Next one passes close to that mighty collonade of rock called Palisades, and second to none in beauty and colors.

Resting on the west end of palisades is that mighty emblem of Volstead, the camel, who seems to have found in its last resting place a haven of peace, watching the river flow on forever.

These are but a few of the many works of nature near here and which would delight the eye of the traveler.

Besides the work of nature, we have the works of man in the many graves of old timers and settlers who have been killed in battle with the Indians or who passed on in their battle to find gold in California. Many of these old land marks have been lost and obscured by time, but the few left would be more interesting, if marked out, than is the Custer Battlefield.

Green River has one of the most interesting histories of the early settlements in Wyoming; but, what history we have, is slowly getting lost with the passing of those pioneers who were the first settlers here.

Let's tell the world of the wonders of Green River, and while Northern Wyoming is Nature's Play Ground why not make this certain part of Southern Wyoming, Nature's Art Shop.

❖

Prohibition, Cathouses and Green River

by James W. June

PROHIBITION – RED DOG – GIN MILLS – CATHOUSES – "JOHN BARLEY SENT ME!"

Prohibition is generally looked upon by Westerners as an abomination imposed upon them by sanctimonious Easterners.

When one mentions prohibition, one thinks of the 18th Amendment (Volstead Act) and the era of 1919 to 1933. "Anti-drinking" legislation in America is as old as drinking itself. For over 200 years, "demon rum" and legally enforced abstinence were engaged in a running seesaw battle, with now "likker" and now water coming out on top - a long drawn-out groin-kicking and eye-gouging fight that is not over yet.

Westerners made their own "likker," both before, during and after Prohibition. Wherever whitemen went, whiskey and beer went with them or soon followed after. Ashley's beavermen and the mountainmen made their own trade whiskey (in a class by itself - in a very low class). The Indians called it "fire water" because a little of it was thrown into the fire to make a flame, "so the Indians knew it wasn't just plain river water." The raw alcohol in kegs was transported to the West and then the mountainmen made their whiskey on location. The following recipe was from one of Ashley's mountainmen journals:

One barrel of river water.
Two gallons of raw alcohol.
Two ounces of strychnine to make them crazy.
Three twists of 'baccer to make them sick, cause Injuns
won't believe it's good unless it makes them sick Five
bars of soap to give it a bead

1/2 pound of red pepper to give it a
kick. Boil with sagebrush until brown.
Strain through barrel.
Wall, that's yer injun whiskey.

In the 1660s, the Massachusetts legislature passed blue laws closing tavern taprooms on the Sabbath, but with the wise proviso that "the faint and sick could be served their medicinal gill or dram at any time or day." This resulted in people feeling very poorly on Sunday and having their constitution strengthened with a stout toddy.

In 1780, the General Conference of the Methodist-Episcopalian Church condemned both the making and drinking of distilled spirits.

In 1789, Connecticut parsons preached not merely temperance but at least partial abstinence.

In 1812 at Lychfield, Conn., Rev. Lyman Beecher reinforced his anti-liquor sermons by distributing a little work by Doctor Ben Rush, Physician: Inquiry into the Effects of Hard Spirits Upon the Human Mind and Body.

By the 1830s more than 6,000 branches of the temperance movement were busily spreading the creed.

The first Wyoming Territorial Legislature in 1869 provided for Sunday closing of saloons, but the 1871 Wyoming Territorial Legislature repealed the poorly enforced statute. The 1882 Wyoming Territorial Legislature ordered the saloons closed from 10 a.m. to 2 p.m. on Sunday in towns of 500 or more people and made it unlawful to sell or give away liquor between sunup and sundown on election day.

The prohibition movement became a women's movement, a mass movement, the main feminist movement between 1875 and 1915, taking precedence over the drive for women's suffrage. A forerunner of the sit-ins and demonstrations of the 1960s and 1970s, the militant women of the 19th and early 20th centuries marched upon the saloons, trying to pray and shame them out of existence first and later wrecking them when the nonviolent approach failed.

Temperance workers first attracted attention in Laramie, when the Sons of Temperance established a division in 1875, and a branch of the Murphy Temperance Union was organized in April 1877. Frances Willard, National Temperance leader, came to Cheyenne in April 1880 to organize a chapter of Women's Christian Temperance Union (WCTU). Later that year Chapters were organized in Laramie and Evanston.

Temperance workers in the 1886 Wyoming Territorial Legislature tried, but failed, to extend Sunday closing beyond the four-hour period of 1882.

In 1888 prohibition sentiment was strongest in Laramie and Evanston. Rawlins, Carbon, Rock Springs, Green River City and the new towns in central Wyoming were wide open and very wet.

The drys had sent many petitions to the 1915 Wyoming Legislature, and a few prohibition bills had been introduced without success. By 1917, the national trend toward prohibition had become stronger. In 1915, the WCTU and the Anti-Saloon League (ASL), with help from the churches, presented the 1915 Legislature with petitions bearing 10,000 signatures and asking for submission of the question to a vote of the people. No action was taken in that session. The wets were on the defensive thereafter, as Colorado did so in 1914, Idaho in 1915, Nebraska, South Dakota and Montana in 1916 and Utah in 1917.

In 1918 it was said that as the one wet spot in the Rocky Mountain region, Wyoming had become the dumping ground for shady characters and ladies and was the supply depot of "likker" for the surrounding dry states. Crime was said to abound in the bordertowns of Evanston, Cheyenne, and Sheridan.

Wyoming went dry on July 1, 1919, "de jure" but not "de facto."

Many men who had no caches of bonded stuff soon prepared substitutes. Three weeks after prohibition began, 42 men and women were arrested in a raid on a disorderly house in west Cheyenne.

After prohibition went into effect on July 1, 1919, events soon indicated that the state's notorious aridity did not extend to the alleys, cellars, parlors and brothels. Hundreds of raids turned up liquor and stills in all sorts of places, some in cities, some in rural areas far from settlements. Since the 1920s were tough times, many smaller ranchers who were otherwise law abiding citizens, in order to make ends meet, turned to the business of making moonshine...and most of it was a pretty good brand of drinking liquor.

After one year, there were fewer drunks and fewer arrests than before prohibition, yet anyone who wanted a drink could find it: First there was the old stuff that had been kept but cost a small fortune; then there was the home-made stuff; and then came the perfumes, hair tonic, bay rum, flavoring extracts (vanilla and lemon) and patent medicines such as Hostetter's Bitters, Dr. Sweet's Infallible Liniment, Limerick's Liniment, Indian Snake Oil, Doctor Von Vonder's Golden Elixir, Chickasaw Chill Cure. These pro-

Moonshine equipment taken by officers in various raids in Sweetwater County during the prohibition era in the 1920s. In the photograph are stills and jugs of "white lightning" that had been seized. Left to right are Courthouse Custodian Bill Hutton, Sheriff Al Morton, and Deputy Sheriff Chris Jessen. (Photo courtesy Marna Grubb)

duced some peculiar results and made some men wild. That was what the Westerner drank before, during and probably after Prohibition.

On these concoctions a man got drunked up or pickled, painted his nose, blossom-nosed, rusted his boiler and struck with bottle fever. He looked down the neck of a bottle until he was affected with the tremors. He went booze-blind. He went on a high and lonesome. He drank pulque and became a walking whiskey vat. He roostered until somebody stole his rudder. He was drunk as a boiled owl. He slept his jag off and woke up feeling as if a cat had kittens in his mouth or as if he had breakfasted with a coyote.

The alcoholic spirits used before, during and after Prohibition were known by a variety of names. They drank **Red Dynamite** guaranteed to blow "yer" head off. There was **Brave-Maker,** which made a hummingbird spit in a rattlesnake's eyes. And there was **Joy Juice,** a single nip would tempt one to steal his own clothes, two would make you bite off your own ears, while three instilled you the desire to save your drowning mother-in-law.

The **Bumblebee Whiskey** was a drink with a sting which made one's ears buzz. There was **Brigham Young Whiskey,** one jolt and you're a polygamist seeing double. There was **Dust Cutter** for those dry enough to spit cotton. **Red Disturbance** raised a blood blister on a rawhide boot.

Block and Tackle made a man walk a block and tackle anything. **Taos Lightning** struck a man on the spot. **Tongue Oil** induced a man to talk his head off. **Corpse Reviver** made the dead rise. **Tangle Leg Whiskey** tied the drinkers feet up in knots, and was made of tobacco, molasses, red peppers, and raw alcohol.

Snakehead Whiskey had a rattler's head nailed to the inside of keg "for flavor." **Lamp Oil** kept a man well-lit. **White Mule** had a mighty kick. **Who Shot John?** felled a man instantly. **Miner's Friend** would outblast any other explosive. **Torchlight Whiskey** was a concoction with a main element of cheap gin.

Red Dog Whiskey was a powerful malignance from Tucson. **White Mare's Milk** was the "fightingest liquor" to come out of a bottle. **Roockus Juice** made a mule grow horns. **Base Burner** was "hot as a she-mink." **Creepin' Whiskey** "creeps up behind you and knocks you down." **Mormon Whiskey or Valley Tan** was sodcom barefooted; one man drank a pint of it, went home and stole one of his own plows, hid it in the woods and didn't know where it was when he was sober and had to get drunk again to find it.

Other names applied are Moonshine which was thought to be one answer to Prohibition, Field Whiskey, Farm Whiskey, White Lightning, Blue John, Crock Beer, Mountain Dew, Purple Jesus, Sneaky Pete, Cow Whiskey, and Scorpion Juice. Which of these a man drank depended on "where you're headed from and what church you went to."

One of the most famous moonshine was **Kemmerer Moon,** which was transported throughout this region and back east to Kansas City and Chicago.

Green River was famous for its beer brewed at the local brewery from 1872 until 1919. The Volstead Act killed the business, which never began again at the end of Prohibition.

Before and during Prohibition what was called rye or bourbon often bore no resemblance to the genuine article. The best grade pure whiskey was doctored as soon as it arrived at its destination. Saloon keepers diluted their whiskey to make one barrel into three by means of additives that gave it an artificial kick. This "inventive whiskey" was definitely poisonous, brought on the DT's and "left a fellow so shaky he couldn't pour a drink into a barrel with the head out." Cheap wines became "Irish Whiskey" when a pint of creosote was poured into it. A pound of burned sugar in grape juice, an ounce of sulfuric acid "to make it "convincing" and a plug of "chawing baccer" to give it a bead, also made a powerful if not altogether satisfactory mixture. There were some who did not use any whiskey at all in their concoctions, no real, clear alcohol. They dosed creek water with any, several, or all of these: tartaric, citric and sulfuric acids, fusel oil, ammonia, black bone meal gun powder, molasses, oak bark, oatmeal, cayenne pepper, tobacco, snake root, juniper berries, creosote, and turpentine.

The Noble Experiment, the Volstead Act, became a reality at 12:01 a.m. on the morning of Jan. 16, 1920, and the last of the old saloons shut down its batwing doors.

In December, 1921, federal officers announced that in Sweetwater County they had completed the biggest and most successful raid of its kind. They arrested 62 persons in Rock Springs, Green River, and Superior and confiscated 1,400 boxes of raisins, 3,000 gallons of "Dago Red" wine, and 1,000 gallons of other intoxicants. Those arrested pleaded guilty in Federal court in Cheyenne and were fined $200 each for possession.

In 1922, federal agents made 208 arrests for illegal manufacture and 548 for illegal sale. Many other arrests were made by state law enforcement, county sheriffs and city police.

The *Green River Star* reported on May 18, 1923 the capture of a big still on the south side of the tracks in Green River and the arrest of the operator, Ed Darvell, by federal officers and County Sheriff officers.

On October 9, 1925, the *Green River Star* reported the find by officers of a twenty gallon still, 300 gallons of mash and two gallons of the finished product that made jack rabbits fight bears belonging to Guno Flanini of Superior.

The *Green River Star* reported on January 15, 1926 the find of the largest operation in Wyoming. Two stills of 250 gallons capacity each, 88 barrels of mash or 50,000 gallons and 100 other empty barrels were found in a well-hidden dugout under Cedar Mountain. The Stills were still warm when found, but the attendant was not around. The sheriff was sure of his identity. The stills were brought to Green River and the dugout and plant were burned.

Bootleggers, officers and innocent persons were killed in gunplay. Three state agents near Laramie in September, 1919, riddled a passing automobile and killed an innocent rancher, whom they mistook for a bootlegger; and the three agents received long penitentiary sentences. In June 1923, county officers lay in the sagebrush near a moonshine cache four miles north of Cody. Two unarmed Greybull men approached, the agents fired, killing one and shattered the leg of the other. The Rock Springs Miner reported the killing of Federal Officer Capen by a bootlegger on May 11, 1928.

The 1920s have been called the "Roaring Twenties," the "Lawless Decade," and "Era of Wonderful Nonsense." All three designations are appropriate in view of some of the transactions in Wyoming.

Heavier penalties were tried as a deterrent in the late 1920s and imprisonment for first offenders in 1923. In 1927, the possession of a still was subject to a three-year penitentiary sentence. In 1929 the Federal Jones-Stalker Act ("Five and Ten Law") authorized penalties up to five years in the penitentiary and fines up to $10,000 for illegal possession of liquor. During 1929, some 425 persons were arrested in Wyoming by federal agents on charges of violating federal Prohibition laws, as compared with 393 in 1928 and 806 in 1922.

In 1930, a poll showed Wyoming and Montana were the wettest states in the region, and both were wetter than the nation as a whole.

The Prohibition agents were not always lily white and were regarded with suspicion. William C. Irving, state law enforcement commissioner (11/27-12/28), was sentenced to serve 18 months in federal prison after being convicted in February 1930 on charges of conspiracy to violate national Prohibition laws. Speakeasies at Rawlins paid him $50 each per month, and operators of a large still at Thermopolis paid him one dollar per gallon of liquor produced.

The end of Prohibition was celebrated with excitement reminiscent of the last Pre-Prohibition hours. In Wyoming, 3.2 beer became legal at midnight May 19, 1933. The 3.2 beer proved disappointing, and the public had to wait for the legalization of stronger stuff, which came to Wyoming in April, 1935. The Legislature chose to establish a State Liquor Commission, which would engage in liquor wholesaling.

Prohibition, however, changed drinking habits. For one thing, it made drinking popular and respectable among women. While the Pre-Prohibition girl had said, "Lips that touch liquor shall never touch mine," during Prohibition, the flat-chested, short-skirted, Charleston-dancing flapper inquired of a prospective date if he was well provided with inspiring potables and what kind of speakeasy he was taking her to.

During the 1920s, the latest trinket was an ankle flask. The women could carry liquor in them and tuck the ankle flask in their boots so no one could see them. Also during this same period, the hip-flask came into wide and common use.

When discussing the use of stills, World War II G.I.s will remember its use. When a unit was stationary for two or more days in one place, the first thing that was set up was the unit's still. Many of the G.I.s also had individual stills made from canteens, its cup, the little coils of copper tubing, and heated cans of sterno.

When discussing alcoholic spirits and prohibition, one has to talk about the saloons. The saloon has one stereotype in particular. The image: a smoke-filled room, men sitting at tables with wide brimmed hats on and playing cards, while painted cats in rustling silk or velvet, their hair adorned with ostrich feathers, are gadding about. To the left, the bar is busy with drinkers and to the right are the swinging doors. Cowboys rest their spurred, high-heeled boots on brass rails. The blond blue-eyed hero emerges on the upstairs landing with guns blazing. The neatly drilled, black-dressed villain hurtles through the splintering railing, crashing with a heavy thud to the floor below, and bites the dust on the saw-dust covered floor. The hero jumps from the landing onto the chandelier fashioned from a wagon wheel. He swings himself, orangutan fashion, over onto the bar, his belly hardware still sputtering with an inexhaustible stream of bullets. The mustachioed bardog bobs up and down from behind the bar like a freaked-out yo-yo. Fanning his hogleg, the blond hero severs the rope by which the chandelier is suspended. It crashes down upon the heads of a half-dozen more swarthy villains, burying them for good. The sawdust is covered with broken glass and blood. The blond hero nonchalantly blows away the smoke from the muzzle of his six-shooter, an absolute must. Silence! The bit players stand transfixed like Lots' wife turned to a pillar of salt. The blond demigod backs out defiantly through the swinging doors. His faithful steed whinnies joyfully. The barkeeper rises from behind the counter, his scared voice ringing out: "Belly up to the bar, gents, the drinks are on the house!"

This has stereotyped the Western saloon, the rip-roaring whiskey mill, the proverbial den of iniquity of the past. The Western saloon's life was short. The Western saloon is a controversial subject. Every statement made about it has been contradicted by another; the saloons were all the same and looked the same.

Actually the Western saloon existed because it filled a basic human need, which is now hard to imagine. It was a place of comfort, refuge and even a place of refinement where one could rub elbows with a fellow human being. It was a place where they spoke cow talk, where miners could relax and communicate with fellow miners and nesters could talk with each other about the hails and dry spells.

The saloon was also a place to dispel the loneliness of a month on the range, two months in the back country with the sheep or mining the claim. There were some people who spent most of their sleeping hours in saloons. The saloon was all things to all men. Besides being a drinking place, it was an eatery, hotel, a bath and comfort station, a livery stable, gambling den, dance hall, cathouse, barbershop, courthouse, sports arena, undertaker's parlor, library, news exchange, theater, opera, city hall, employment agency, museum, trading post, grocery and ice cream parlor. A saloon might fulfill none or several of the above functions at the same time.

The saloon was often the first substantial building in a new settlement and the last to crumble when the settlement turned into a ghost town.

The saloon was known by many names: bughouse, jughouse, whiskey mill, whoop-up cantina, water hole, pouring spot, sala, hop joint, doggery, grog-shop, gin mill, gin point, snake ranch, jugtown and watering trough. A bit house was a saloon where every drink cost a bit or twenty-five cents. At short bit houses, the drinks cost half that. A barrelhouse dispensed whiskey from open barrels so delicately balanced that a child could pour from them. A shebang house was a saloon of green lumber with some sawdust to stand on but no chairs or tables. A deadfall was a drinking place of evil reputation. Pretty waiter saloons had girls in short skirts who induced lonely miners and cowboys to buy a drink for them. A fandango house was a dance hall saloon. A day and nite saloon never closed. Hell on wheels were rolling saloons, transported on trains, following the railroad building crews from place to place. A company saloon was a drinking establishment owned by a mining company, recycling the miners wages back into its own pockets. It was sometimes called the place "where a rattlesnake wouldn't take his mother."

During Prohibition, the saloon became a grocery store, cafe, restaurant, ice parlor, candy and cigar store, and billiard parlor. There was a backroom where the main sale item, however, was booze and accessed by a password at the backdoor.

Also during this period there were numerous speakeasies, roadhouses and brothels where the spirits were sold and, in which, admission was by password only.

The old saloon did not come back with the end of Prohibition. Over the years it had acquired the ignoble reputation as symbols of evil, and "saloon" became a dirty word. As a result, what came back after repeal was not the old familiar thirst parlor, but the bars, cocktail lounges, ye olde taverns, taprooms, cafes, and clubs.

Two types of saloons specialized in providing the right kind of female companionship: the hurdy-gurdy house or "pretty waiter saloon," and the variety saloon disguised as a theater.

Hurdy-gurdy houses were essential fixtures of mining and cow towns. The word "hurdy-gurdy" comes from an old-time German musical instrument, a sort of hand organ; and in the most primitive dance hall saloons, a hurdy-gurdy man provided the only music and the name stuck. The hurdy-gurdy house existed to sell drinks. The girls existed to keep the wet goods moving. They were known as hurdy-gurdy girls, honky-tonk gals, beerjerkers, box rustler, or pretty waiter girls. Some of them were prostitutes, but most of them just danced with men for a living. They were considered a cut above the fallen angels. They were there to entertain, to please men, and, most important, to make them buy drinks at outrageous prices. They had their own places to live and sleep in. They might be snubbed by the so-called better element, and they were seldom virgins. They took lovers freely and defied convention by living open-ly with their paramours, but most of them were not whores and resented it if treated as such. They were proud that they picked or rejected their lovers as they pleased. They worked for saloon owners and not for madams or pimps. What the girl drank, for a dollar a shot, bore of course no relation to what was written on the label. The label might say champagne, but what the girls got was weak tea or colored sugar water. The average pay of pretty waiter girls was twenty dollars a day. They also received a commission on the booze they sold and half the earnings from the sale of their bodies.

The women of easy virtue were known by many names: giddy ladies, painted cats, fair but frail, scarlet ladies, come-on girls, fallen angels, "boarders," ladies of the evening, easy women, fast women, fancy women, fair belles, sportin' gals, owls (nightwalkers), crib women (lowest in their profession), shady ladies, daughters of joy, celestial female, chiledo, chola, chippy, and sisters of misery.

The houses of prostitution were known by various names. Brothel originated from the Old English word brothen, meaning ruined. Bagno's origin is Italian. They were also known as Bawdyhouse, Boarding House, Bordello, Bull-Pen, Cathouse, Cow-Yard, Crib (a small dwelling for a prostitute), Gooseberry Ranch, Goosing Heifer Den, Hog Ranch, Old Ladies' House, Parlor House, Resort, and Sporting House.

The areas that had brothels were known as the Red Light Districts, which originated from a custom of railroaders leaving their red brakemen's lanterns hanging outside the door of their girl of the evening to discourage intruders. They were also known as the Line or the Tenderloin. One of Wyoming's most famous districts was the Sand Bar in Casper. The brothel was operated by a Madame and most houses had a bar and dance area. The floor where the ladies lived was known as the monkey hall - officially off limits for the guests. The daughters of joy received a monthly check-up from the local doctors and were grounded if they didn't get a clean bill of health. Each brothel paid a local "tax" to the city coffers, and they purchased all their necessities at the local stores.

Prohibition forced most of the girls of the evening to the brothels. Green River had its own brothels: Green House, Oxford Rooms, Pandora Rooms, Teton Rooms and Y-Bing Rooms. With the close of the brothels, the fancy women then moved to the trade of the hooker, streetwalker, and the call girl to apply their virtues.

In reviewing all that has been told, an important question becomes apparent: Can government legislate behavior?

❖

Green River had a Sawmill

by James W. June

The Green River sawmill with the logs being piled outside to be sawed into lumber. In the foreground are some of the ties still in the river. (Photo courtesy Sweetwater County Historical Museum)

Green River had a sawmill from the time of the origin of the town in 1868 and operated up until 1920 when the Union Pacific Railroad expanded its railroad yards to the east. The sawmill was located on the north bank of the Green River just above the mouth of Bitter Creek.

There were five enterprising men that could foresee the future of the local area. In 1867, Charles Deloney contracted with the Union Pacific Railroad Company to furnish ties for the railroad. He began his timber operation in the fall and winter of 1867-68 in the upper Green River country. He made the first tie and saw timber drive down the Green to Green River City in the spring of 1868.

Three other enterprising men, H.M. Hook, mayor of Cheyenne, James Moore of Cheyenne and S.I. Field were the leaders of the squatters at Green River City. These men obtained the land at this location from the Overland Mail Company. They said the mail contractors had secured, from the U.S. Congress in 1862, a land grant which ante-dated the Union Pacific Railroad Acts of 1867. S.I. Field then platted and laid out the original town that is known as Green River No. 3. The construction of Green River City began the first of July, 1868.

The other enterprising man was Judge Carter of Fort Bridger, who built two sawmills, one on Black's Fork near Fort Bridger and one on the Green River near the mouth of the Bitter Creek. He could see the need for lumber in the building of the railroad and the construction of towns and for the need of mining timber in the coal mines. These sawmills were steam operated.

The original Green River City buildings were constructed of adobe brick which were made at a site near the present location of the Zumbrennen Tire Service, Inc.

The *Frontier Index* of August 11, 1868 reported that "music of the carpenter's tools are everywhere heard above the din and bustle of business. The two sawmills of Judge Carter, on the Black's Fork and another on the Green River, do not supply the demand for finishing lumber alone."

The *Frontier Index* also reported Green River City's first election on August 11, 1868, the incorporation of the Green River City, Carter County, Dakota Territory on August 26, 1868, that Green River City had a population of over 2,000 on September 11, 1868, and the arrival of the Union Pacific Railroad tracks on October 1, 1868.

As reported in the *Green River Star*, the tie and saw-log drives came down the Green River every spring to the boom at Green River to supply the Union Pacific Railroad Company with ties and saw-logs for the sawmill. These drives came from upper Green River region, which included the Horse Creek, Cottonwood Creek, Piney Creek, LaBarge Creek and Kendall areas.

The *Green River Star* also reported that logs and saw-timber were hauled into the Green River sawmill from the Little Mountain and Pine Mountain areas in south central Sweetwater County. This is very evident at the present day, when one travels in these areas. These old cut-over areas on Pine and Little Mountain can be observed today where these areas are being revegetated naturally with fir, pine, aspen and understory brush. Also old stumps and logs can be found.

The Green River sawmill furnished the area with the finished lumber to build many of the early homes as well as the mine timbers and lumber for area coal mines until 1920.

The *Green River Star* reported the Union Pacific Railroad extending the east yards in 1920 and moved the channel of Bitter Creek to the south next to the bluff at its present day location. The Green River sawmill was demolished and the site destroyed to increase trackage for the Union Pacific Railroad yards to the east.

Green River did have a lumber and sawmill industry in its past history.

❖

Sickout

by Sherry Espeland

March 15, 1973 may not mean much to some of us, but it is a day that teachers of the Green River Education Association will always remember. March 15, 1973, was a day known as a "Successful Sickout."

As the fourth quarter of the 1991-1992 school year begins, the Green River Education Association and the Sweetwater County School District No. 2 School Board collaborate on negotiations for the corning school year. Negotiations have changed immensely since that spring day in 1973.

As I began learning about this day, I spoke with two individuals involved with the sickout. Mr. Byron Stahla, president of the GREA then, and Mr. Bill Thompson shared insight into what the day was like for the school district. Both stated that the day was "not an attack on the administration, but a way of communicating the wants and needs of the association." The following is a brief description of March 13, 1973:

Frustration over the lack of negotiations with the school board, and meeting after meeting, the GREA met one more time to ask the association to "call in sick" the next day. Fifty to seventy percent chose to "call in sick."

On the sickout day, many met at Byron Stahla's house for support. Stahla recalls one woman who was physically sick sitting on his living room floor. The stress during the negotiations had overwhelmed many of them. This day was no different.

Around lunch time, the association met once more. The place: Mansface Church. After listening to various speeches, the group decided to go back to their classrooms that afternoon. One teacher even stated, "I'm sure now the board will begin listening to the wants of the association." The teachers returned.

As the lunch bell rang, the classes that had been doubled up with substitute teachers, or custodians, now had their regular teachers back. Teachers discussed with their students what had happened that morning. Teachers felt they needed to communicate to students the issues behind the "Sickout."

The day ended.

As historians, we can relate to the statement, "we lost the battle, but we won the war." The "Successful Sickout" was the beginning for negotiation agreements with the GREA and the School Board. Since that day, we are witness to better communication between the GREA and the School Board - each organization with the same goal: student success.

❖

Green River's First Recreation Area

by James W. June

Green River's first recreational area or park was the Island. The Island has been known by various names since the settlement of Green River City. It has been known as the Island, Johnson Island, Island Park and Expedition Island. The island was in private ownership until Green River City purchased it in October 1909.

The Island

The Island was claimed by S.I. Field when he platted Green River City in early 1868. In 1872, the plat of a claim filed by S.I. Field, founder of the present day Green River, claimed the island, stating that the island was a half mile long, south of the railroad tracks, with an irrigation canal as its northeast boundary.

Efforts made by Mr. Field in which he was quite successful in 1875, was a crop of potatoes, cabbage, turnips, radishes and other "garden truck" products.

Johnson Island

W.A. Johnson purchased the Field property in 1872. The island then became known as Johnson Island. Johnson Island, still in private ownership, was becoming an area of recreation and family outings. Although there was no mention of city organized offerings of July Fourth activities on Johnson Island, the town council permission was given to sell beer on the Island July 4, 1892.

The town council received a proposal to purchase Johnson Island in June, 1895, but this fell through when no funds were available for real estate purchase.

In April, 1908, a move was made by a local company by the name of Musgrove and Company to transform Johnson Island into

In 1908 Johnson Island was transformed into a beautiful pleasure ground by erecting an open-air dance pavilion, a merry-go-round, launches for river trips, and a new wooden wagon bridge. (Photo courtesy Sweetwater County Historical Museum)

a beautiful pleasure ground by erecting a lighted, open-air, dance pavilion, a pleasure merry-go-round, various other amusing features and two gasoline launches for river trips. A new wooden wagon bridge was built to the island off of south second East Street (Cedar Street), the location of the present bridge. A baseball park was built on a plot of ground just opposite the island, which was donated for that purpose by W.S. Hodges of Western Alkali Company. The town of Green River bought Johnson Island for $2,000 in October 1909 from Western Alkali Company.

Island Park

Johnson Island's name was changed to Island Park in June 1910, with a free concert and dance given by the Green River Band. In the spring of 1910, the town built a steel bridge to replace the wooden wagon bridge for a cost of $2065 and this bridge is still used today.

The Island Park became a very popular outing spot for the Sweetwater County residents. The island was operated as an amusement park by concessionaires. There was a beach from which sun bathing and swimming could be enjoyed when the flood period was over. River trips up and down the island were enjoyed by many.

The Island

In 1930, the town of Green River built the present indoor pavilion and a town outdoor swimming pool on the location of the old baseball park just opposite the island, at a cost of $25,000. The pavilion over the years has been used for a dance hall, public gatherings, roller skating rink, National Guard Armory, "Teen Town" and Flaming Gorge Days activities.

The heavily wooded area at the center of the Island Park was cleared in 1955-56 to make way for the lawn area which exists today.

In 1976-78, the pavilion was restored at a cost of $256,412. The preservation of the Island Pavilion was not recognized for its own historic value because it was built 40 years after Powell. It was envisioned as a community center to have a historic place more usable and enjoyable to the public.

Expedition Island

The Island Park's name was changed to Expedition Island on May 24, 1969. The island name was changed to Expedition Island to honor John Wesley Powell's Green-Colorado Rivers Expedition in 1869 and 1871.

The 1869 Powell Expedition took off from the north bank of the Green River just below the Union Pacific Railroad Bridge upstream a half mile above Expedition Island. The 1871 Powell Expedition took off from the head of the first island above Expedition Island.

Expedition Island was named as a National Historic Landmark by the Secretary of Interior commemorating Major John Wesley Powell's two expeditions down the Green and Colorado Rivers in 1869 and 1871. Expedition Island is recognized only as the appropriate site to commemorate both expeditions. The only Powell Expedition that left Expedition Island was the reenactment of the Powell Expedition by the Sierra Club of California on May 24, 1969.

❖

A Woman's Work: Female Labor In and Out of the Home

by Ruth Lauritzen

> I have done most of my cooking at night, have milked seven cows every day, and have done all the hay-cutting, so you see I have been working. But I have found time to put up thirty pints of jelly and the same amount of jam for myself.... I have almost two gallons of the cherry butter, and I think it is delicious.
>
> –Elinore Pruitt Stewart
> *Letters of a Woman Homesteader*

In the late 1800s and early 1900s all women were "working women." Though few were employed outside the home or in traditional "male jobs", women labored each day as long and as hard as their male counterparts. In most cases a woman's work was in the home as chief housekeeper, seamstress, cook and childcare specialist. This included many labor intensive duties such as scrubbing and ironing laundry, cooking on coal burning stoves, and hand-sewing clothing and household furnishings.

In the years before the advent of modern conveniences such as electricity and indoor plumbing, even simple housekeeping chores could be a major undertaking. From hauling and heating water to hanging the clothes on the line to dry it generally took one whole day to do a family's weekly laundry. This did not include ironing which took most of the next day as well. Treadle sewing machines were the norm as were hand powered butter churns.

Fortunately for Green River women modern conveniences came quite early. In 1871 the Green River Water Works was incorporated and during the next several years businesses and residences

Maggie Riley and her companion supplied milk to many Green River residents in the early 1900s. (Photo courtesy Sweetwater County Historical Museum)

were put on line with water from the Green River. Rock Springs was not so fortunate. Residents had their water delivered by tanker cars on the railroad to be sold for 25 cents a barrel until a water line from Green River was finally installed in 1887. Green River "got the electric" in 1892, but only at night. It was not until several years later that round-the-clock service was available.

If women were earning outside income frequently their jobs were an extension of their daily housekeeping chores. It was not uncommon for women to run boarding houses, eating establishments or hotels. The wife of entrepreneur S.I. Field was in charge of cooking meals at the eating house Field ran during Green River's very early days. Mrs. Caroline Eggs ran the Big Hom Hotel which was located on the south side of the tracks. A 1901-02 city directory lists a total of four businesswomen: Mrs. Eggs; Mrs. M. Nolan, restaurateur; Mrs. H.H. Campbell, druggist; and Mrs. Sarah Ware, dressmaker.

Other women took on more non-traditional roles in the community and some met with considerable resistance. A prime example of this was Dr. Charlotte Hawk. Charlotte Gardner Hawk came to Green River in 1896 in the company of her husband Dr. Jacob Hawk. They were employed as surgeon and assistant surgeon of the Union Pacific in Green River. Charlotte was a graduate of medical

A former slave, Nancy Phillips came to Green River in the late 1860s with the S.I. Field family. She was a community midwife and dressmaker. (Photo courtesy Sweetwater County Historical Museum)

school at the University of Illinois and had encountered much prejudice there as a woman in a traditionally male field.

Upon her arrival in Green River she found that the prejudice continued. For several years she served only as a nurse to her husband because many of their patients had strong reservations about being treated by a woman doctor. Dr. Charlotte, as she was called, eventually found her niche in Green River society as the local obstetrician and gynecologist. She delivered many babies and performed the monthly inspections on the "girls" at the Green House, the local house of ill repute.

Prostitution was a traditional but socially unacceptable line of work that women could go into. Depending on the location and situation the work could be fairly pleasant and lucrative or brutal and dangerous. Women who worked in brothels were a great deal safer and more comfortable than those who worked the street and "administrators" such as madames or pimps made a great deal more money than the common prostitute.

Isabelle Burns, a madame in a brothel in Kemmerer around the turn of the century, described her experience as a positive one in spite of some still discernible moral dilemmas. "I have been informed that sewer workers become immune to the smell and stench that surrounds them and that was the way I felt when I hustled. I went into prostitution as a way of life. I was lazy and not trained for other employment available in the few openings for women. I enjoyed the pleasures of the flesh and the daily love from many men. The pay was good .... "

The concept of working women is not a new one, it is just that the jobs women fill have changed over the years. By the turn of the century there were some serious rumblings among women for more rights, including the right to vote. While Wyoming women had been given that right in state and local elections, in 1920 the nine-teenth amendment to the Constitution guaranteed women that right on the federal level.

These activities and the two World Wars influenced society enough to allow more and more women to work at professions formerly reserved for men. Unfortunately this new freedom did not necessarily award women equal opportunity and pay, but just the chance to join men in the workplace. These issues continue to be addressed even now, over seventy years later.

❖

At Green River "The Country Changes for the Better"

by Marna Grubb

The Desert House was a hotel located north of the railroad tracks shown in the foreground. (Photo courtesy Sweetwater County Historical Museum and enlarged from a photograph of Green River dated 1875)

When George Eckman, Green River's mayor from 1991 through 1994, returned from one of his trips to Halifax, Nova Scotia, where he would visit his brother, he brought back several books, two of which were historic books of our area, which he had found at a used bookstore. Knowing these would be of interest, he shared these books with me - and - I would like to share with you.

One treasure he found was a cloth, stiff-cover copy of J.R. Bowman's *The Pacific Tourist,* published 1882-83. This was a complete traveler's guide of The Union and Central Pacific Railroads. Illustrations were beautifully done by Thomas Moran, who more than any other artist, drew sketches of the Wonders of the West (our buttes west of Green River were one of his favorite subjects), and Albert Bierstadt, one of the most celebrated painters of American Scenery at that time.

The Pacific Tourist reported that "at Green River you will find the dining room entrance fairly surrounded with curiosities and the office filled with oddities very amusing" and "at Green River you will always get nice biscuit."

Green River was reported to be "a regular eating-station, breakfast and supper, and is now one of the best kept hostelries on the road. This place will eventually be a popular resort for those who are seeking for fossiliferous remains and those who delight in fishing. Mr. Kitchen is able to provide for all, in elegant style, at reasonable prices. Here, also, he has on exhibition and for sale the specimens alluded to - such as beautiful moss agates, fossil fish, petrified shells and wood, with others which we are not able to name."

Bowman further reported that "Being the end of a division, Green River has a large roundhouse with fifteen stalls, and the usual machine and repair shops. The railroad bursts into the valley through a narrow gorge between two hills, then turns to the right and enters the town, crossing the river beyond on a wooden truss bridge. The old adobe town, remains of which are still visible, was on the bottom-land directly in front of the gorge."

At that time, he informed that "Green River is now the county-seat of Sweetwater County, Wyoming, and has a population of nearly 500 persons. Efforts have been made by Mr. Field and a few others to reclaim the soil, but thus far with indifferent success, though Mr. Field was quite successful, in 1875, with a crop of potatoes, cabbages, turnips, radishes, and other 'garden truck'."

Also, "Stages leave here for Big Horn, Sweetwater, and other towns tri-weekly. The Desert House is the only hotel, a pleasant place with its flowers, ferns, and pictures."

Another cloth, stiff-cover book found in Nova Scotia was *Our New West,* published in 1869 – just one year after the railroad arrived in Green River and Green River became an incorporated town in the Dakota Territory, Carter County. This book is a record of travel by Samuel Bowles, whose traveling companion was Schuyler Colfax, Speaker of Congress and Vice President of the

United States who he portrayed as "trusted and beloved above all other public men by the American people."

Bowles reported that his trip from Laramie to Green River was very desolate. "No living streams are found in it, few living springs have been discovered; and in building the Railroad through it, water had to be brought up from behind, not only for the workmen and animals to drink, but for the locomotives to make steam. The water found on or near the surface is unfit for either purpose; but deep wells will probably in the future relieve this difficulty. A high, rolling, desert country is this, with scarcely any vegetation but the rank, coarse sage brush, and the soil a fine, alkali-laden dust. To all slow-traveling emigrant trains and stage passengers, this region is a memorable pain. The eye has no joy, the lips no comfort through it; the sun burns by day, the cold chills at night, the fine, impalpable, poisonous dust chokes and chafes and chaps you everywhere."

As the railroad marched rapidly across our broad continent, rough and temporary towns spring up at its every public stopping-place. As this was changed every thirty or forty days, these settlements were constructed of the most perishable materials. "Restaurant and saloon keepers, gamblers, desperadoes of every grade, the vilest of men and of women made up this 'Hell on Wheels,' as it was most aptly termed."

Then he reported that "The country changes for the better as the road crosses Green River, and enters upon the third section of the Mountain Pass, which ends with the Salt Lake Valley at Ogden. Nothing on the whole line rivals this section in grand and picturesque scenery. It has also, with the same exception, been the hardest part of the road to build."

❖

The Overland Stage

by James W. June

The Overland Stage was started in 1861, running between St. Joseph, Missouri and Placerville, California, following the Oregon Trail route. The first daily stages left St. Joseph and Placerville July 1, 1861. Both coaches reached their destination on the 18th. The Overland Stage had the U.S. Mail contract and also carried passengers. In September, 1861, Atchison, Kansas, which was fourteen miles further west, was made the starting point. Late in 1861, Ben Holladay purchased the mail route and he became "Stage King" and owner of the route of the "Overland Stage Line." By late 1861, after Holladay purchased the contract and transportation facilities, the Indian problems were so bad along the Oregon Trail route, that he changed the route. In 1862, Holladay secured a land grant for the Overland Mail Company from the U.S. Congress for its stage stations. He then moved the route to the south along the Cherokee Trail, which was renamed the Overland Trail, to avoid the Indians. It proved to be a more effective route, and it was over this path that the Transcontinental highways provided the vital gateway to the West and was the famous Lincoln Highway route. Holladay employed the most skillful stage men in the country; he bought the finest horses and mules suitable for stabling; he purchased dozens of first-class Concord coaches; he built additional stations, and added other features to make the long tedious overland trip (2000 miles) a more pleasant one. After five years (1866), he sold out to Wells Fargo and Company who operated it until the iron rails were stretched across the continent in 1868-69.

Passengers paid cash, usually $200 from Atchison to Placerville, or 10 cents per mile, for their transportation and were allowed forty pounds of luggage. On the other hand, government mail was carried at a flat rate, and when the stagecoach was over-

Green River Stage Station showing the buildings on the south bank of the Green, looking to the southeast. The Game and Fish building has been built where the southeast corner of the structures are shown. The Jaycee Park was later located where the west barns or sheds are shown. (Photo courtesy Sweetwater County Historical Museum, Reed Album)

crowded, mailbags were often left at the wayside stations to give passengers preference.

A stagecoach trip was not a pleasurable excursion. The stage rolled along both day and night on the eighteen to twenty day trip and passengers found all attempts to sleep periodically interrupted by the jolting of the coach on the rough roads. An alternative was provided by stopping at one of the "home stations" to sleep, but one risked being unable to resume his journey if the next stage that came along was overcrowded. Travelers complained constantly about lack of toilet and bathing facilities, the miserable and expensive food, the extensive use of whiskey both by fellow passengers and stage attendants, and the drunken and profane stage drivers. As noted in one passenger's diary at the Salt Wells Station, "We arrived at 4 o'clock, made some cakes of flour and water, fried some antelope meat and this with some Salt Wells water coffee, constituted our bill of fare."

The Green River Stage Station was on the south bank of the Green River, on the Overland Trail where it crossed the river. The Green River Stage Station was 1066 miles from Atchison, Kansas. It was 15 miles from the Rock Springs Stage Station to the east; and 14 miles to the Lone Tree Station to the west.

In December, 1862, federal troops were garrisoned at each station along the Overland Stage Route with the Fort Bridger troops. In 1864, a mounted patrol accompanied each stage, and at each station there was a corporal, or another non-commissioned officer, and up to 10 privates who went along as a mounted escort to the next station.

The Green River Stage Station was a "Division Station" and also a "Home Station." The "Division Stations" were spaced about every two hundred miles. The agent of a division station was responsible for the smooth functioning of the line for the whole two hundred mile distance. He kept the books, kept records on the employees and kept all of the gear in repair. In addition, there were two kinds of traveling repairmen at the division station. One was equipped as a traveling blacksmith, and the other was a harness maker and leather mender. The station was comprised of a large main building which included a number of rooms - sleeping quarters for women, a kitchen and dining room. Other buildings were a blacksmith shop, bunk house for men, barn and corral and the Division Points. The division station usually had two attendants and two stock tenders. The original stage station and shop buildings were constructed of native sandstone.

The State Game and Fish District building and the city Jaycee Park have all but obliterated the site of the Green River Overland Stage Station, that was abandoned upon the arrival of the Union Pacific Railroad in 1868.

The Overland Stage would ford the Green River when it could, from the north of the stage station, coming upon the bench to the station, up the draw to the east of the station. A portion of this ascending trail of the stage road can still be seen in the mouth of the draw, back of the Game and Fish Department office.

When the Green River was not fordable, the stage coaches were ferried across the river, at a point east of the stage station and the ford downstream, where the City Horse Corrals start. Part of the steel cable used on the ferry can be seen on the south bank of the river.

The west-bound Overland Stage road from the stage station ran along what is now Astle and Riverview Streets and up Telephone Canyon. This route up Riverview Street and Telephone Canyon was also used by the Lincoln Highway until the 1920s when the Wyoming Highway Department built a bridge across the Green at Jamestown, and then the Lincoln Highway went through town on North First Street (Flaming Gorge Way).

❖

A Year in the Social Life: Green River – 1904

by Ruth Lauritzen

In the early twentieth century the town of Green River was a small place with a citizenship of about 1400. The happenings in the town; births, deaths, marriages, church and social events, and all other things which made up the fabric of community life were chronicled in the local newspaper, the *Wyoming Star*, predecessor to the *Green River Star*. Then as today the *Star*, edited by O.O. Davis, reported mostly local news. However, a major difference is the editorial license taken by Davis who had a personal comment on many things he reported on. What follows is a compilation of social events and entertainments gleaned from the pages of the 1904 volume of the *Wyoming Star* which show a life in many ways different from, but sometimes surprisingly similar to the Green River of today.

1904 was a leap year and in celebration of that unique circumstance several young ladies formed the Leap Year Club. A leap year traditionally means that a woman may ask a man to a social event or even to take her hand in marriage, something nearly unheard of for girls of the day. The first club activity of the year was a Leap Year Ball held in January at the Opera House. The Opera House was on Railroad Avenue on what is now the parking lot between the former KUGR office building at 165 E. Railroad Avenue and the old First National Bank building at 131 E. Railroad Avenue. This building was the location of many community social and cultural events. The admission to the dance was one dollar for ladies and free for gentlemen. A "dainty and most toothsome" supper was served at a cost of twenty cents. Editor Davis described the event in the January 8 issue:

> The ballroom was beautifully decorated in the club
> colors, while the floor was in excellent condition

and the music furnished by Adam's orchestra could not have been better, in fact there could not have been a more enjoyable arrangement than that given by the young ladies, and the attendance was the best ever given a ball in this city.

All, in all, it was a most delightful pleasure producing event, and the public awaits with patience for the ladies to give another of their leap year dances.

Apparently not ones to rest on their laurels the club sponsored another ball later that same month. This dance was staged as a curiosity and called a Bloomer Ball. There was much discussion in town on whether the girls would wear bloomers to the affair. Bloomers were very full pants which were gathered at the ankles and worn under a short skirt. They were the namesake of an early female activist, Amelia Bloomer who had controversial opinions on women's dress reform and suffrage. When the appointed evening came:

...it was a large and curious crowd that gathered at the opera house to witness the girls as they appeared on the ball room floor dressed as many supposed, in those horrid bloomers. But how the faces changed when to their surprise and awe in march a line of Green River's fairest young ladies modestly dressed for the evening, wearing instead of those horrid bloomers, large and beautiful bouquets of imitation chrysanthemum, and seated themselves very modestly long {sic} the west side of the hall. Well, all opera glasses and eye glasses were immediately replaced in the pockets of those who came through the curiosity than the idea of enjoying a dance, and with the help of the sweet strains furnished by Adam's orchestra enjoyed a most delightful evening tripping the light fantastic.

The young men in town also had a club, the Twentieth Century Club, which competed with the Leap Year Club in putting on gala events. February found these gentlemen sponsoring a Masquerade Ball. Apparently it was a very successful event. The Opera House was:

A summer day in 1903 caught this group of merrymakers at a picnic on the Green River. Sitting from left; Pete Gras, Celia ?, Ted Bishop, unknown. Standing from left: Charles Viox, Alida Peters, unknown, Nellie Peters, unknown, Nellie Dankowski, Mattie Mundt, unknown, unknown, unknown, Joseph Gras, unknown, James Thomson. (Photo courtesy Sweetwater County Historical Museum)

...packed from the doors to the stage and every character represented was cleverly carried out and merriment reigned during the entire evening. James Metcalf as the country gawk, was the course of much laughter, while Harry Kelley as the flashy colored gentleman was there with the goods and cleverly sustained his part.

It appears that in 1904 it was better for women to be heavily clothed and unassuming than creative as Davis indicates in his report. "The ladies were all modestly and tastely {sic} costumed and it would be hard to say which was the better as they were all so good."

These two groups continued to put on a series of dances and entertainments throughout the year. They also sponsored events together as indicated by this July 29 report:

The Leap Year Club and the Twentieth Century Club gave a joint party at the opera house

Tuesday evening which was pronounced the best entertainment of its character given this season. It commenced as early as 8 o'clock in the evening and lasted until the early hours of the following morning when all who attended retired to their homes worn and tired with their unlimited enjoyment. The evening was spent in dancing, cards, conversation and the partaking of refreshment, which had been crefully {sic} prepared by the young ladies. Prizes were awarded the most efficient lady and gentleman card players, while a beautiful cake was to have been awarded to the best lady and gentleman waltzers, but someone who no doubt is partial to cake, took the cake without effort, and the contesting parties are hot on the trail of the fellow who swipped {sic} the prize.

Other organizations held dances as well. The Green River Opera House hosted the Trainmen Ball in May. The event was sponsored by a union organization, the Brotherhood of Railroad Trainmen, and included visitors from Rock Springs and many other points along the rail line. The dancers partook of a midnight supper at the Overland Hotel on the south side of the tracks and then returned to dance "...until the streaks of dawn appeared in {sic} east."

Certain social events in Green River had a definite intellectual bent. Green River had a Literary Club made up of an older crowd of women intent on increasing the level of culture in town. Meetings of the Literary Club consisted of various presentations and discussions about a certain author. A biography of the chosen author was presented as well as a character sketch and recitations of his or her work. Selected authors for 1904 included Robert Browning and Nathaniel Hawthorne.

These more intellectual entertainments may today sound odd, if not downright boring, as demonstrated by the case of a party given by Mrs. H.V. Hilliker. The amusement was a flower guessing contest. The name of the flower was presented in a rebus, a riddle in which words or syllables are presented in the form of pictures or symbols.

Other popular entertainments were card parties. Progressive high-five and euchre were two games favored by adults and more youthful groups. Young ladies frequently held card parties for their friends while adults often attended as couples. These events frequently included musical selections and refreshments. It is perhaps somewhat apparent which of these parties were attended by Editor

Early twentieth century members of the St. John's Episcopal Church Ladies Guild pose with their children beside their church building which still stands on the corner of Second North and First East. Much of Green River's social life in 1904 centered around the churches in town. (Photo courtesy Sweetwater County Historical Museum)

Davis as there are much more detailed descriptions of the "clever hostess" and the "dainty and toothsome refreshments....".

Musical events played an important role in the social life of the town, as indicated by the presence of vocal and instrumental selections at events of all sorts. Indeed, entire evenings were dedicated to music. There must have been considerable actual, (or perceived) talent in the community because all of the entertainment at a January "musicale" was provided by local party-goers.

One of the most delightful social events of the winter was the Musicale given by Mesdames Richard Charnney and David Hodges at their home on Second South Street Wednesday evening. About sixty guests assembled at the invitation of these charming and delightful entertainers, and safe within the comfortable home speedily forgot the wild winter wind that was wildly raging without.

A solo was rendered by O.O. Davis himself along with numbers by E.A. Gaensslen and A.C. Werner. Several other guests performed piano numbers and Mrs. Hugo Gaensslen recited two pieces. The highlight of the evening was "...the cornet solos fur-nished by Mr. O.L. Fultz and the violin solos by Mr. W.V. Cassidy. These gentlemen are rare performers upon these instruments, and the heartiness by which they were encored showed the appreciation with which their music was received."

Occasionally a musical "expert" was brought into the community. A Musico-Literary recital was presented by Professor William ApMadoc in August. Davis described it as "... a departure in the cause of literary and musical education that we have never had so thoroughly presented to us before and the plea for intelligence in music, was a strong feature of the entertainment."

As frequently happens, the public response to this "education-al" event was poor. Davis lamented the light attendance:

> ...everybody should have heard him when
> they had the chance. The fact that more did not
> hear him will have no effect upon his reputation
> and standing as an instructor and entertainer, but it
> is simply our loss.

Some social events centered around church organizations. In 1904 church activity in Green River centered around three major congregations, the Union Congregational Church, St. John's Episcopal Church and the Immaculate Conception Catholic Church. The Ladies' Aid societies of these churches sponsored many events including an "Oriental Tea", Ice Cream Festival and assorted suppers and bazaars. The Congregational ladies seemed particularly adept at putting on unusual events. In August they sponsored a shoe social at which the price of admission to supper was determined by the measurement of one's foot. The following month was the left-hand social. The left hand was to be used during the whole party and those caught using their right were subjected to a fine and the laughter and teasing of all present.

As today, summer was the season for vacations. Visits to fam-ily in other areas were frequently undertaken as were trips to National Parks such as Yellowstone and Rocky Mountain. Davis offered some suggestions for the local teachers on how to best use their summer.

> We have not yet learned just how our teachers
> have planned to spend their vacation, but we are
> sure that it will be in some profitable way. A few

months at some nature's wonderful park, or a short
course in some specialty at some of our colleges, is
a wonderful help to the teacher already exausted
{sic} by the cares and monotony of the school
room...it is hoped that they may all be able to
return to their work built up for another year's
good labor.

Indeed it seems that Professor Wendt, the head schoolmaster
took his advice. Wendt returned from a holiday in Nebraska "looking well", and Davis indicated that "The professor will be able to
come down on the kids with several pounds more beef than usual
when school opens."
Outdoor events were also summertime fare. There were numerous picnics at Johnson (Expedition) Island and day trips out of
town were enjoyed by many. The July 1 issue reported:

A jolly crowd of twenty-five young people
went several miles up the river last Sunday and had
a very pleasant outing. The day was spent in hunting, fishing, target shooting, eating the delicious
lunch prepared by the girls, and having a good time
in general.

Some things never change as indicated by the fact that in 1904
summertime ball games were an abiding obsession for some.
Furthermore the most hotly contested games were those played
with Rock Springs teams. "We Skunked 'Em" proclaimed a
headline in the June 10 issue. The Green River baseball team
with the support of about fifty residents defeated their
Rock Springs opponents in what Davis proclaimed as "... the
most interesting game of the season....". The editor's partisanship
is very apparent in the following description from the June 10
issue:
It is certainly putting it mildly to say that the
game throughout was a hot affair ... but the Green
River lads were too formidable for the unfortunate
Rock Springer's and when the game closed it was
found that the visitors had completely routed
them .... when the game was finished the Rock
Springs boys looked as if they wished there had
been no witnesses of the game.

Davis also picked sides in defeat as demonstrated in a June 24 report:

> It is sufficient, however, to state that the Green
> River boys had four different men, players who did
> not play with the team when they put it all over
> Rock Springs two weeks ago. Had there been no
> misunderstanding, and the same boys had played
> which took part in the game at Rock Springs,
> Green River would have won hands down.

Holidays were always a reason to celebrate. Independence Day 1904 dawned to the accompaniment of firecrackers and gun and cannon shots. Davis waxed poetic in his description of a flag flying on top of Castle Rock:

> It was a beautiful sight to behold, stirring with-
> in us all the highest emotions of patriotism and
> love of country. No wonder no one dares to fire on
> that emblem of liberty, when it stirs the deepest
> emotions of the human heart.

The day's activities were sponsored by the local fire department and included a program, a parade of the citizenry led by a band and hose carts, horse races, a ball game, foot races for all ages, an egg race for women and a wheel barrow race for men. A boys band reminiscent of the one in the movie *Seventy-Six Trombones* had been created that summer and this event was their premier. Davis commented:

> The music furnished by the band before and
> during this program was appreciated by all and did
> great credit to its members and leader. But few
> could detect the fact that this band had only been
> organized but a little over a month.

With the coming of autumn the hunt became the activity of greatest interest. Several notices appear in the November 18 issue concerning the various successes of hunters. One man, Jesse Hardin, was so successful that he "...is wearing a larger hat now-a-days."

As the year drew to a close social events moved indoors and the holidays were celebrated with some of the same winter time activities seen at the beginning of the year. The Twentieth Century Club held a Thanksgiving dance and a masquerade ball during the week between Christmas Day and New Years Day. The Leap Year Club sponsored their last event with a dance on December 30. Davis warned:

> ...it being the last chance for the girls for four years every young man who attends will be in danger of a proposal. Well I guess the boys will all be there and run the chance of their lifetime.

The social round of Green River in 1904 doubtlessly provided citizens with a great deal of enjoyment, but it would be a mistake to consider that the entire life of the town. All too often history, viewed through the haze of nostalgia, becomes something it was not, the unfailingly "good old days."

Next month's *Echoes From the Bluffs* will examine a year in the "real" life of Green River 1904, the other side of the fun and frolic of a year in the social life.

❖

A Year in the Real Life: Green River – 1904

by Ruth Lauritzen

Last month we visited the social whirl of Green River in 1904 as viewed through the pages of the local weekly newspaper, the *Wyoming Star.* This activity was just a part of living in Green River. Editor O.O. Davis also chronicled the more practical, day-to-day concerns of life at the turn of the century.

A big news story in 1904 was the movement of the terminus of the Oregon Short Line to Green River. In the 1880s the Union Pacific built a branch line to the northwest to hook up with the Oregon Short Line, a line which extended into the Pacific Northwest. The terminus of this line was at Granger. The UP bought out the line and in March of 1904 Green River was named as the new terminal station. This meant considerably more switching took place in the Green River yards which created many new jobs and increased the town's importance as a rail center.

This good news created a fresh round of boosterism. The May 13th edition reported a rousing speech made by Robert C. Morris in support of seeking funding for a library from the Carnegie Foundation. In praising Green River's future he said:

> ...I want to say a few words about Green River. Unfortunately, it has been too much the habit of many people maintaining that Green River did not amount to much, and that sooner or later the railroad division would be moved to Granger or some other more desirable location. Recent events, however, encourage us to believe that Green River is going to be more of a town. Its definite location as the terminal station of both the

Union Pacific wrecker foreman Charles Lenhart poses with his equipment and crew in the early 1900s. The wrecker from the Green River yards responded to several 1904 train accidents. (Photo courtesy Sweetwater County Historical Museum)

> Union Pacific and Oregon Short Line railroads makes our city an important railroad division, bringing with it increased population and general improvement.

It was a bad year for the beleaguered town of Granger. Not only did they lose their designation as a railroad terminal but in June they suffered a fire which, Davis said, "...almost puts an end to a town that once was thought by many would be a division point of the Union Pacific...." Two saloons, a hotel and two houses were destroyed at a loss of $6000.

In May the *Star* reported improvements were being made in the running of the Green River post office. After much public complaint closing time was changed from six to seven p.m. and it was agreed to expedite the transfer of the mail from the railroad to the post office so that citizens would not have to wait "... a half hour or more ...." to get their mail.

The turn of the century was a time of great social reform in the United States. These ideas came to Green River in the form of the presentation of Ten Nights in a Barroom at the Green River Opera House. The play addressed the evils of drinking alcohol. According to Davis the presentation "...is endorsed by the clergy and the press. It is pure, moral and instructive. Every mother, father, young man, sweetheart and child should see this production played just as it was written."

Any news about the railroad was a big story in town. There were reported train wrecks at Hallville, a rail stop about fifty miles east of Green River; Carter near Fort Bridger; and in the town's own railyard. The last incident resulted in the loss of two cars and some freight but no injuries were reported. Davis gave warning, "The train was moving no faster than an ordinary walk and it is a caution how such damage could be done considering how slow the train was moving." This tale of caution was not one to be taken lightly in a town split in half by an unfenced railyard.

An indication that the West was still quite wild was a note in the May 27th issue which stated that guards were being placed on express trains to prevent hold ups. It seems that this was a wise precaution as just four years before the famous outlaw Butch Cassidy attempted a robbery at Tipton in the eastern part of Sweetwater County. According to the legend after blowing up the express car the bandits found only $50.40 in the safe. Cassidy and his Wild Bunch were just one of many gangs operating in the area in the early 1900s and robbery and rustling were still quite rampant.

In August there is mention of a fake robbery attempt perpetrated by a railroad employee, James Utley. He claimed that he had broken up a robbery attempt and in the process was shot from a distance by the would-be outlaws. Because of suspicious powder bums on his skin and the lack of any evidence to indicate the presence of outlaws his story was proved to be a fabrication in an attempt to gain prestige and perhaps an award for himself.

The newspaper also reported tragedies of a more personal nature. Townspeople experienced everything from fire cracker bums on the Fourth of July to the loss of a limb due to a railroad accident. There were deaths from consumption (tuberculosis) and scarlet fever. On the more joyous side, recoveries from serious illnesses and accidents were reported as well as numerous marriages and births. There was even good news from the sporting front. An item appeared in the December 9th issue which stated "Foot-ball is certainly moderating - only three players were badly hurt in Chicago last Sunday and but one is reported dead in Iowa."

Green River of 1904 was a town of triumphs and tragedies, very much like the town today. Situations and incidents have most certainly changed, but as history often shows, the human condition remains very much the same. ❖

A Lady Named Grace

by Marna Grubb

Throughout our community one finds many people who contribute to making Green River a great place to live. One such person is Grace (Gravelle) Gasson. Grace is remembered by many as the friendly, efficient personality who worked for many years at the Sweetwater County Library in Green River, formerly the Carnegie Public Library.

Grace has lived her entire life in Green River, the daughter of Mr. and Mrs. George G. Gravelle, Jr. (deceased). She has an older sister, Mareese (Gravelle) Morck of Monroe, Washington, and an older brother Gail Gravelle of Boise, Idaho (deceased).

Grace's grandfather, George G. Gravelle, Sr., came from France to Canada and then to the United States. He came to Green River

Grace Gravelle Gasson retired in 1986 as Director of the Sweetwater County Library System, a position she held for 25 of 39 years of service.

George G. Gravelle's apothecary shop was built in 1872 and was located at 45 East Railroad Avenue. The store which carried a full line of medicine and "notions" was later renamed Campbell Drug. (Photo courtesy Grace Gasson)

from South Pass, when they moved the county seat, and opened an apothecary shop and drug store in 1872 at what is now a vacant lot at 45 East Railroad Avenue, where he administered his professional skills as a druggist. George Sr. married Martha (Scott) Baker in 1876 who recently had been widowed. But the marriage was short lived as George Gravelle, Sr. died in 1878 of a kidney ailment.

On July 10, 1876, the *Laramie Weekly Sentinel* reported that "On Saturday last we were at Green River and spent a pleasant time among our numerous friends in that thriving village. It is making some progress and growth in the way of substantial improvements and building. Material is being got upon the ground for the new Court House which will be a fine building."

The *Sentinel* continued with "Capt. J.W. Ward is building a first class hotel which will soon be completed and in full blast. In fact it is in full blast now, judging by the number of guests and patrons who repairs there for rations."

Also, "Judge Fields is doing a good mercantile business, besides farming, stockraising, etc. Green River is already a favorite stopping point for tourists and pleasure seekers. The scenery around it is grand and it furnishes abundant sport for hunters and fishermen."

Then it reported in 1876 that "Dr. Gravelle keeps a drug store well stocked, not only with drugs but miscellaneous goods and notions. Though he only professes to be a druggist and chemist, he is compelled to do all the medical practice in that region, which gives him his hands full."

George Gideon Gravelle, Jr. (Grace's father) was born on October 15, 1877. His father, George Sr., died in 1878, when George Jr. was only three months old; therefore, he never really knew his father. George Jr. completed his schooling in Green River and then journeyed to the University of Wyoming for training to become a druggist.

Martha (Baker) Gravelle learned the drug business and served the public from 1878 to 1910. After George Sr. died, she married Henry Campbell in 1881 and the business was changed to the Campbell Drug.

Shortly after T.S. Taliaferro came to Green River from Virginia, he and Mrs. Campbell began the nucleus of St. John's Episcopal Church. They began the construction of old St. John's in 1892 and it was completed for Easter Sunday 1893. Bishop J.P. Spaulding held the service. This beautiful church is still standing at 27 W. 2nd North. Mr. and Mrs. R.H. Lawrence had sold Lot 6, Block 5 for $175 on December 1891 for the construction of the church.

Martha (Baker) Gravelle had four children (one each from her first two marriages and two from her third marriage). In 1873, while married to William Baker, she had Martha Baker who married Dr. John Gilligan in 1891. In 1877, as mentioned previously she had George Gravelle, Jr., who married Grace's mother in 1902. In 1882, while married to Henry Campbell, she had Hattie Campbell who married William Hutton in 1903; and, in 1885, she had Madeline Campbell who married Bernard Kincaid in 1906. These four marriages would have fascinating stories of their own.

Henry Campbell died in 1894. George Gravelle, Jr. came back to help his mother with the drug store. Mrs. Campbell died in 1910.

George Gravelle, Jr. married Mable Rumble in 1902 and they had three children, one of which was Grace. George Gravelle, Jr. died in 1918 at the age of 40.

Grace began working part-time at the Library during her last two years of high school. She went full-time when she graduated - a total of 39 years. She retired in 1986 as Director of the Sweetwater County Library System, a position she held with great esteem for 25 of those years.

In 1951 Grace married Franklin Gasson. They had one son, Walter, who now lives in Cheyenne. Walter married Kim

Greenbaum, also formerly of Green River. Grace now has three grandchildren - Jennifer, Elizabeth and Sarah. Grace's husband, Franklin Gasson, died in 1967.

Franklin Gasson had an uncle, Henry Franklin, who was one of the large sheep and cattle operators in Sweetwater County. He was a major stockholder in the Green River State Bank and also of the First National Bank, which it was called after its name change in 1915. He served on the Board and as Vice President of both banks. He served on the Green River town council and owned numerous properties in Green River. His home, built in 1889, was located at what is now 11 E. 2nd N. It was a Sears, Roebuck & Co. mail order house. When Franklin died, his wife, Ida married Jack Grundell, a locomotive engineer from Evanston. Ida and Jack were avid rock hunters and decorated their yard with petrified wood, geodes and various other rocks from this area (which is still an attractive display at this location). Some of these were made into bird baths with half geodes on top for the bath. When the Grundells died, the house became the property of Franklin and Grace Gasson. This is where Grace (Gravelle) Gasson lives today. The interior is very attractive and well kept. A bay window extends from the living room on the west side of the home.

Grace, along with her ancestors, have played an interesting and important part of Green River history.

CCC Camp Green River

by James W. June

The first CCC units from Wyoming were drawn from Laramie, Platte, Goshen and Albany counties. Conservation projects included improvement cuttings in forests, insect control, trail building, road construction and maintenance, campground improvements, fence building, fire fighting and other related work.

One Wyoming project was the gathering of wood ticks for a study to help develop the serum for Rocky Mountain tick fever.

The CCC camps received young men who enlisted for a six-month period, with the option of re-enlistment up to a maximum of two-years. The enrollee was paid $30 per month of which $25 was sent to his family. The remaining $5 could be used for personal expenses. At a time when cigarettes were 10 cents a pack and roast beef 10 cents per pound, a five-dollar bill fit comfortably in the wallet.

The Federal Government provided housing, food, clothing, medical care and tools.

Ratings were given men who had shown capabilities in certain fields and in leadership. Two red chevrons on a man's right sleeve indicated that he was rated as an assistant leader. Three chevrons indicated he was a leader, the highest rating possible to an enrollee in the CCC.

The Green River CCC Camp was authorized April 1, 1938. Lieutenant Hardman of the Farson CCC Camp inspected the Green River site located on the land of the Wyoming Soda Products Company in the southeast part of the city. This site was located north of the river, north and west of the Wagon Bridge, and east of what is now South Third East Street.

During late April of 1938, work was started on cleaning the grounds of weeds, debris, etc. and laying sewer and water lines for buildings to be erected. The camp, established with the members of

In 1938 the Green River CCC Camp was established southeast of the Green River. The Wyoming Soda Products Company light and power plant can be seen in the background. (Photo courtesy Sweetwater County Historical Museum)

CCC Company 3699, arrived at Green River CCC Camp in July, 1938.

The camp had approximately 188 men. It was composed of men principally from Chicago. The average age ranged from 17 to 20 years old. One hundred thirty-three of them were recruited at Camp McCoy, Wisconsin, on July 11, 1938. The camp was formed of an experienced group of 33 men from Marseilles, Illinois, who came to Green River on July 21, 1938. The Camp Commander was Lt. Van Oosten, assisted by junior officer, Second Lt. Mueller who also was in charge of the mess.

The camp consisted of four barracks housing 48 men each. The officers buildings were for the commander, assistant commander, chaplin, and other leaders. There were two bath and toilet houses, mess hall and kitchen, chapel, club house building, medical and dental building and storage buildings.

Second Lt. Mueller, who was in charge of the mess, was assisted by four cooks and a mess steward, who had charge of preparing the food. The cook's pay was $36 or $45 per month depending whether he was a second or first cook. Two cooks, a second and first cook worked on alternating days. The cook's day began at 3:30 or 4:00 a.m. and worked from 14 to 15 consecutive hours. It took 3 to 4 hours to prepare a meal.

The cook's sole responsibility was to feed the entire company, direct K.P.s in the kitchen and dining room, and to keep the kitchen spotlessly clean. The cook prepared meals according to a fixed ration allowance which was 42 cents per man per day.

The principal work at first was camp construction and improvement. Stone walks were laid, buildings improved, ground cleared of all debris, pipe and sewer lines completed, installation of roads and general beautification was done.

One of the Green River CCC Camp projects in 1938 was the construction of an ice skating pond just east of the CCC Camp and north of the Utah Power and Light Plant.

In January, 1939, the Green River CCC Camp started dismantling the old county bridge across Black's Fork River. This bridge was the old Lincoln Highway Bridge crossing Black's Fork. This bridge was hauled to the Green River crossing site in northwestern Sweetwater County. The last of this bridge was re-erected by the Kemmerer CCC Camp, which started construction of the bridge abutments in January, 1938. This bridge was for the access to the Little Colorado winter range by stockmen.

While dismantling of the old county highway bridge in 1938, the Green River CCC company built a wooden bridge across Black's Fork River at the Paravicini Ranch for easier access to the old Lincoln Highway and to Green River.

Other projects of the Green River CCC Camp included building a reservoir at Spring Creek for water storage along the stock driveway between Manila and Green River and improvement and construction of the Blue Rim road. They surveyed and built the White Mountain Road from Green River to U.S. Highway 187 at Fourteen Mile Hill, which followed the historic old Green River-Lander stage road. They did road improvements south of Green River and Rock Springs, built reservoirs for water storage, and trail improvement for livestock for Taylor Grazing (BLM). They worked on reforestation, trail and campground construction in forest areas. They also fought range and forest fires.

When Pearl Harbor was bombed on December 7, 1941, the beginning of World War II, the members of the CCC Camps went to serve their country with honor and distinction. The Green River CCC Camp and other camps were officially out of business on June 30, 1942. Everyone, including the critics of the CCC, had to admit that the CCC served its country well.

❖

Green River Wagon Bridge

by James W. June

The site of the city of Green River has provided a natural camping and crossing area of the Green River for ages, being first used by the Indians. The Green River at this location had gravel beds on the bottom which furnished stable foundation and low waters for crossings. Jim Bridger knew of these Indian Trails and crossings and showed Howard Stansbury this area in 1852.

With the establishment of the Overland Stage Route in 1862, all the Transcontinental, Overland and Southern traffic crossed the Green River by using the Overland Stage ford and ferry until 1896. These were downstream and east of the old wagon bridge site. The traffic then followed the Overland Stage route up Telephone Canyon to the West.

This was the first wagon bridge to be built across the entire width of the Green River. The first bridge to span the Green River was the Union Pacific Railroad Bridge built in 1868. It was not until 1910 that a wagon bridge spanned the Green River at Green River, Utah. Also in 1910, the Big Island Bridge was built across the Green River at Big Island above the Town of Green River. In June, 1911, a bridge was also built across the Green River at Jensen, Utah.

In March, 1896, the Town of Green River received a proposal from Sweetwater County to construct a bridge across the Green River to the south of town. The county proposed that the county and the town each pay $2,000 towards the total cost of the bridge. The Town of Green River later paid an additional $675 because an added span length was found necessary to be added to the bridge.

On April 20, 1896, the Sweetwater County commissioners called for bids for construction of a two-span bridge across the Green River at the Town of Green River, Wyoming. The bid was awarded to the Wrought Iron Bridge Company of Clinton, Ohio.

The 1896 Wagon Bridge at Green River, Wyoming on June, 1950, looking north from the south side of the bridge. (Photo courtesy of Fern Gaensslen)

The bridge was a single lane, two-span, iron structure with a wooden deck and wooden through truss, reinforced with iron rods. A through truss bridge is one that the traffic is carried along the bottom chords of the structure and one appears to travel through the truss. Truss bridges are characterized by a structural assemblage of many relatively small members joined together in a series of triangles that interconnect to form the bridge. The truss bridge was popular because of the comparative ease of fabricating, hauling and assembling the individual members. The north bridge abutment was and can still be seen at the end of South Fifth East Street, which was the highway or road to cross the bridge. The south bridge abutment can be seen on the south side of the river just south of the piers. The piers were filled with concrete and reinforced with iron rods, remnants of which still can be seen in and along the river.

In 1913, with the use of the automobile and the establishment of the transcontinental travel, the wagon bridge was used by the Lincoln Highway, which was later designated as the U.S. Route 30, until 1922. The Lincoln Highway entered the town in the east and came on North First Street (Flaming Gorge Way) to Elizabeth Street (North First East Street), then south crossing the railroad tracks to South First Street (South Second Street), then east to East Fifth South Street to the bridge.

In 1954, Sweetwater County demolished the old Wagon Bridge because it had become unsafe and a hazard to the public. (Photo courtesy Sweetwater County Historical Museum)

In 1922, the Wyoming State Highway Department built a new highway bridge across the Green River west of the Town of Green River. They then changed the route of the Lincoln Highway (U.S. 30) west through the town on North First Street (Flaming Gorge Way), past Tollgate Rock to the new bridge.

The 1896 Wagon Bridge also provided better access from the Henry's Fork and Lucerne valleys to the railroad and the Town of Green River. It also helped to the development of the trans-Uinta mountain road to the Ashley Valley and Vernal. The bridge continued to serve the Ashley, Henry's Fork, Lucerne, Burntfork and the south country areas until 1951.

The Wyoming Highway Department in 1951, built the Wyoming Highway 530 Bridge across the Green River, east of the Wagon Bridge site.

In 1954, Sweetwater County demolished the old Wagon Bridge across the Green River because it had become unsafe and a hazard to the public.

The remains of the old 1896 Wagon Bridge are the north and south bridge abutments and the remnants of the bridge pier. The north bridge abutment exists on the north bank at South Fifth East Street. The south bridge abutment exists on the south bank, south of the bridge pier. The bridge pier can be readily identified in the river during low water. The bridge pier serves as a gauge for water flow in the river for the local residents, when it is covered with water, the river is at the high water stage.

❖

Remembering Days Gone By with Dale and Ethel Morris

by Marna Grubb

In each community there are some people who do not ask what their community can do for them, but what they can do for their community. One such couple is Dale (Peggy or Peg) and Ethel Morris who have given much to Green River and have enjoyed doing so.

One of the first questions that comes to mind is, "Why is Dale known by many as Peg or Peggy instead of Dale?"

Dale said that when he was about seven years old he teased Francis Viox about having a girl's name, so Francis and Dr. Gaensslen gave Dale his nickname of "Peggy" - since the song "Peggy O'Neil" was popular at that time - and the name has followed him throughout the years.

Dale Morris was born in Missouri in 1916. He moved to Green River when he was three years old with his family - stepfather Al Morris and mother Nina Morris. They first lived in the house on the corner west of the Brewery with his grandmother Morris. They had no electricity and used coal oil lamps.

When 12 years old, Dale walked around town delivering bakery goods for Johnny Saleen. Dale had one half sister and three half brothers. He graduated from Green River High School in 1936. He was employed by the Union Pacific Railroad for 40 years and was Yardmaster when he retired in 1975.

In 1918, Ethel Hill was born in Rock Springs in a house behind the Elk's Home on "D" Street. Her father and mother were Robert and Mary Hill.

Robert worked for the water company owned by the U.P. Coal Company. When Ethel was two years old, her family moved to Kanda (which was a pump station for the water line to Rock Springs and a section for the Railroad).

St. John's Episcopal Church choir in 1942 on steps of their first church on Second North. Left to right, top row: Dale Morris, unidentified, and Doug Johnson. Second row: Catherine Callahan, Mary Burnaugh, Gladys Casteel, unidentified, unidentified. Third row: Betty Waechter, Thelma Thornhill, Clara Jensen, Ethel Morris, and Margaret Lenhart Logan. Fourth row: Reverend C. L. Callahan, Herb Lewis, Bud Burnaugh and Jimmy Lowe. (Photo courtesy Dale and Ethel Morris)

Ethel's sister, Edith, was born at Kanda. When Ethel was five years old, the family moved from Kanda to Green River. They first lived by the Water Pump Station in a house which has since been moved to South 2nd East and currently is used as a training house by the Green River Volunteer Fire Department.

Ethel attended schools in Green River and graduated in 1936 from Green River High School. Dale and Ethel started dating the summer before their senior year. Dale was class president and Ethel was vice president. Dale reports that, since their marriage, "the roles have changed!"

Ethel had five sisters (twin sisters died as babies) and two brothers- Glenn Hill, Green River's Fire Chief from 1965 to 1995, and Robert Hill of Caldwell, Idaho.

Remains of Green River High School after fire destroyed the entire building, except the gymnasium, in October of 1940. (Photo courtesy Sweetwater County Historical Museum)

Dale Morris married Ethel Hill in 1936 and raised three daughters. Their middle daughter, Barbara, died in 1958 from surgery complications while she was a student nurse in Denver. The other two daughters - Marilyn (Morris) Casteel and Karen (Morris) McDaniel - are married and live in Texas. Dale and Ethel have three grandsons.

Ethel also worked for the Union Pacific Railroad. She was employed in 1956 and retired in 1980 for a total of 24 years. At the time of her retirement, she was district clerk in the Mechanical Department.

When Dale and Ethel were married, they wanted to buy a house on North 5th West, so they visited Mr. Chrisman at the First National Bank for a loan. The price of the house was $1700 and they needed $200 down, which they didn't have. So Mr. Chrisman said, if they could borrow the $200 from Mrs. Chrisman, they could get the loan - so that is how they paid the $200 down. House payments were $25 per month.

While their girls were growing up, Ethel was a Girl Scout leader for 15 years and a 4-H leader for approximately six years. She is a Past Matron of the Eastern Star.

While Ethel was a Scout leader, she noticed information in a magazine regarding the selling of Girl Scout cookies as a fundraiser. Thinking this was a good idea, Ethel spent $50 and ordered cookies, storing them in their basement until the girls could pick them up for selling.

Then they had a water leak and the water came to within two inches of the cookies, although she reports that not one of the cookies was destroyed. This was the beginning of Girl Scout cookie sales in Green River.

Ethel was active in the Altar Guild for St. John's Episcopal Church for approximately 20 years and a member of St. John's Guild for 20 years. She has helped with St. John's Thrift Shop since its startup in 1964 by Mrs. C.L. Callahan in its original location west of the Teton Cafe building.

Dale was a member of the Green River Volunteer Fire Department for 15 years in the 1930s and 1940s when Roy Cameron (Manager of the Telephone Company) was chief. Whenever there was a fire, the railroad fire whistle blew and all the firemen ran for the fire truck. They received $2 a call.

Dale's most memorable fire was the night the Green River High School burned in October of 1940. Dale lived close to the High School and when he was called, he looked out the door and could see the school was flaming high in the night sky.

Before the night was over, three fire departments (Green River, Union Pacific and Rock Springs Station No. 2) and dozens of volunteers battled against unbeatable odds - and the Green River High School was gone - all except the gymnasium, which is still there today.

Dale and Ethel have been faithful members of St. John's Episcopal Church for many years. They have sung in church choirs and served on committees. Dale helped with the Shrove Tuesday pancake supper, and he is general handyman and helper for St. John's Thrift Shop. Dale served on the Vestry for 23 years.

Dale and Ethel are members of the Sweetwater County Historical Society. Dale is a Past President of the local Society and served as President of the Wyoming State Historical Society from September 1991 to September 1992.

Dale has served the City of Green River on the Planning and Zoning Commission and the Board of Adjustment. He was honored in 1987 as Green River's Outstanding Citizen.

Dale was elected three times to the School District No. 2 Board and served 12 years. He also was appointed twice to fill vacancies until the next regular election. He served as clerk for six years.

He has been an active member and past president of the Green River Lion's Club. He was active in their public assistance programs and fundraisers, such as pancake breakfasts and popcorn sales.

For several years, at the beginning of its development, Dale was a member of the Mansface Terrace Board of Directors. He also is active in the Golden Hour Senior Citizens, having been a member of the Board of Directors for several years and past president. He helped with the Center's monthly public breakfasts. (Pancakes seem to play an important part in Dale's life!)

He is a former Scoutmaster for Boy Scout Troop #1, a member and former Green River Finance Chairman for the American Red Cross, a member of the Board of Directors and Past President of the Union Pacific Old Timers Club.

Dale is a member and Past Master of Mt. Moriah Lodge #6 and various other Masonic bodies. He has been a Shriner for 48 years. Dale recently served three years on the Castle Rock Medical Center Board.

For 25 consecutive years, Dale performed as Jolly Old St. Nick for various families, churches and civic organizations.

Dale and Ethel reminisced of their many fond memories of growing up in Green River.

"There was the Meadow Brook Dairy with Mr. Dillon and the horse-drawn wagon making the daily delivery of bottled milk and picking up the empty bottles.

"Sweetwater Brewing Company cut ice from the river and stored it in the ice house on South 5th West. In the summer, they sold ice. If you wanted it you put a sign 'ICE' in your window and the ice truck supplied you with how many pounds you needed.

"Grocery stores had home deliveries. You could call the store, order your groceries and they would be delivered to your home. Most people charged their groceries and paid the bill at the end of each month. When you paid your bill at the store, the owner gave you a bag of candy.

"While growing up, there were no shots to prevent contagious diseases. However, to keep an epidemic from spreading, the doctors quarantined the houses with a sign. White was for measles; red was for scarlet fever and diphtheria. Everyone respected the signs and they kept diseases from spreading.

"When Peg was 10 years old he got coal and wood in for several people, then took the ashes out. For this they would give him 5 or 10 cents.

"This job came to an end in 1929 when natural gas came to Green River. Many people converted their stoves to gas. The gas company put the gas burner and 'doughnuts' in the old stoves - no more coal, wood and ashes, just open the valve for heat to cook and heat."

Dale and Ethel both have many beautiful memories of growing up in Green River, with many cherished relatives and friends. They have seen many changes, such as the "slow down" of the Union Pacific and the birth of the "Trona Mines."

And - their plans for the future - "Even though retired, we choose to stay in our beloved Green River."

Valentines from the
Past Relived

by Ruth Lauritzen

As the most romantic of holidays, St. Valentine's Day, quickly approaches lovers may take heed to the proven methods of the past for winning the heart of their beloved. What follows is an article reprinted from a February 1918 issue of the *Green River Star.*

A cynic once remarked that the two most irritating days on the calendar were those consecrated to Saints Swithin and Valentine, because, said he, the first often brought with it a strain; for, of all strains in the world, he argued, the worst was that imposed by having to read a silly lot of foolish and useless valentines.

The cynic probably does not stand alone in his opinion of Saint Valentine's day. There are thousands of men like him who believe that the day had degenerated; that, where once Cupid conquered hearts through loving missives sent on February 14, he now merely yawns and fails to heed.

But does he? Have the old valentines, as love messages, really lost their power? Or have new kinds of valentines succeeded the flimsy lace kind of other years? And are they at all effective?

The printed chronicles of the last several years reveal numerous cases that go to disprove the statement of the cynic and his followers.

On Saint Valentine's day, 1908, Arthur Trumbull of Oswego, N.Y., sent a young woman named Alice Cayvan, whom he had been courting with indifferent success for several years, a large heart fashioned out of crimson cardboard.

Through the heart he had stuck a papier mache arrow. On it he had written the single interrogatory word "Hopeless?" The next day the heart was returned to him by mail; but the arrow had been removed and the hole in the center had been patched up with a bit of white paper on which Miss Cayvan had written a clearly legible "Yes." They were married soon after.

Not less productive of result was the effort of Albert Hildrummel of Topeka, Kan., who, according to an article printed in Western newspapers, sent the young woman he loved, Clara Sedgwick, a blank marriage certificate on last Valentine's day with these verses on the back:

> *This is my idea of a valentine,*
> *Practical, indeed, but true.*
> *If you'll write your name on it,*
> *It will be a valentine for two.*

It is interesting to note that the recipient did as directed. An odd valentine was that sent two years ago by Francis Everlin of Chicago to Sarah Collins of Toledo, Ohio.

Everlin had asked the latter to marry him on numerous occasions; but the young woman had always asked him to refrain from regarding her otherwise than "a sister." Everlin had no such intention; however, and, biding his time till Valentine's day, sent her a valentine made up to resemble a ballot such as is used in municipal elections.

At the top of the ballot was a pen and ink picture of a house, and beneath appeared Everlin's name opposite all the offices to be voted for, viz., rentpayer, bundle carrier, loving husband, and so on.

A slip was appended asking the voter to vote the straight ticket. Whether it was the humor of it or something else is unknown; but the fact remains that Miss Collins put the matrimonial X under the house.

The "missing-line" puzzle craze gave Herbert Randall of San Francisco his valentine cue in 1907. To his sweetheart, Vera Salison of the same city, he sent this incomplete stanza, asking her to fill out the last line. The verse ran:

"It might have been" are saddest words
In world of woe and love and strife;
For thee, these are the gladdest words:"

The stanza was returned the following day with this line: *"Yes, dear, I now will be your wife."*

One of the most peculiar valentines on record was the one sent a year ago by Allen Straw of Pittsburgh to Louise Rovayer of Erie. It was nothing more or less than a large roll of white silk, bearing the words: "This is for a wedding dress. Please valentine me with a 'yes'." The silken valentine was effective.

On Valentine's day three years ago two men sent their sweethearts railroad timetables to Niagara Falls, and another man sent his lady love a trunk tied with white ribbons and strewn inside with rice.

John Thomas Ray of Omaha won a wife through a valentine sent to a young woman living in St. Louis. Ray's valentine took the form of a big red apple, to the stem of which he had attached a card reading: "Love me and a world of happiness shall be yours. Love me not, and all that you will have will be this apple. It is big and red and pretty, but it will not last any more than will the semihappiness you believe you are enjoying while single."

The popular jigsaw puzzles were used as valentines by several wooers last year. One man, named Shaw, of Atlanta, sent one to his sweetheart in the same city and with it the lines: "I've puzzled my brain to guess your answer. Won't you put me in shape again with a 'Yes'?"

The girl sent the valentine puzzle back with a note that read: "I do not want this puzzle. I'll give you myself. I have been a puzzle, I admit; but I'm going to solve myself for you."

Another man, Stanley Lemoyne of Denver, sent one of the puzzles as a valentine to Rhea Knowles of the same town, with the note: "This will help pass away the dull hours for you in case you refuse to marry me." The girl married him.

Old valentines, these, indeed: but odder still the valentine sent in 1906 by Reynolds Touhey of New York to May Lindstrom of Brooklyn, a valentine that succeeded in leading the latter to the altar. Touhey's valentine was a Dresden doll baby, and attached to it was a card reading: "Imagine having nothing more real than this all your life!"

– The Sunday Magazine.

❖

Steamboat Comin'
The Comet

by James W. June

The Green River Navigation Company was formed by some Green River and Linwood businessmen on March 18, 1908. The company set up a steamboat line to carry passengers and freight between Green River, Wyoming and Linwood, Utah. Their certificate of incorporation stated "...the object of carrying on and conduct of a general transportation by water upon the Green River, a tributary of the Colorado River."

The stockholders of the Green River Navigation Company were Marius Larson, Niels Pallesen, George Solomon, J.H. Crosson, J.W. Chrisman, Oscar Engberg, O.O. Davis, and Hugo Gaensslen.

Linwood stockholder M.H. Larsen brought his brother, Holger Larsen, who was a steamboat builder in Germany, to build the steamboat. Holger inspected the river and stated that steamboat travel was feasible, and he could build the boat.

He went to Chicago and purchased the engines, boilers, and materials. Upon returning to Green River, he set up a ship yard on the bank of the river.

By late May, 1908, the iron frame had been completed, which was a point of interest and pride to the residents of Green River.

Work on the new steamboat progressed rapidly and by the Fourth of July, 1908, the craft, at a cost of $25,000, was christened the "Comet." Crew members and passengers were invited to board the new steamboat to look at the boat. It was reported by the *Star* that "she proudly and gracefully moved out into midstream with the Green River Band playing lively air, and the crowds on the banks cheering loudly at her good behavior."

The Comet, a stern-wheeler steamboat, voyaged down the Green River in 1908. (Photo courtesy Sweetwater County Historical Museum)

The Comet was a stern-wheeler steamboat, 60 feet in length, 12 feet in width, with a 40 ton stern wheeler, a 60-horsepower boiler and two 20-horsepower engines.

The boat was so arranged for ample room for the pilot house, cabin, passenger and freight departments, compact and every convenience necessary for plying the waters of the Green River.

On July 7, 1908, the Comet set off on her maiden voyage down the river to Linwood, Utah. Round trip tickets were $5.

The crew included Holger Larsen as the pilot; M.H. Larsen, purser; J.H. Crosson, coal detective; J.W. Chrisman, chief engineer; Oscar Engberg, assistant engineer; George Solomon, anchor man; O.O. Davis, diving bell; Hugo Gaensslen, wireless operator; and Mrs. A.O. Neilson, chief of the commissary.

There was no record of the anchor or the diving bell being used. The wireless operator kept the crew and passengers informed of William Jennings Bryan's successful bid for presidential nomination at the Democratic convention in Denver.

The chief of commissary served very delicious meals and was kept busy replenishing the crew and passengers with beer from the Sweetwater Brewing Company.

Eight hours after casting off, the Comet was moored at the Linwood landing.

The next day, the Comet departed Linwood on the return trip to Green River, but it took 33 hours to reach its destination. The Comet had to be winched over many sandbars and barriers.

Several times passengers had to help unload cargo to lighten the load to cross sandbars. On the return trip, the Comet ran out of fuel several times and had to wait for fuel to be hauled to the steamboat.

The coal detective and crew members had to leave the steamboat and commandeered pack horses and coal from ranches and farms along the river to replace the fuel supply.

The *Star* hailed the steamboat a success and the Green River as navigable, even if the return trip from Linwood took 33 hours actual running time. Plans were made, at various points, to establish coaling stations and other improvements for the freight and passenger business along the route.

The Comet made several trips with passengers and freight to Linwood, Utah, during the summer. The company, later in the summer, supplemented its freighting revenue with all-day excursions, with the passengers furnishing their own lunches.

The Comet crew had dwindled to three. Trips on the Green River were long and arduous and the passengers were called upon to unload and load the cargo to lighten the steamboat across sandbars.

After a very difficult pleasure excursion up to Big Piney in the fall of 1908, the company decided that the Green River was impractical for a steamboat.

The Comet was stripped and the hull sank into the river on the north bank below the present Wyoming Highway 530 Bridge and above the "tie booms".

The Comet's ship bell was salvaged by J.H. Crosson, the ship's coal detective and kept in his family. Later the bell was donated and used by the Green River Lion's Club. The club would ring the bell to signal the start of its meeting.

The bell was destroyed in a fire that swept through the club's meeting place, the Covered Wagon Inn (Sweetwater Martha's), which was four miles west of the Town of Green River, in October 1962.

❖

Old GR Cemetery
Once Located
at Library Site

by James W. June

The first cemetery of the Town of Green River began in 1868 and was used until 1913 when the town established the Riverview Cemetery. This photo was taken between 1921 and 1926. The homes in Virginia Circle in the upper left corner were built in 1921 and the cemetery was moved in 1926. (Photo courtesy Sweetwater County Historical Museum)

Green River's first cemetery was at 300 North First East Street, formerly Elizabeth Street, now the location of the Sweetwater County Library.

A cemetery was started in 1862 on the south bank of the river, east of the Green River Stage Station, which was used until the establishment of the Green River City in 1868.

S.I. Field established the lots for a cemetery in the city on his original plat of the town. There are no records existing of the burial ground because the records of territorial Green River are missing from the town files.

It is assumed that they were destroyed in the fire of 1917. The city records from 1891 on were saved from the fire.

In 1892, the Town Council records of March, show that the council ordered a new survey of the cemetery to be made, approved a road to it, and also a water line to the cemetery.

With the growth of the town, and the need for additional burial space, the 1913 Town Council records show the council passed a resolution to purchase 80 acres of land from the U.S. Government for a new cemetery. The Riverview Cemetery has been in use from 1913 to the present day.

In 1926, the town, with funds from a federal CWA project, transferred the bodies and old grave markers from the old cemetery to the Riverview Cemetery. A 1926 ordinance adopted by the Town Council shows that they wanted to remove all graves.

The area was to have been "cleared of every obstruction" the ordinance reads, "so that the said streets and alley may be used without let or hindrance as public highways of said town."

Thus all of the known graves and grave markers were moved to the present cemetery. Also, many unmarked graves located during this project were put into common graves, there are several with 13 to 14 bodies in a grave site.

The old cemetery site was used as a park after the removal of the graves until 1944.

During 1944 with veterans coming home from World War II, a temporary housing project was built on this site for the returning servicemen and their families to live. During the construction of the project, eight to ten graves were found and moved to Riverview Cemetery.

The identities of the bodies were unknown. Marna Grubb relates seeing one of the bodies, which was just a skeleton, wearing an old western style, fringed leather jacket and still having a red beard.

Edward Taliaferro told of the time when one of three children were out playing and brought home a human skull. The children lived in Virginia Circle which is just east and next to the cemetery site.

In 1978, the county purchased the site to build a new Sweetwater County Library. During the construction of the library, 12 bodies were found in unmarked graves. Also during construction, a skull with tufts of brown hair was found, these remains were also re-interred in the Riverview Cemetery.

During structural work that was necessary to the library building in 1985-86, a coffin with a child's body and several other bone remains were uncovered. Again, these were moved to the Riverview Cemetery.

When the construction of the new library in 1978 started, tales and rumors of historic tragedy mingled with superstition of medical science fiction created speculation about the site. Records of the original burials and attempts to relocate the bodies were not available, but the memories of long-time residents provide some clues.

One of the rumors was that reopening the graveyard by the con-struction would release germs buried with epidemic victims, which occurred during 1868-1900. These germs or epidemics varied from smallpox, black smallpox, scarlet fever, "those germs," etc.

An area in the cemetery called "Grader's Row" purportedly gave railroad workers the various epidemics during work around the unmarked graves. Some old timers say the graves were not moved because city workers were afraid to "touch them because of the danger of some of the germs coming back to life."

The graves may have been too hard to find.

When the rumors first surfaced, the Wyoming Department of Health and Medical Service said the germs "have long since died." Some inexplicable occurrences have resulted following each of the construction periods at the library since 1985.

❖

County Seat Changes Appearance, Locations

by James W. June

Sweetwater County Seat and Courthouse

The county seat for Sweetwater County (known as Carter County before December 1869) was located first in South Pass City. Gold was first found in the area in 1841, but its discoverer was killed by Indians.

The first to file a claim was Henry Reedal, who discovered the Carissa Lode in 1867. Shortly after, the Miner's Delight Lode was discovered. These finds attracted an onslaught of miners, and by the fall of 1868 the town of South Pass City had mushroomed into Wyoming's largest town with 3,000 residents.

The discovery of gold at South Pass helped the effort to make Wyoming a territory separate from the Dakota in 1869. There was a movement to make South Pass City the county seat of Sweetwater County, the Wyoming Territorial capital.

At this time South Pass City included six general stores, three butcher shops, several restaurants, two breweries, seven blacksmith shops, five hotels, and dozens of saloons and "sporting houses".

S.I. Field had designated Block 8 of the Original Plat of Green River for county offices. The location was known as the county block.

The Wyoming Territorial legislature passed an act (Laws of Wyoming 1873, Chapter 38, Section 1) changing the county seat from South Pass City to Green River City and ordering that all county records be moved to that place. But a Section of that act stated that the county seat could be removed from Green River by vote at the next general election. The county commissioners held their first meeting in the new county seat December 22, 1873. The county commissioners at their meeting in Green River on April 26,

The 1876 Sweetwater County Courthouse with the second floor serving as a community room for meetings and dances as well as court. Central heat was not included as is evident with the numerous chimneys. (Photo courtesy Sweetwater County Historical Museum)

The 1907 additions to the Courthouse with the added wings, vault built onto the old courthouse. (Photo courtesy Sweetwater County Historical Museum)

1874, decided due to the weather, road conditions, etc. it would be impracticable to move the county records from South Pass at that time. At the county commissioners meeting in Green River on July 18, 1874, the commissioners made the motion and moved the county records from South Pass City to Green River, the county seat.

At the general election, September 1, 1874, the citizens disagreed with the legislated change. South Pass City received the greatest number of votes, the commissioners directed that all of the county records, county clerk and probate judge move to South Pass City by October, with as little delay as possible. The county commissioners' meetings were held in South Pass City from November 21, 1874, until June 15, 1875.

At the January 15, 1875, county commissioner meeting in South Pass City, County Treasurer James P. Brennan was requested to bring all his records before the commissioners. He claimed he could not bring the records for the books had been stolen the preceding October while enroute from Green River to South Pass City. They gave Brennan until the first of February to produce the records, agreeing to keep the matter from the public until that time. The commissioners investigated the problem of the county records on February 2, 1875. On February 9, 1875, the commissioners officially announced due to the loss of the county records, they could not give a statement of county affairs. Record books reported stolen were: Records of County Warrants; Cash Book; Records of Deed, Book 5; and Index Book.

The Wyoming Territorial officials decided to settle the problem of the county seat. Court proceedings "Territory of Wyoming vs. Board of County Commissioners of Sweetwater County" on May 10, 1875, directed the commissioners to hold all their meetings in Green River, and to move all county records there by June 15, 1875. The case was heard and order issued by Judge J.M. Carey.

To correct the loss of the county books, the Wyoming Territorial Legislature, on March 6, 1884, passed an act (Law of Wyoming, Chapter 91, Section 3) authorizing the county commissioners to advertise that all deeds recorded in Deed Record Book E, Entry 16, from August 10, 1870, to December 23, 1874, be sent to the county clerk for recording, since said book was lost, stolen or destroyed.

The first courthouse in this county was erected in Green River in 1876, when the Territorial Legislature authorized the county commissioners to bond the county for the sum needed, not to exceed $20,000 on December 11, 1875. Plans, drawn by Solon Burgress for the courthouse and jail were approved, and a contract

The Sweetwater County Courthouse with the 1929-30 additions of added wings and heating plant. Landscaping began in 1907. (Photo courtesy Sweetwater County Historical Museum)

Present day   The Courthouse as it now appears was dedicated August 13, 1967. (Photo courtesy Sweetwater County Historical Society)

of $18,974 was awarded to James East of Cheyenne on March 28, 1876, however he failed to furnish bond.

The contract was given to J.L. Atkinson of Evanston for $22,250 on May 10, 1876. The first courthouse was built with kiln dried adobe brick made locally in Green River. When the building was completed in 1876, the contractor would not accept "script" in payment, because he did not consider the county good for the amount due.

Green River businessman and rancher Pat Barrett, loaned the county the money, delivering it in cash to the contractor at the site. It is said that Mr. Barrett brought the money in a basket - others say a gunny sack.

The sheriff's residence was in the jail section of the courthouse. The sheriff's quarters was provided for by the Wyoming Law.

In September 1885, the Sweetwater County Courthouse was the scene of a Grand Jury investigation of the September 2 Chinese Riot and Massacre in Rock Springs. The Grand Jury was unable to return indictments of the investigation.

In the 1900s, additions were made to the courthouse with wings on the north side and a vault on the south side. The courthouse was heated by separate heating units, as seen by the numerous chimneys rising above the building in the old photographs.

The grounds around the courthouse were barren until 1907, when Mr. W. Hutton Jr., custodian, started planting trees, shrubs and grass about the courthouse.

In 1929, the need for expansion of the jail facilities was realized. The jail was remodeled and expanded with a new sheriff's residence being built to the west of the courthouse on the courthouse block. Also, an additional wing was built on the south of the courthouse for office space, and a heating plant was added.

In 1964, the walls of the main building were held upright by long bars and eyebolts; the walls were cracking and buckling, floors were sagging; the jail area was unsuitable and not sanitary; and valuable records were inaccessible because of lack of adequate storage. On April 28, 1964, the voters approved the proposed new $1,450,000 Sweetwater County Courthouse.

The county commissioners awarded the bid to L.M. Olson, Inc. of Rawlins on May 18, 1965 for a sum of $1,294,800. In June 1965, the sheriff's house was moved west from its site across the street to make way for the new building.

The first stage phases of the courthouse were completed in June of 1966. The old courthouse came tumbling down in June 1966 and the remaining east wing of the new building was built on the same ground on which the old courthouse once stood.

The new Sweetwater County courthouse was completed and dedication ceremonies were held August 13.

❖

Palisades Park –
The Original Greenbelt

by Bill Thompson

"Let's go to the Park for a picnic today!" probably was stated in various ways by the residents of Green River most likely from the town's founding up through the "teens", the "twenties" and into the 1930s.

As the photographs show, the Park was west of town along the Green River within easy walking distance for the residents. "As teenagers we would build a little fire by Tollgate Rock and cook breakfast," recalled Mae Wright. "Sometimes the family and I would walk out there and along the river we would collect berries. We later made jelly from them." Rodney Rollins remembers how he and other kids went from the Park up through Horsethief Canyon and explored the cave they found high in the rock bluffs. Mae said that although the girls went some distance up the canyon, she didn't recall "any of us going up and into the cave." When asked about finding snakes there Mae Wright said that "We never saw a snake on this side of the river until about 1940; on the other side though, by Mansface, it was another matter."

Gwynn Dickinson and her friends would walk to the Park for an outing and would also meander up the canyons north of the river. "Once Ralph Gaston fell off the Palisades and bounced around some ...." On a more placid note, Gwenn related how she and her friends would climb on top of Tollgate Rock enjoying the view and wave to passing motorists (see photo of rock and the condition of the road at that time).

In 1924 a new highway was constructed which followed the old South Pass Stage Road. This encroached somewhat on the area. It was at this time that the bridge across the Green River was built (present day Jamestown Road).

Palisades Park west of Green River. (Photo courtesy Rudy Gunter family collection)

Dale (Peg) Morris has fond memories of family picnics and relaxing times spent at the Park, but times change and sometimes overnight it seems. Peg remembers that "The road needed to be widened as the 'new' highway was being straightened. So in 1941 they blew up the Rock (Tollgate)." The river channel was dug out and moved to its present location. As a by-product of moving the highway away from the Palisades, an area between it and the Palisades became a nice ice skating pond.

This road was the major end of the Park as the residents knew it. There had been a gradual eroding of the pastoral setting through the years. A small business had set up operations ...came and went.... This was covered in a previous "Echoes" article. The Hines Plant sold stock and raised money for an oil shale refinery. Basically it was a scam. Some of the foundations are visible on the Hugh Crouch property today.

But the attraction of what was left of the Park was not lost on the stepfather of Kurt Hoffman. "He would come from Rock Springs to picnic and just lie on the grass. He loved it." Later in the 1940s Kurt "went deeply into hock" to purchase the area.

The cliffs west of Green River. (Photo courtesy Rudy Gunter family collection)

Residents of Green River continued enjoying the ice skating pond there. Kurt worked at keeping it usable for everyone and their families. He became known as an accomplished skater as he went through skilled maneuvers that he had developed years before.

Then in the 1960s the Twin Tunnels punched through the foundation of Castle Rock for the "new" interstate (I-80). The pond was covered and paved over with highway. For Green River residents the last Palisades gathering place for a relaxing outing was gone.

There are others that have stories about the Park but for one reason or the other they could not be reached. Perhaps they might wish to share some of those stories in a letter to the *Green River Star.* We hope so.

The pictures for this article were selected from the Spence-Gunter collection, and as many of you know, outstanding historical pictures of this area are hanging in City Hall, thanks to the efforts of Marna Grubb. There are others filed in our County Museum. Why not pay a visit soon?   ❖

Green River Schools
1876-1963

by Bob Edwards

Soon after the completion of the Union Pacific Railroad, Green River was established as a townsite because of the abundance of water provided by its river, plenty of land to build on and also because of the railroad itself.

Early education in Green River consisted of children being home schooled, if taught at all, but in 1869, the first Wyoming Territorial Assembly passed a law forbidding children under 14 years of age from working in the mines.

This coupled with the increasing population, provided the need for the first formal school, established during the 1870s.

Although the child labor laws helped to boost attendance in the schools, most of the male children had left school by the eighth grade and found jobs for themselves.

The first Superintendent of Education was H.G. Nickerson (1870-1871), followed by A.O. Dibble (1872). Through the Education Act of 1873, the county superintendent had the power to examine and certify teachers for Sweetwater County and by 1918 teachers were granted certificates by either examination or credits earned at a standard normal school or university.

By 1922, all teachers were required to be high school graduates. The first formal school house was built on the corner of North 1st East and Flaming Gorge Way in 1876. Basic teaching materials were: maps, charts, dictionaries, flags, globes, blackboards, and desks, and a piano was also given to the school. Noted in an article, by Paul Rideout, Superintendent of Education, in 1891, there was only one teacher provided for 142 students.

Therefore, Mr. Rideout assisted by teaching primary school in the morning and grammar school in the afternoon. (Sheddon, 1890, p .53)

Also of interest, was a night school, established after the turn of the century, which was provided for those children who were not able to attend school in the daytime.

The first school building was only in use for two years and because of the tremendous growth, soon became inadequate and the first grade was moved to North 1st West and the second grade was then located across the alley in a house on the same street. The third through eighth grades were in the original building (Elizabeth St. School), which is still standing on East 2nd Street.

By 1891, there was a great need for an even larger primary school. A new two-story building, now known as the Masonic Temple, was completed that year.

The new school had three finished rooms and there were 158 students attending a 10-month school term. First and second grades were together and the third, fourth and fifth were located in the sec-ond room. Sixth through ninth grades were in the third room upstairs.

In 1904 the school board decided to add a 10th grade and by 1912, 11th and 12th grades were also added. Ruth Lenhart had the distinction of being the first four-year graduate in 1912.

School would begin at 9 and dismiss at noon for lunch. Often students ate their lunches brought from home, at the Green River Mercantile, since they were not allowed to remain at school during lunch hour. There was, at this time, no playground equipment so children played around the entire Castle Rock area at recess.

Primarily the basics were taught, which included reading, writing, arithmetic and spelling in the first three grades. Fourth grades also included hygiene and language; fifth grades added geography and physiology and sixth grade - history.

Seventh graders studied reading, arithmetic, language and history in the first half and spelling, arithmetic, grammar, geography, physiology and algebra, the second half. Eighth grade students had basically the same curriculum but also included Latin and full-time algebra.

The only addition in ninth grade was second year Latin, algebra and bookkeeping. Spelling bees and ciphering were a regular Friday afternoon event and the principal sport was baseball.

Other buildings, such as the old Rex Theater or the Library auditorium were used for additional functions, such as school plays and graduation.

During World War I, there were several changes in the regular course of studies, including the addition of a Junior Red Cross program, emphasis on democracy and war within English and history courses and students learned to make items such as surgical dressings, bandaged foot socks, hospital robes, pillows, hot water bottle covers, helmets, mufflers, socks and scarves, to be sent overseas.

Prior to the War, German was offered, but was dropped in 1918 and French and Spanish were offered instead.

In 1923, the first girls and boys basketball teams were organized and in 1924, a football team was added.

When overcrowding again became a problem, the first high school building was built in 1921 by the Evers Brothers, at a cost of $95,000. This became known as the first Lincoln High School.

In 1926 the old school site was bought by the Masons. The bell tower of the Masonic Hall was removed and the school children were given the opportunity to say what should be done with the bell, through poems of their own. The student with the best poem was rewarded with $5 *(Green River Star,* Jan. 29, 1926).

In 1932, a gymnasium was added to Lincoln High School. The basement was used for the west end grade school students, although Washington School was built in December 1925 for the east part of town. In September 1940, the west end was also given its own school.

In October 1940, Lincoln was destroyed by an early morning fire, which gutted the structure and caused approximately $155,000 worth of damages. Once again, grade school children took up classes in the basements.

❖

Wyoming Frontier Education in the Early 1900s

by Marna Grubb

I have always been fascinated with a photo of a school room at Cherokee, Wyoming, back in the early 1920s. Teacher Esther Wiggen recorded on the back of the photo that "This is a picture of

Esther Wiggen (Photo courtesy Marna Grubb)

"Sleep and taught school in the same room." (Photo courtesy Marna Grubb)

my room at Cherokee. Sleep and taught school in the same room. You can see how they had mud on the inside between the logs, the darkest logs were covered with grease and dirt. I had a paper placed over the window."

Cherokee was one of the many railroad sidings which sprung up along the Union Pacific Railroad and, according to a Union Pacific map, it was located between Wamsutter and Rawlins (close to Creston). These towns along the UP were close together and the smaller ones just housed the section crews who worked on the tracks in the area. Cherokee is just a memory now. UP Historian Jim Ehernberger, former Secretary to the Superintendent and later train dispatcher out of Cheyenne, reports that, when traveling with the Superintendent in 1972, they had been called to Cherokee for a derailment which had damaged the siding - and that was the end of Cherokee.

The teacher, Esther Wiggen, was born in Rock Springs on January 19, 1902 and graduated from Rock Springs High School with the class of 1920. When she taught at Cherokee, she would stay in Rock Springs with her family on weekends, then catch the train to Cherokee to teach during the week. She later worked for the U.P. Coal Company in Rock Springs.

Esther met Chris Jessen from Green River and they were married May 14, 1924. As reported in the May 16, 1924, *Rocket Miner,* "The groom is Undersheriff of Sweetwater County, and is one of the live wires of our neighboring town in Green River." He later became Sheriff and was Chief of Police for the Town of Green River for 30 years (1933-1963).

Esther worked several years as a postal clerk at the Green River post office, especially during World War II. Esther passed away in 1974. Chris preceded her in death in 1970. They had one daughter. These were my parents.

❖

The Town U.P. Did Not Build

by James W. June

Green River's future was seen by five enterprising men, Charles Deloney, Judge Carter, H.M. Hook, James Moore and S.I. Field.

Charles Deloney contracted with the Union Pacific Railroad Company to furnish ties for the railroad in 1867. He began his tie and timber operations during the fall and winter of 1867-68, in the upper Green River country.

He made the first tie-timber drive to Green River City in the spring of 1868. These drives were annual affairs - the timber drives until 1919 and the tie drives until 1941.

Judge Carter of Fort Bridger foresaw the need for lumber in building of the railroad, the town, and for mine timbers in the coal mines. He built a steam-operated sawmill on the north bank of the Green River above the mouth of Bitter Creek in the summer of 1868.

H.M. Hook and James Moore, both of Cheyenne, and SJ. Field were the leaders of the squatters at Green River. These three men obtained the land at the location from the Overland Mail Company. They knew the Union Pacific Railroad was going to cross the Green River in this area. The mail contractor had secured a land grant from the U.S. Congress in 1862, which pre-dated the Union Pacific Railroad Acts of 1867. Field then laid out the original plat of the city on July 1, 1868.

In July 1868, the building of Green River began in Carter County, Dakota Territory. Green River at this stage of time was referred to as Green River No. 3.

Green River No. 1 referred to the small settlement with a stage station and post office in 1856, which was 345 miles north on the Green River and the Oregon Trail.

Brigham Young, president of the Church of Jesus Christ of Latter-day Saints, was encouraging settlement of this location, which he called "Green River."

This region was known as Green River Country, Utah Territory, with Fort Bridger as the county seat.

Green River No. 2 was the Overland Stage Station on the south bank of the Green River where the Game and Fish Department building is now located; this was established in 1862.

The *Frontier Index,* the "Press on Wheels," set up shop in Green River with Editor Leigh Freeman, and printed the first newspaper on Aug. 11, 1868.

The *Frontier Index* reported on Aug. 11, 1868 "that music of the carpenter's tools are everywhere heard above the din and bustle of business."

"The two sawmills of Judge Carter, on the Blacks Fork and another on the Green River, do not supply the demand for furnishing lumber alone."

The original Green River city buildings were constructed of adobe brick and were made at a site near the present location of Zumbrennen Tire in Green River.

The Aug. 11, 1868 *Frontier Index* reported the first city election on Aug. 6, 1868, in which five councilmen were elected: Joseph Binns, James W. Bank, F.H. Buzzard, John L. Terry and James B. Brown. Thomas J. Smith was elected marshall; Harry Owenson, clerk; W.H. Dixon, treasurer; and L.L. Burns, assessor.

Joseph Binns was elected by the council as president of the council.

The ordinances and tax measures of Green River City, Carter County, Dakota Territory, were published in the Aug. 11, 1868 issue of the *Frontier Index.* The Coe Library at Yale University contains the copies of the original ordinances, which contain nine chapters and were signed by Binns as president of the council.

The ordinances prohibited carrying or discharging firearms or other deadly weapons, public intoxication, any disturbance of the peace or fighting and indecent public exposure.

Provision was made for construction of streets and alleys with provisions that prisoners unable to pay fines should work these out on street work. Licenses were required of auctioneers with a monthly fee of $10; merchandise wholesalers a monthly fee of $20; feed stables and butchers a monthly fee of $10; retail merchandisers a monthly fee of $10; restaurants, public boarding houses, hotels, lodging houses a monthly fee of $5 to $20.

Gambling was prohibited, as were houses of prostitution. A speed limit of six miles per hour was set up, covering the riding or driving of horses or mules within the city limits. Special provision was made that no filth or filthy substances be allowed in city streets or alleys or other premises where these would be offensive to the public.

The ordinances also created the office of city attorney. The *Frontier Index* of Aug. 11, 1868, also reported on "Pugilistic, on Sunday night Aug. 9, 1868, was a very entertaining and successful sparring exhibition given by Jimmy Dwyer, champion of lightweights of the Mountains. Next Wednesday night, another similar performance will take place at Kinston's Dance Hall, between Billy Bennett, Patsey Marley, Billy Reed, Jack Ryan and several other noted pugilists.

"Jimmy Powers will give a club dance during the evening and the exhibition will wind up with a friendly set-to between Bennett and Marley. On Sunday, the 15th inst., Jimmy Dwyer and Billy Bennett will take the ring in a prize fight for a stake of $300. The fight will take place on the island."

The *Frontier Index* of Aug. 21, 1868, reported the incorporation of Green River. The incorporation established a town site slightly in excess of 175 acres and apparently north of what was in a few weeks to become the Union Pacific Railroad right-of-way.

The description is based upon "Front Street," which is hard to identify from the description but may be presumed to be the general route of today's Railroad Avenue. This notice was signed at South Pass City by W.D. Matheny, president of the Board of County Commissioners of Carter County.

John T. Reynolds was named the first Postmaster for Green River, which was established on Aug. 26, 1868. The Post Office was discontinued on Dec. 1, 1868, and the mail was sent to Bryan Post Office. The Green River Post Office was re-established Dec. 7, 1868.

S.I. Field constructed one of the first wooden frame homes in 1868 and it was located on the south side of the railroad tracks. The house was a single story structure at 100 East Second South, and was a general merchandise store, restaurant and residence for Field.

The general merchandise store in 1868 was the forerunner of the oldest existing business in Sweetwater County, the Green River Mercantile. In 1872, W.A. Johnson purchased the Field property, moved and continued in the general merchandise store.

Johnson made this his residence, making the yard into a show place, with a huge landscaped lawn. The property was purchased by the Mountain States Telephone Company in June 1977, and the structure was torn down for a warehouse that was never built. The Riverside Nursery and Greenhouse occupies the site today.

The *Frontier Index* of Sept. 11, 1868 reported Green River had a population of more than 2,000 and substantial adobe buildings were erected, and the town presented a permanent appearance.

The tracks of the U.P. Railroad Company had been laid as far as Green River by Oct. 1, 1868. With the arrival of the railroad in Green River, much to the U.P.'s displeasure, they found a town already established.

The Union Pacific Lot Company, who had the privilege of selling lots in any town that grew up along the railroad; nevertheless, demanded from $70 to $250 for each lot.

After ten days of fruitless discussions, the Green River citizens offered to pay the price demanded for the lots if they could be assured that Green River would be the winter terminus for passenger and freight trains. The Union Pacific's reply was: "We cannot accept the proposition of the citizens, as we cannot state where the winter terminus will be."

In had been intended that Green River would have been a division point, but the railroad was miffed, and it proceeded at once to bypass Green River by laying out a new town, Bryan (for a while known as Corinne) on the Black's Fork 12 miles west of Green River, and making it their division point.

Green River had but 100 residents by early November 1868, after the Union Pacific by-passed it, moving the division point to Bryan, the adobe brick buildings were abandoned.

The *Frontier Index* of Oct. 6, 1868, recorded the arrival of the train.

"Looking eastward to see an 'Iron Horse' snorting and pushing a string of construction cars around the bluff at the east end of town.

"Gen. Casement and four trains of cars were right in the heart of Green River City at 11:45 a.m. of this date Oct. 6," the *Frontier Index* reported. "Seventeen trains had arrived a few hours later and at 5 p.m. three tracks each a mile long, filled with trains. Bells are ringing, whistles blowing, the train has charged to the North and snow will fall tonight!"

The first census of the Wyoming Territory, 1869, indicates that Green River had a population of 101 people. The 1879 census figures showed that Green River had a total of 106 persons.

The winter of 1871-72 had a heavy snow blizzard so that trains were blocked off from December 1871 to April 1872.

The earlier expectations of being the division point for the UP were realized by Green River when the water supply on the Black's Fork at Bryan proved inadequate. The railroad company came back in 1872, establishing a roundhouse, depot, and machine shops at Green River. Thus, Green River was reborn and this became known as Green River No. 4.

In June 1877, R. Blackstone surveyed and drew a map of the lands of S.I. Field showing the original plat of Green River, consisting of 36 blocks. These were laid out by Field as early as 1868, but were not surveyed and drawn until June 1877.

The 1880 census showed Green River with a population of 327 people.

The winter of 1886-87 had repeated hurricane blizzards, heavy snow fall and chilling rains which combined to kill off a third of all range cattle and sheep and block trains off and on during the winter.

According to the 1890 census, Green River had a population of 723 people.

The Green River Town Council minutes showed that the town of Green River was incorporated under the laws of the newly formed State of Wyoming on May 5, 1891. Green River's first election after the town's incorporation under the laws of the State of Wyoming was on July 15, 1891.

Edward J. Morris was elected the first Mayor for a one-year term. The town council consisted of Dr. John M. Gilligan, Walter S. Powell, Jacob F. Snyder and Thomas F. Carey, with two serving a one-year term and two serving a two year term.

❖

Meet Me At The Fair:
The History of the
Sweetwater County Fair

by Ruth Lauritzen

Celebrating the agricultural lifestyle, county fairs frequently had their beginnings in rural farming and ranching communities. Thus it was only appropriate that the fair movement in Sweetwater County got its start in Eden Valley, one of the major agricultural areas in the county.

In 1914 residents of Eden Valley sponsored Harvest Home Day at the University of Wyoming Experimental Farm. Events included displays of canned goods, baked goods, fancy work and crops; speeches, greased pole climbing, bronco busting and sack races. The festival was truly a community celebration with everything from the prize ribbons to the food at the potluck supper provided by the citizens of the valley. However, attendance went far beyond the community level. A sizable portion of the 300 people at the fair had motored up from Rock Springs for the day.

The next year a Sweetwater County Fair Association was formed and filed articles of incorporation with the Wyoming Secretary of State. This association was described in a 1915 *Rock Springs Miner* article, as "an institution which is to receive state as well as county support in developing the agricultural, livestock and other resources of the county." In spite of the formal incorporation, things did not change much with Eden Valley continuing to hold small community fairs through the 1920s, '30s and early '40s. These events went by various names including the First Annual Eden Valley Fair of 1928 and the Eden Valley 4H Club Fair in 1938.

By 1946 it was decided that a formal Sweetwater County Fair should be organized. The location was moved from Eden Valley to

Rock Springs where the early fairs were held at the Old Timers Building (Rock Springs Civic Center). They were known as "slab fairs" because the corrals, pens and other outdoor structures were built from slabs of wood donated by a local lumber mill. Not much livestock was exhibited at the early fairs. During the first fair in 1946 only eleven calves and five lambs were brought in and they were housed in tents outside while the building was used for exhibit space.

In 1948 a committee was formed to look into building a community park in Rock Springs to be used for ball games and other such outdoor activities. Land was purchased north of the existing town, (presently south of I-80 near the Elk Street exchange), and work began on the Community Park in 1949. By 1953 the park was determined to be the ideal place for the fair to be held, and buildings were constructed for that purpose. Parades, horse shows, street dances, stock car races, soap box derbies and sports such as horseshoe pitching and bocci bolli began to be a part of the fair during this time.

Under the leadership of George Graf and John S. "Jack" Logan, Green River agriculturalists made a great showing in the fair over the next several decades. George Graf was involved with the fair in some capacity from 1947 until his death in 1966 when his wife Louise took over for him. Jack Logan also served on the board and as Green River community chairman for many years. According to a contemporary newspaper article these men were responsible for the "...exceptional accomplishment to place Green River prominently in the fore-front of garden work in the County...to these two gentlemen go much of the credit for the unusual Fair record established this year at the Fair. They spent a great deal of time in working up the entrys and promoting a well-rounded display."

In a character sketch in the collection of the county museum, De Ette Thrasher Trappe wrote about her neighbor George Graf's devotion to gardening and to the fair, "His goal is to make the agriculture section of the fair bigger and better each year, and to win as many ribbons and trophies as he can. I have had to chuckle many times as I've watched him baby along a row of barley which he grows precisely for the purpose of winning the blue ribbon from the farmers who raise barley as part of their living. It is worth every minute of the time he spends on his garden for him to be able to see the products of his work on the shelves with blue ribbons, and to walk proudly along teasing the farmers in his good-natured way."

After twenty years the fair outgrew its facilities in the Community Park. A site for a new fairground was chosen, buildings

John S. "Jack" Logan tends the Green River Community booth at the 1948 Sweetwater County Fair. (Photo courtesy Sweetwater County Historical Museum)

were constructed and in 1977 the fair was held at the present fairground for the first time. Over the years many other activities have begun to use the fairgrounds such as parimutuel horse racing, rodeo, auto racing, cultural and craft festivals and private parties. This prompted a change of name for the facility in 1991 to the Sweetwater Events Complex. However, in spite of the increasing diversity of activities at the complex the premier event continues to be the fair. Today's Sweetwater County Fair with its concerts, carnival and special competitions is far removed from the tiny Eden Valley events of yesteryear, but in many ways still allows an increasingly urbanized and industrial area to experience the agricultural lifestyle which makes Wyoming famous.

❖

Lynching in Green River

by Bill Thompson

"No person shall be deprived of life, liberty or property without due process of law."

5th Amendment U.S. Constitution

"In all criminal prosecutions, the accused shall enjoy the right to a speedy trial, by an impartial jury...."

6th Amendment U.S. Constitution

Wyoming Day – December 10th. Commemorated by appropriate ceremonies in schools, clubs and similar groups.

Wyoming Official Directory

As Joel Wodson stepped up to the Union Pacific lunch counter at Green River, Wyoming on the morning of December 10, 1918, his focus was on ordering breakfast. It is doubtful that Wyoming's holiday entered his thoughts. Wodson, a janitor at the Union Pacific Social Hall, found the short walk from his room in the Social Hall to the lunch counter convenient for obtaining a meal.

It became evident though that irritation was in his mind as he stared at the dried mush that the waitress had brought him. In no uncertain tones he told the waitress that he had ordered sausage. She claimed that he had ordered the dried mush. She left and shortly brought him an order of sausage. It did not end there. Wodson continued to berate the waitress. Finally when he called her a "Damned Liar" she picked up several salt shakers and threw them at him.

Two switchmen, Miller and Curtis who were at the counter could not help but overhear and see the situation. Edward Miller had been a resident of Green River for some months. In that period of time he had become well liked by his fellow employees and townspeople. He had acquired some very staunch friends. Miller

The 1918 lynching of Joel Wodson. (Photo courtesy Bill Thompson)

rose and went over to the black janitor. He escorted him to the door and, slapping Wodson on the back, told him to get out and save everyone trouble.

Wodson went immediately to his room at the U.P. Social Hall, got a gun and returned to the lunch counter. A friend of Miller's (Curtis?) saw that Wodson had a gun in his possession and told Ed Miller about it. Miller is quoted as saying, "Well I better get out and save trouble." So Miller and his friend Curtis left the lunch counter by the end door. Wodson seeing this then hurried out the side door of the lunch counter. By this time Miller and Curtis had stepped out into the archway where Wodson accosted them stating, "You will never lay a hand on me again!" He fired at Miller, one shot entering the heart, the second about four inches above the first shot, which dropped Ed Miller in his tracks. When Curtis started to enter the depot Wodson shot him through the wrist and Curtis fell to the pavement. Wodson fired again but missed.

Fleeing the scene Wodson was soon captured near Peter's Garage by Special U.P. Officer Matt McCourt who hurried him to the county jail. Ed Miller was moved to the lunch room where in a few minutes he died. Curtis was rushed to

---

the Green River Pharmacy and given medical attention. He was then sent to the Wyoming General Hospital at Rock Springs.

The news spread quickly throughout Green River that Miller had died and a large angry crowd marched on the jail demanding Wodson. A well known Attorney, T.S. Taliaferro, spoke to them pleading law and order, justice and reason. "But the infuriated crowd was beyond reasoning, the negro being discovered in the coal hole of the heating plant of the jail, where he had been hidden by the officers, he was seized and dragged to the depot and hanged to a light pole in front of the depot, where it (sic) hung until the arrival of the coroner from Rock Springs .... Ten minutes after the hanging the town was quiet and no further demonstration was made."

On December 13, 1918, Fred W. Johnson, the County Attorney, stated that he would call a grand jury to investigate as to who (sic) had a hand in the lynching and that he would probe the matter to the fullest extent. Nothing came of it. ... no one was brought to trial ... in regard to arrests, indictments, trials, etc. – nothing happened.

The body hung in full sight of our World War One troops riding the Union Pacific ... returning from a war that was fought, "To make the world safe for Democracy" and Justice.

Basic information for this article was obtained from *The History of Sweetwater County* by James W. June.

❖

Early Wyoming Travel Daring, Perilous

by James W. June

Green River's portion roughest part in state

Fame for the Lincoln Highway with part of its route through Wyoming really did not come into fruition until a few not necessarily successful road races came to pass. However, many changes and lots of travelers later, the Lincoln Highway came into its own.

The 1908 New York to Paris Automobile Race left the starting point in Times Square in New York on Feb. 13, 1908. There were six cars in the 1908 race.

The American car for the 1908 race was the Thomas car. The automobile was furnished by Edwin Ross Thomas of the Thomas Automobile Factory in Buffalo, N.Y.

The Thomas car was a 60 horsepower, four-cylinder model. Mortague Roberts was hired as driver; and George Schuster, an employee of Thomas Automobile Factory, served as mechanic and driver.

The German car was the Protus. It was built by the Protus-Motorenbau Company in Berlin. The Protus was a large four-cylinder, shaft-driven car, weighing 4,000 pounds plus, and when loaded was capable of traveling fifty miles per hour.

The driver was Lt. Hans Koeppen and two factory engineers, Hans Knape and Ernst Mase.

The Italian car was the Zust. The Zust was a forty-horsepower, four-cylinder car driven by Giulo Sirtori and Antonio Searfoglio. Henri Haaga was the mechanic.

Built by Marquis de Dion, the French car was the DeDion. It was a thirty-horsepower, four-cylinder engine, with a four-speed transmission. It was equipped with steel-studded Michelin tires.

It also used steel flanged wheels to run on railways when necessary. M. Bourcier se St. Chaffray was driver and M. l' Autran mechanic. The DeDion car dropped from the race at Vladivostok, Siberia.

The second French car entered in the 1908 race was the Motobloc, a forty-two horsepower, four-cylinder motor vehicle that could travel 42 miles per hour.

Baron Charles Godard was the driver, with Authur Hue and Maurice Livier as mechanic and drivers. The Motobloc car dropped out of the race after leaving Wyoming.

The third French car was the Sizaire-Naudin, which had a 15-horsepower engine and could travel a top speed of 50 mph. M. Paul Pons was driver with Maurice Bertyhe and Lucien Deschamps as other crew members.

The Sizaire-Naudin dropped out of the race before it reached Wyoming because of mechanical difficulties.

The race cars reached Wyoming and traveled through during March, 1908. The Thomas car was the first to reach Cheyenne on March 8. The Protus, the German car, was the last to reach Laramie March 22, 1908.

The Protus car reached Paris first, but the race committee disqualified the German car because they had shipped their car over part of the Rocky Mountains from Pocatello, Idaho, to Seattle in a railroad car in order to sail with the Thomas car for Siberia.

The Thomas car arrived in Paris two days after the Protus car and won the 1908 New York to Paris Automobile Race. The Zust car was awarded second place in the race.

The Transcontinental Auto Race of 1909 started June 1 in New York and ended in Seattle. The start of the race on June 1 was the opening of the Alaska-Yukon-Pacific Exposition at Seattle. The race's route in Wyoming was Cheyenne and Laramie to Granger, then northwest through Idaho, Oregon and Washington.

The Wyoming Highway Association in 1911, published a Road Guide. This guide was from Cheyenne to Green River to Granger to Evanston. That portion from Green River to Granger was not described in the road guide, but it followed the Overland Stage Road to Granger.

The Lincoln Highway crossed southern Wyoming. It was so named because it was authorized in 1912, the centennial anniversary of the birth of Abraham Lincoln. It began on the East Coast in New York City, N.Y., and ended on the West Coast in San Francisco, Calif.

The French Entry in the 1908 New York to Paris race pictured here in southern Wyoming with its driver and mechanics. Most did not finish. (Photo courtesy Sweetwater County Historical Museum)

The Lincoln Highway signs were band of color red, white and blue; with capital LH in the white band. It was the nation's first coast-to-coast motor vehicle route.

In 1913, Sweetwater County built a bridge across the Black's Fork River, just below Bryan and the Lincoln Highway road from there to Granger, which was south of the stage road and the U.P. railroad tracks. The Colorado Bridge and Construction Company built the bridge at a cost of $5,895, with a span length of 150 feet and a roadway width of 14 feet 9 inches.

It was a pin-connected, Pratt Through Truss type bridge patented in 1844 by Thomas and Caleb Pratt, which was a popular type bridge of this period.

In 1913, a group of highway minded men made a tour to San Francisco on the West Coast from Indianapolis, Ind. They started from Indianapolis on July 1, 1913. All of the automobiles finished the trip.

The party included 19 vehicle makes which were a Marmon, 2 Marians, 1 Pilot 60, 2 Haynes, 2 Americans, 1 McFarland, 2 Appersons, 2 Hendersons, 1 Empire, 2 Premiers, 1 Pathfinder, 1 Brown Truck, and 1 Premier Truck, which carried camp equipment, repair parts, supplies and extra tires.

Lincoln Highway, authorized in 1912, shown here west of Green River. (Photo courtesy Sweetwater County Historical Museum)

Equipment specified to be carried on each car included one shovel, one pick, one sledge, one steel stake three feet long, one pair of tackle blocks, 600 feet of 3/4 inch rope, one lantern, 12 mudhooks, one set of tire chains, four African water bags, one envelope type tent and chocolate bars in cans, beans, canned goods.

Before 1924, the Lincoln Highway entered Green River from the east at the east exit of the interstate into the city. It entered under the bluff, north of a swamp area to the corner, where China Gardens is located, of East Second North Street and North Fifth East -Wyoming - Street. Then south on North Fifth East Street to - the present stop light - East First North - East Flaming Gorge Way -Street.

Then west on East First North - East Flaming Gorge Way - Street to - the second stop light - North First East - Elizabeth - Street. Then south on North First East - Elizabeth - Street cross the railroad track to East First South - East Second South - Street to South Fifth East - Wyoming - Street crossing the river on the old Wagon Bridge to the Overland Trail road - Riverview Street.

Then west on the Lincoln Highway - Riverview Street - to Telephone Canyon and Lincoln Highway to Peru Hill and the Black's Fork below Bryan. This route for the Lincoln Highway was used until 1924, when the Wyoming Highway Department built a new bridge across the river.

The Lincoln Highway Association, in 1915, produced a transcontinental tour on the Lincoln Highway in moving pictures. It started in New York City and ended in San Francisco at the Panama-Pacific Exposition, where the film was first shown. The official Lincoln Highway Caravan consisted of five cars, and left New York May 15, 1915, expecting to reach San Francisco Sept. 1, 1915.

The caravan consisted of five cars. The lead car was a 1915 Stutz car, presented by the Stutz Motor Car Company. It was painted white, with wheels and running gear royal blue, the hood red, white and blue, the Lincoln Highway colors.

In the lead car was H.C. Ostermann, consul-at-large of the Lincoln Highway Association; Edward A. Holden, secretary to Mr. Ostermann; and Civil Engineer C.W. Thomas, camera man.

In the Packard car was L.C. Halker, technical representative for the Packard Motor Company, Mrs. H.C. Ostermann, Mrs. O.P. Canaday, and C.W. Reiling, official statistician.

In the Studebaker car was J. Meinzinger, technical expert for the Studebaker Company; and R.C. Sackett, publicity man for the Studebaker Company.

In the Oakland car was O.P. Canaday, representative of the Wayne Oil Tank and Pump Company.

In the Little Giant Truck was LeRoy Beardalay and Earl Phillips, representatives of the Chicago Pneumatic Tool Company of Chicago.

On Tuesday afternoon, Aug. 3, 1915, the official Lincoln Highway Caravan arrived in Green River. Accompanied by Mr. and Mrs. T.S. Taliaferro, the party journeyed up along the Green River, photographing the views near Castle Rock. The party continued along the river to the Big Island Ranch where they photographed the elk located there. A supper was served at the ranch.

On Wednesday morning, Aug. 4, 1915, further pictures were made, including scenery... the public square, banks and other buildings in Green River. The party left at 2 in the afternoon for Fort Bridger and continuing on to Evanston the following day.

Hugo Gaensslen received in the second week of October, 1915, the Lincoln Highway feature film, in which Green River was featured. It had been shown the first time to the public at the Panama-Pacific International Exposition in San Francisco. The film proved to be a big success.

In 1916, the Lincoln Highway markers consisted mainly of red, white and blue colors painted on poles, fence posts, stakes or rocks to mark the highway's route.

In 1916, Henry B. Joy, President of the Packard Motor Car Company and the head of the Lincoln Highway Association camped on the Continental Divide on the Lincoln Highway.

The Lincoln Highway symbol appeared on road maps as early as 1918.

In 1920, the Overland Economy Run was routed from New York to San Francisco on the Lincoln Highway.

In 1920, 3,000 metal or porcelain trail markers with the Lincoln Highway symbol were placed along the route at a cost of $10 per marker.

❖

1949 Blizzard

by James W. June

The 1949 Blizzard had the most severe storms in the Rocky Mountain area in the past four decades. The following chronological order will let you realize what the winter of 1949 was like.

NOV. 18, 1948. A severe winter storm with blizzard conditions started in Nebraska, South Dakota, Kansas, eastern Colorado and eastern Wyoming. This storm was severe enough to close the highways and strand travelers on that date in most areas. Nebraska and Kansas were hit the hardest with this storm. The snow drifted deep enough to stop the railroad in western Nebraska.

NOV. 19, 1948. The storm finally quit, snowplows had cleaned highways and normal travel was resumed, but the early winter conditions and high winds had drifted many areas with deep drifts, which put a hardship on much of the livestock early in the winter in these areas.

The weather then turned warm. Huge snow drifts began to melt and the travel got back to normal.

DEC. 1948. In December the weather turned warm and the snow melted. Things got back to normal. Livestock losses were assessed, the holiday travel for Christmas was building with the trains being crowded and the highway travel increased to celebrate the Christmas and New Year's holidays.

No thought was given that the November storm was a prelude to one of the worst blizzards in three decades. The weather forecasters could see nothing but snow flurries in the offing. The balmy days felt like spring.

DEC. 31, 1948. Wheatland 4:30 p.m. Return trip by author with family to Laramie and University from Sheridan. Had eaten supper and started 57 miles to Bosler on Wyoming Highway 34 up Sybille Canyon. Had started lightly snowing with 4 inches on the

Workers try to clear railroad track during the Blizzard of '49, one of the most severe in history. (Photo courtesy Sweetwater County Historical Museum)

ground. Upon reaching the head of the canyon and U.S. Highway 30 at Bosler, we were breaking drifts of snow as high as the headlights. At Bosler the highway had been plowed, but it was snowing very hard. Reached Laramie at 10:30 p.m.

JAN. 1, 1949. Upon getting up in the morning, there were drifts of snow throughout the town from 8 to 14 feet deep.

The Denver KOA radio station in Denver was predicting another nice day with snow flurries.

Snowdrifts where already piling upon the highways where the bushes and banks stopped the wind. By afternoon it was snowing quite hard.

JAN. 2, 1949. The snow continued with the wind whipping the snow and visibility zero. The snow was covering vehicles, buildings, trains and drifts up to 14 feet deep. Ranches, farms, trains and highway travelers were being completely isolated.

JAN. 3, 1949. Cheyenne. The morning was beautiful. The bus to Denver, Colorado on U.S. Highway 85 about 20 miles from Cheyenne hit a roar and a holler and could only make 10 yards per hour. The bus picked up several motorists marooned in snowbanks.

They came upon a light and had reached a small tavern and a few houses along the highway. Four hundred and sixty-five persons

Clearing the tracks during the blizzard of '49. (Photo courtesy Sweetwater County Historical Museum)

were caught there in the storm. Two hundred stayed at the tavern and the others stayed in the two stalled buses. Snow was so deep that entrance to the buses was by the windows only.

Green River. In the morning there were 1200 railroad passengers marooned in Green River. The storms and winds in eastern Wyoming resulted in the worst rail blockade in Wyoming in three decades.

Blizzards that closed the Union Pacific railroad over Sherman Hill and eastward to Sidney, Neb., resulted in total cessation of rail traffic east of Green River by late afternoon of the 3rd.

Two freight trains were enroute between Rawlins and Green River. Train No. 38 - a section of the Pony Express and Train No. 18 left the night of the 3rd. No. 38 made it to Laramie and No. 18 made it to Rawlins and could go no farther.

The streamliners, the City of Portland, the City of Los Angeles, and the City of San Francisco, as well as The Utahn, Los Angeles Limited, and the Pony Express were held in Green River.

JAN. 5, 1949. The snow blockade was broken late in the evening and the Pony Express left Green River, followed at safe intervals by the other trains. Also the highways were opened.

JAN. 9, 1949. Blizzard conditions again made all types of travel hazardous and drove highway travelers off the roads. No snow fell but sub-zero temperatures and 50 mile per hour winds made it impossible to travel.

JAN. 12, 1949. The rail and highway travel resumed. Some of the county roads were open to travel.

JAN. 13, 1949. All local hay as far as Bridger Valley, Farson and Pinedale had been used to feed the livestock. It was costing $300 per day per band of sheep to feed. Hay was being shipped in from Laramie, Centennial and North Platte, Nebraska.

The roads in the range were badly covered with snow, with feed deeply covered with snow. The winds have buried the grass and browse very deep with snow. Feeding will be necessary for anoth-er six weeks.

Antelope are being killed by the trains, with as high as 250 at one time in the Red Desert area.

JAN. 16, 1949. The high temperature at Green River was 4 above zero.

JAN. 17, 1949. The high temperature was 21 below zero.

JAN. 18, 1949. The high was 1 below zero.

JAN. 19, 1949. The high was 26 below zero.

JAN. 20, 1949. The high was 6 below zero.

JAN. 21, 1949. The high was 16 below zero.

JAN. 22, 1949. The high was 6 below zero. An east wind blizzard hit southern Wyoming in the evening with visibility to zero due to snow and wind. Huge drifts were piling up.

JAN. 23, 1949. The high was 2 below zero. Snowing and high east winds piled drifted snow up to 10 to 14 feet deep. Again the road and rail travel was halted. Travel on the U.P. was slow and erratic and no travel on the highways was possible.

Stockmen were having a very hard time feeding their sheep and cattle.

JAN. 24, 1949. The high was 15 below zero.

JAN. 25, 1949. The high was 30 below zero.

JAN. 26, 1949. The high was 30 below zero.

FEB. S, 1949. Severe blizzard conditions again tie up rail and road travelers.

County Commissioner George Stephens opened a road up the LaBarge road and brought out a ranch family.

FEB. 6, 1949. Again 2,000 travelers were stranded in Green River. Food demands taxed the business houses to supply the passengers with the meat supplies almost completely gone.

Members of the Sportsman's Club, Fish and Game Commission, National Guard, Civil Air Patrol and a number of local residents made strenuous efforts to reach antelope in serious conditions 10 miles up the LaBarge road. Headed by two snow plows, a caravan of 25 cars attempted to reach the antelope, but the drifts that had been opened the day before could not be reopened and the caravan was forced back.

FEB. 8, 1949. New food supplies arrived by special trains from Ogden, Utah. Homes, business houses and institutions began to feel the effects of the hard, long winter with heavy frost sinking ever deeper into the ground, freezing water mains and sewer lines. Many places could not be unfrozen until spring due to the frozen ground.

Drifts of snow on the U.P. right-of-way between Wamsutter and Rawlins were 20 feet deep. The drifts were a half mile long. Highways were drifted, closed between Wamsutter and Rawlins and west from the Green River to Salt Lake City. Trains with passengers returning to the west were routed by the southern route.

An Emergency Red Cross Office was set up in the old VFW building on Railroad Avenue to aid strandees and meet the needs of the community.

FEB. 10, 1949. The Green River National Guard unit - Co. "C" 141st Tank Battalion was called in service to help get to the isolated ranches in the area. A truck and jeep were employed to break through to the Casey west of Green River. It took the four guardsmen 12 hours to reach the Casey house and return to Green River with the family. They were found to be without food and fuel.

FEB. 11, 1949. Two 30-ton medium tanks, a truck, and jeep were dispatched south to Buckboard and Holmes Ranch area to contact the families in that area to learn of their condition and situation regarding the storm. No one from this area had been heard from for more than two weeks. All were faring well and had sufficient fuel and food for another two weeks.

FEB. 12, 1949. Two tanks, six by six truck and jeep were sent to Antelope Springs 40 miles east of Rock Springs, to rescue Dick Carpenter who required medical attention. It required one and one-half hours for the first tank to reach Bitter Creek from the highway. The second tank required five hours to negotiate this two-mile stretch. The blizzard was so bad they had to stay the night in Bitter Creek.

FEB. 13, 1949. The trip was resumed in the morning and the unit reached the Carpenter place, made their rescue, and was enroute back within half an hour. The wind was so strong and the blowing snow was so thick the tank tracks made thirty minutes earlier could not be seen at all. It took about 8 to 10 hours for the return trip.

FEB. 15, 1949. Green River Sportsman's Club were feeding 200 antelope near the Korean Gardens, four miles west of Green

River. Two dogs shot and five antelope disposed of by the Sportsman's Club following dog-molestations of the antelope.

The sportsmen warned people having dogs in the vicinity of the antelope to prevent them from molesting the animals. Any dogs caught chasing or snapping at the game would be shot at once.

Rawlins, Wyoming, had been marooned for over two weeks, and it was still impossible to get into the town. There were 12-foot drifts of snow across the highway west of Rawlins.

A weasel and a guard truck was sent to Fort Bridger to rescue a marooned party on Bigelow Bench, 8 miles west of Fort Bridger.

FEB. 20, 1949. The first passenger trains were passing through Green River after a 15 day tie-up. Highway travel was started back to normal.

FEB. 22, 1949. The trains were moving regularly on schedule and highway travel was back to normal.

MARCH 3, 1949. The February "operation snow bound" in Green River required $1,200 of Red Cross funds to meet the emergency needs.

MARCH 15, 1949. Another blizzard hit the same troubled areas, which caused additional heavy losses to the calving and lambing livestock within the blizzard area.

APRIL 1, 1949. Chinook winds hit and the snow melted as if under a blow torch. Flooding followed resulting in a quagmire of mud within the states of the 1949 Blizzard. The results tie up the rural people. But the temperatures were more moderate.

On Jan. 24, 1949, President Harry S. Truman put into effect "Operation Snowbound." The Army put the C-82 flying boxcar and C-47s (D-C3s) in the snowbound areas. They flew dropping feed to snowbound livestock, animals and supplies to the snowbound ranchers, farms and towns through the end of March. Many small planes, private and federal, were used to take supplies to the snowbound and rescue sick people.

The total overall loss within the states of the 1949 Blizzard were estimated at $190 million. Seventy-six lives had been lost in the blizzards. There were 119,000 cattle and 134,000 sheep killed valued at $19,600. Crop losses were put at $108 million. Property damage at $10.7 million. Damage and revenue to the railroads was $50 million.

The 1949 Blizzard was a real boiler. When will the next one occur?

❖

"Oh, Christmas Tree..."

by Ruth Lauritzen

While an almost universal symbol of the American Christmas of today, the Christmas tree is a relative newcomer to the holiday scene in the United States. The tradition of bringing a decorated tree into the home for the holidays came to the United States in the mid-to-late 1800s through two avenues; German immigrants and the widespread adoption of Victorian English fancies.

The originators of the custom, the Germans, brought the practice with them when they immigrated. According to *The Christmas Tree Book* by Philip V. Snyder the earliest recorded Christmas tree in America appeared on Christmas Day 1747 in the German Moravian church's communal settlement at Bethlehem, Pennsylvania. As more and more Germanic peoples arrived in this country the decorated tree became more common, but remained pretty much an ethnic oddity throughout most of the United States until the late 1800s when its use was popularized by the tastemakers of Victorian America, the English.

By the mid 1800s the Christmas tree was very popular in England, due in part to the influence of Prince Albert, the German husband of Queen Victoria. The trees he decorated for his children were widely publicized in periodicals of the day. Always eager to ape what they perceived as their more sophisticated cousins across the sea, upper class Americans soon adopted the Christmas tree. However, in a twist that was uniquely American, the evergreen sat on the floor instead of a table as was the custom in Europe.

In spite of this difference the Christmas tree retained much of its European influence. Most of the purchased trims such as glass, metal and wax ornaments, tinsel and candle holders continued to be imported from Germany. However, in many American homes, especially those of more modest means, it was perfectly acceptable, even desirable, to make tree decorations. Chains of popcorn, cranberries and colorful paper loops festooned the branches as well as paper cones full of candies, tissue paper flowers, home-baked cook-ies, and decorations made from blown out eggs and even prunes. Contemporary publications such as *Godey's Lady's Book* and *Peterson's Magazine* were full of ideas and instructions for such decorations.

The tree tradition first came to Sweetwater County and Green River through the German influence. This area's extremely ethnically diverse population had its share of German families who brought the custom with them. According to Mrs. Roy Soulsby, whose reminisces of early day Rock Springs are found in the information files of the Sweetwater County Historical Museum, her German immigrant family always had a tree.

> The children were put to bed early so that their parents could decorate the tree with strings of pop-corn and cranberries and decorations made out of bits of paper, yarn and other things which had been saved by their mother during the year. To these were added candles in holders clipped to the branches.

In a 1972 *Green River Star* article Louise Spinner Graf recalled how trees were incorporated into the Christmas celebrations of the German families in Green River. A group of six German families, including the Spinners, Eggs and Gaensslens, special ordered trees each holiday season. Graf remembered the trees of her youth were decorated with the beautiful glass, metal and paper ornaments brought from the old country as well as the more simple trims of home-baked cookies and ropes of cranberries and popcorn. She said that Christmas was a time of visiting and hospitality when visitors, after viewing the tree, took a cookie of their choice from its branches when they left.

According to Graf the custom of the Christmas tree was not widely adopted in Green River until after World War I. This was not uncommon in regions of the western and southern United States which were far removed from the "cultural centers" of the large eastern cities. However a glance around the city today confirms that the notion, once adopted, has taken a firm hold on Wyoming Christmas traditions.

❖

The Oldest Working Bank in the County

by James W. June

In 1888, Mr. Robert Morris and Mr. Hunter established the Morris and Hunter Bank and operated it in conjunction with the Hunter & Morris General Merchandise, which was located in block 20 in the Railroad yards on the north side of West Second South, across from the present apartments at 95 South Second West Street.

The Morris brothers, Robert and Edward, purchased the Hunter & Morris General Merchandise and the Morris Hunter Bank, forming the Morris Mercantile Company and changing the name of the bank to the Morris State Bank in 1890.

The Morris Mercantile Company built a new brick building on the comer of West Railroad Avenue and North Center Street and moved into it in 1891. The Morris State Bank was located in the north end of the building on the alley.

When the State of Wyoming established its first banking department in 1895, the Morris State Bank received its charter.

In 1915, T.S. Taliaferro Jr. was elected as president of the Morris State Bank.

When the Green River Mercantile Company purchased the Morris Mercantile Company and the Morris State Bank in 1916, the bank was reincorporated under the name of State Bank of Green River.

On March 25, 1917, the Green River Mercantile building (the Old Morris Mercantile Company building) was completely destroyed by fire and also the State Bank of Green River with only the vault surviving the fire.

The day after the fire in 1917, the State Bank of Green River was open for business at 33 Elizabeth Street. This is the parking lot behind the Ember's Restaurant and where Nick's Barber Shop was located.

In 1919, when the First National Bank of Green River moved from the Green River Mercantile Company building into their new building on East Railroad Avenue, the State Bank of Green River, established in 1907, moved into that location in the Green River Mercantile Company.

When the new Hotel Tomahawk building was open in 1921, the State Bank of Green River moved into the first door south of the Hotel Lobby.

In 1932, the State Bank of Green River moved back into its old location off the alley in the Green River Mercantile Company building.

The State Bank of Green River built and moved into a new building at 79 West Flaming Gorge Way in 1960.

Again the State Bank of Green River built a new building and moved to 125 West Flaming Gorge Way in October, 1977.

The State Bank of Green River merged with the First Security Bank of Wyoming in October 1993, and became the First Security Bank of Green River. The bank has served continuously the residents of Green River and Sweetwater County for 106 years.

The original Morris and Hunter Bank vault is still in use and can be seen in the office of the Green River Mercantile Company.

❖

Oldest Continuous Business in Sweetwater County

by James W. June

In July, 1868, when Green River City was being built, S.I. Field built a wooden frame, single story structure on the south side of the railroad tracks, which included a General Merchandise Store, a restaurant, and residence.

This site was located on the south side and at 100 East Second South Street, opposite the over walk across the railroad. John Wesley Powell Expeditions were serviced at the Field store and restaurant in 1869 and 1871.

The Field Store was the voting precinct for south of the railroad right-of-way in the 1870 General election. In 1872, W.A. Johnson purchased the S.I. Field property and store.

W.A. Johnson used the S.I. Field building for his residence and developed the house and yard into a show place, with landscaping and lawn. The property and house was purchased by Mountain States Telephone Company to build a warehouse in June 1977, tearing down the house but did not build the warehouse.

The property was later sold and a greenhouse was built on the site.

In 1872, W.A. Johnson changed the Field General Merchandise Store to the W.A. Johnson Mercantile Company and moved its location two blocks to the west on the north side of West Second South Street.

The Johnson Mercantile sold clothing, groceries, wagons, etc. The W. A. Johnson Mercantile Company was the depot for the Big Piney Stage Line, which had the U.S. Mail contract and carried passengers.

The stage left Green River every Monday morning for Fontenelle, La Barge, Calhounville and Big Piney and returned to

S.1. Field general merchandise store, restaurant and residence, south of the railroad tracks in 1868. (Photo courtesy Sweetwater County Historical Museum)

Green River every Saturday morning. The W.A. Johnson Mercantile Company was purchased by Mr. Robert Morris and Mr. Hunter in 1887.

In 1887, the name was changed to the Hunter and Morris General Merchandise Company. They sold clothing, groceries, rubber goods, coffins, wagons, etc. The Morris brothers, Robert and Edward, sons of Esther Hobart Morris, purchased the Hunter and Morris General Merchandise Company in 1890.

The Morris Mercantile Company was formed in 1890. The Morris Mercantile Company moved into a new two-story brick building on West Railroad Avenue, east of the Brewery in 1891. They sold clothing, dry goods, groceries, harness, saddles, wagons, buggies, buckboards, hay, grain and building materials.

The Green River Mercantile Company was incorporated in 1910 and purchased the Lawrence and Hoadley General Store. In 1910, the Green River Mercantile Company also had a Big Island Branch Store at Bridge on the Green River. It was a store, hotel, shearing corral and wool house.

In 1914, the Big Island Branch Store was made a voting precinct. In mid-1920, the federal government had the Branch Store torn down because it was on federal land.

In 1913, the Green River Mercantile Company established a meat market, sold groceries, clothing, up-to-date fabrics, hay, grain, wagons and buggies.

W.A. Johnson establishment (S.I. Field general store, restaurant and residence) torn down in 1977. (Photo courtesy Sweetwater County Historical Museum)

In 1914, the Green River Mercantile sold and displayed Ford cars and gasoline to the automotive business.

In 1916, the Green River Mercantile Company purchased and merged the Morris Mercantile Company into their corporation. They then moved into the Morris Mercantile Company building on Railroad Avenue.

In February 1917, fire burned the Green River Mercantile Company building to the ground on Railroad Avenue. It destroyed the Green River Mercantile Company business, the State Bank of Green River, U.S. Post Office and all the offices on the second floor.

The day after the fire the Green River Mercantile Company opened its business in the buildings where Nick's Barber Shop and Edith's Beauty Shop were on Elizabeth Street. This is now the parking lot behind the Embers Restaurant.

The Green River Mercantile Company remodeled and expanded the original building at 79 North First East in 1921 and again in 1926, dealing in general merchandise, groceries, meats and hardware.

From 1922 until the mid-1930s, the Green River Mercantile Company were undertakers and embalmers.

The Green River Mercantile Company is still in business at the present time, being the oldest mercantile business in Sweetwater County established by S.I. Field in 1868.

❖

Unique Greeter at Local Museum

by Marna Grubb

When one visits the Sweetwater County Museum located in the Courthouse at Green River, a photo cut-out of a man is there to greet visitors.

This man is W.S. Johnson II, born in Green River on May 25, 1882, and died in Green River on November 22, 1958. He was a son of frontier businessman and rancher, W.A. Johnson, Sr.

Green River has had three persons named W.A. Johnson - Sr. (1833-1910), II (1882-1958), and Jr. (Willie) who lives in Green River today in the family home at 114 East 2nd South.

W.A. Johnson, Jr. stands next to the cardboard cutout of his father on display at the Sweetwater County Historical Museum. (Photo courtesy the Green River Star)

W.A. Johnson, Sr. came to Green River before the arrival of the railroad. He was an active man in the business world and was county sheriff in 1879-80. In his obituary in the *Green River Star* in 1910, it was reported that "his acts of charity were many, and while not always visible, every day of his life he was doing something for his fellow men." It further stated that, "Through his business shrewdness, he gathered about him valuable and extensive property interests in Nebraska and Wyoming."

Green River's Expedition Island was originally claimed by S.I. Field in 1868 when he platted Green River City before the arrival of the railroad. In 1872, W.A. Johnson Sr. purchased the Field property. The island then became known as Johnson Island.

In later years (1909), the Town of Green River purchased Johnson Island from Western Alkali Company. In 1910, the name was changed to Island Park, and the town replaced the wooden bridge with a steel bridge, which is still in use today. It wasn't until 1969 that the name was changed to Expedition Island in honor of John Wesley Powell's Green and Colorado River expeditions, which began in Green River.

W.A. Johnson II, son of W.A. Johnson Sr., had been a rancher at Bridger Bottom and, in 1907, he entered the contracting business here with J.E. Irvine. Later he operated the town's second movie theater in the days of silent films.

In June of 1909, he was married to Daisy Nellie Vickery of Ogden, who also was a native of Green River. W.A. Johnson built a new home for the couple south of the rail yards, where they lived the remainder of their lives. In 1910, W.A. Johnson II was employed by the railroad, relinquishing this in 1914 when he was appointed as postmaster at Green River.

In 1923, he entered the grocery business when he went into the Selrite bakery and grocery. Between 1933 and 1938 he was deputy state game and fish warden for the area. From 1938 to 1943, he was foreman of the CCC camp at Rawlins. During the war years (1943-47) he was employed at the Stansbury mine as custodian.

W.A. Johnson II was 76 years old when he died in 1958, and his wife Daisy was 98 when she died in 1985. W.A. Johnson II and Daisy had three sons - Gilbert Vickery Johnson who died as an infant (July 4, 1910-July 26, 1910); W.A. (Willie) Johnson, Jr. who still resides at the family home at 144 East 2nd South; and Douglas, who is married with two children and living in Colorado Springs, Colorado.

W.A. "Willie" Johnson Jr. was born in Green River and graduated in 1940 from high school in Green River, the old Lincoln

School before it burned down. He worked for the USGS in Colorado for one year before entering the University of Utah.

In 1942, during the World War II, Willie entered the service and served in England with the 8th Air Force for air/sea rescue. He was out of the service and back to Green River in 1945.

He, along with his brother Doug, built an addition onto the house. He also attended the University of Wyoming for three years prior to 1950, where he studied electrical engineering. During the 1950s he worked for the Union Pacific Railroad as an electrician for nine years. He then ventured to Stauffer Chemical and retired in 1992 after 30 years at the age of 71.

Willie's electrical career had begun when he was six years old. His father was a merchant and gave Willie a Lionel electric train for Christmas so Willie took it apart and this started his interest in electricity.

He also learned much from a big erector set with an electric motor. Through much of his career, he was surrounded by D.C. motors and generators.

While growing up in Green River, Willie said he had many chores to do, such as chopping kindling wood, carrying in the coal, taking out the ashes and pulling weeds. He received an allowance from which he would buy savings stamps at school, plus he saved until he had $35 to buy a bicycle. As for discipline, "Spanking was the way in those days."

For fun, he would swim in the river and at Green River's outdoor swimming pool. He learned to swim by copying Bill and Maxine Spears, the managers of the pool. He also enjoyed playing tennis with Woodrow Hunter on the southside railroad court.

He said he was spoiled on birthdays. It was enjoyed by inviting friends over for cake. His parents' birthdays were not observed.

"They should have been," he added. Also he and his brother would get together with the Larsen and Potts children and sell Kool-Aid drinks on top of old box crates. They enjoyed gun fights with their rubber guns. Solid-wood, model-airplane carving or building was an intensively-pursued hobby for Willie.

Christmas was a fun time for his family. Usually Doug and Willie, and sometimes dad, W.A. Johnson II, went to Little Mountain for a Christmas tree. For many years, candles were used to decorate the tree.

Some of their family friends were Minnie Rasmusen, after whom Minnie's Gap was named, and Emma (1884-1958) and Walter S. Holmes (1860-1942) from the Holmes Ranch located along the river about one mile east from the Buckboard Ferry Crossing, 24 miles south of Green River.

Willie has very fond memories of several dogs he had as pets throughout the years - Texas, Black Silk, Black Satin and Rusty. There was also a cat named Blackie.

Willie remembers an exciting time while on a high school graduation party trip. They were doing a mountain climbing expedition to Sheep Creek cave. He didn't invite his best friend, Bert Nelson, for the climb because the year before one of his legs was paralyzed from the knee down from a football injury - so Bert took off by himself with no one aware of this.

Later they heard him calling and found he had become trapped 65 feet from the ground on the face of the cliff. They were trying to determine how to get him down safely and had to talk him out of jumping. They then tied their 5/8-inch diameter by SO-foot, hemp climbing rope around a rock and attempted to toss it to Bert. After many failures, Tony Kalivas finally made a successful toss and Bert tied off the rope, but the free end of the rope was still 14 feet short of the boulder-strewn ground.

Bert lowered himself down to the end of the rope and, using the face of the cliff for pushing off, he swung himself toward a bunch of bushes and let go, landing upon them without injury, so all turned out well. But. .. back at school, they "got chewed out" by their teacher Edith Peters.

While in Junior High and High School, Willie's hobbies were experimental electrical-device building and chemistry set experiments. From 1955 to 1960, he was uranium hunting; and 1955 to 1970 he also was woodworking. Snowmobiling was foremost in his thoughts from 1970 to 1977. Willie's hobby since 1984 was amateur astronomy.

In closing, I urge you to visit the Sweetwater County Museum where W.A. Johnson II will greet you and lure you in to view some of Sweetwater County's historic past - you'll enjoy it!

❖

Building of the
Union Pacific Railroad

by James W. June

The Union Pacific and the Central Pacific companies were incorporated to build the first transcontinental railroad.

The Central Pacific Company was organized in Sacramento, California.

The Central Pacific building from California, used Chinese labor and pushed construction to reach Utah before the Union Pacific.

The Union Pacific Company used mostly Irish laborers and sped across the prairies of Nebraska, the mountains and deserts of Wyoming from Omaha to win the race to the Utah terminal and the railro,ad route to the West Coast.

On May 10, 1869, a train from the East met a train from the West at Promontory Point, 40 miles from the Great Salt Lake, 1,086 miles west of Omaha on the Missouri River and 600 miles east of Sacramento.

The railroad received 20 sections of land for every mile of track completed. Union Pacific also received mineral rights on the land.

The company was loaned money in government bonds for a thirty-year period, amounting to $16,000 a mile for easy construction, $32,000 a mile for more difficult construction, and $48,000 a mile for difficult construction across deserts and over mountains.

The Union Pacific followed a southern route across Wyoming because of the lower mountain passes and grades which lent to the construction of the railroad. The route followed the coal deposits across Wyoming, and Salt Lake City and Brigham Young had pressed for a railroad route into the Salt Lake Valley since 1852.

The Union Pacific followed the Platte River to the South Platte and then to Crow Creek and across Sherman Hill. The difficulty was finding a pass over the hill with a grade level enough for track.

William H. Jackson photograph of the Green River depot in 1869. (Photo courtesy Sweetwater County Historical Museum)

Grenville M. Dodge separated from his troops in 1865 after an Indian campaign and took a shortcut to reach his companions.

He came upon a pass (Evans Pass over Sherman Hill) through the mountains which led without a break to the Laramie plains.

The pass was marked by a lone tree and Crow Creek. The transcontinental route then went through a second pass at Creston, Wyoming, which is at the southern edge of the great saddleback, while South Pass is in the northern edge, 80 miles to the northwest.

This route also missed the Bridger Pass to the south, thus avoiding the heavy snow conditions of Bridger, South Pass and the snow in passes of Colorado.

The construction of the 540 miles between Cheyenne and Ogden, less than half the length from Omaha to Ogden, cost 70 percent of the entire cost of building the road.

The first engineering problem occurred crossing the summit of Sherman Hill.

According to Union Pacific contract, the grade could rise only 90 feet to the mile, so switchbacks were used to avoid too steep a climb. The second engineering problem was west of Sherman Station at Dale Creek, a chasm from 600 to 700 feet wide and over 130 feet deep.

A high, wooden trestle bridge was built, but later burned and replaced with a steel, spider-web bridge.

When heavy freight and heavier engines made crossing dangetous, a tunnel through the mountain lowered the summit to 8,000 feet and the old bridge was abandoned.

Six million railroad ties were needed, 2,400 ties to every mile. Ties made of oak were shipped from Pennsylvania at a cost of $3.59 each until the tie camps in the mountains were opened.

The tie camps employed thousands of choppers in the mountains. During the winters of 1867-68 a thousand men worked in the Laramie Mountains cutting ties to float down the streams.

Tie Siding near Sherman became an important tie depot. The first tie camps in the upper Green River area were opened in the fall of 1867, and the first tie drive reached Green River City in the spring of 1868 and was an annual drive of 4,000 ties per year until 1941.

Other tie camps of importance were in the Ham's Fork, Smith's Fork and Black's Fork, Bear River areas and ties were floated to the railroad for use in building the tracks.

Food for men and livestock was hauled 200 to 300 miles beyond the end of the track where men were grading.

One construction camp hired Buffalo Bill Cody at $500 per month for 18 months to furnish the camp with the hindquarters of 20 buffalo per day.

The desert water between Rawlins and Green River was tainted with salt and alkali. That surface water was even unfit for use in locomotives.

It was necessary to sink deep artesian wells to obtain water for men and engines. Water had to be hauled to the end of the track and carried in wagons 50 to 60 miles to various construction camps.

From Fort Kearny in Nebraska to Bitter Creek, Wyoming, every mile had to be surveyed, graded, "tied," and bridged under military protection because of Indian problems. At times half of the construction gangs would have to stand guard while the other half worked.

Surveyor's stakes were pulled up and destroyed, stations were raided and burned, and construction trains wrecked.

Protection for the workers in Wyoming were from Fort Russell (now Fort Warren) at Cheyenne, Fort Sanders near present Laramie and Fort Steele near Rawlins.

Coal lands were included in the land grants awarded through the Act of 1864. The Union Pacific surveyed mines at Carbon (1868), Rock Springs (1868) and Almy (1869). Some of the first coal mines in the Rock Springs area were Rock Springs (1868), Black Butte (1869), Van Dyk (1869), Blair (1869), Point of Rock (1869), and Hallville (1869).

The Indians of the region knew of coal deposits in southern Wyoming but did not use them. In 1824-25 when the mountain men came to the area, Jim Bridger first learned of the coal deposits and became interested in them.

He built the Fort Bridger trading post near a coal deposit and used it in his blacksmith shop.

Bridger also guided Fremont in 1843-44 and showed him the coal deposits in Carbon County, and Fremont's report first mentions coal deposits in Wyoming.

In 1850, Bridger showed Captain Howard Stansbury the survey of the Great Salt Lake with its coal beds along the Overland Trail.

In 1862, the Overland Stage was moved and operated along this route, and many of the stations and blacksmith shop utilized the coal in the area. The route was also used by the Union Pacific.

The end-of-track towns moved rapidly with the construction work and were called "Hell on Wheels." Boarding trains for track gangs, bunk cars, kitchen-store-room-office car, and grader's fort (half buried "dug-outs"), for protection from stray bullets during sleeping, strung alongside the grade of these towns.

Then came the "hangers on" which included the tent cities of restaurants, gambling halls, saloons with their "gin mills", and the dance halls with the "daughters of joy", "sisters of misery" and "painted cats".

Huge populations would migrate overnight, resulting in 3,000 people in the town.

This would be short-lived and when the end of track moved on in 60 days, nothing remained.

Towns like Benton, Bryan, and Bear River City were just a few to meet this fate. Other towns like Cheyenne, Laramie, Rawlins, Rock Springs, Green River, and Evanston, survived and became permanent towns along the Union Pacific.

Camp Carmichael was the last of the construction camps before Green River, approximately 4 miles east of town. At this point was the Great Cut at Bitter Creek, one of the longest on the Union Pacific.

On October 1, 1868, the Union Pacific tracks and train reached Green River to find a town of 2,000 people. Green River City was the only town which the Union Pacific Railroad Company did not build.

Green River City was never an end of the track town, but the Union Pacific continued on to make Bryan the end of the line.

West of Green River City existed another cut which was sixty-feet high and a hundred feet long and known as Burning Cut.

A watchman built a fire one night and the wall caught fire burning with a brilliant flame. The flames were used to illuminate night work on the cut.

In 1870, the Union Pacific Company investigated the potential of extracting shale oil. This cut later became known as Peru.

Bear River City was the next end of the track terminal with more than 2,000 people, after Bryan. It became famous for crime, lynching, and a pitched battle in November, 1868 between the townspeople and a construction gang.

Evansville (Evanston) was reached by the Union Pacific December 1, 1868. The Union Pacific continued on to Wasatch for the end of track terminal.

The Union Pacific Railroad Company won the race to Promontory Point and east met west on May 10, 1969.

❖

Price Control and Rationing in Wyoming

by James W. June

On Dec. 7, 1941, wartime scarcity of essential goods brought about price control and rationing. One month after Pearl Harbor, in January 1942, Congress passed an act setting up the Office of Price Administration (OPA) to stabilize prices of goods and services.

A presidential directive gave the OPA the power of rationing scarce goods. Due to the rapidly rising prices in April 1942, the OPA issued the General Maximum Price Regulation - General Max - freezing prices at the highest levels that prevailed in March, 1942, and became effective in May, 1942.

In March, 1945, the OPA issued Maximum Price Regulation 580, which allowed a certain percentage mark-up based on a fair retail margin.

The State of Wyoming set up the Price Control and Rationing Program Dec. 23, 1941, which lasted until post-war. Boards of Price Control and Rationing were set up in each county.

Five days after Pearl Harbor, the government banned the sale of tires and tubes until a rationing program was in place. On Jan. 5, 1942, tires and tubes were released in limited numbers to persons who could establish their need to further public welfare and safety.

Wyoming tire and tube quota varied from month to month. In June 1942, Wyoming was allowed 112 passenger car tires, 681 passenger car retreads, 398 passenger car tubes, 931 truck and bus tubes. The essential users' tire and tube that were to be replaced were examined at official inspection stations.

The tires became scarce and precious. The motorist had to record the make and serial numbers of their tires to aid in arrest of tire thieves. Two Cheyenne taxi drivers were arrested for the sale of tires they had stolen and served six months in jail and fined $25.

The rubber shortage led to new cars with only four tires. In November, 1942, persons with more than one spare tire were required to sell the extras to the government. Those who did not relinquish them were refused gas rationing books. Ten thousand tires were sold in the Casper region.

In 1942, the President requested that a 35-mile mph speed limit be observed. By October, 1942, the various newspapers were publishing car license numbers of those not observing the 35 mph speed limit. In July, 1943, the OPA threatened to check speeds all over the state and to report violators to the local ration boards, which after a hearing, could cancel gasoline ration books.

Automobiles, trucks, tractors, trailers, typewriters and bicycles were added to tires and tubes, which could not be bought without a certificate obtained from the local rationing board. Wyoming's October, 1942, quota was 104 cars and in October, 1944, was only 7.

Gasoline rationing came to Wyoming Dec. 1, 1942. Motor vehicle owners registered and obtained coupon books. Basic ration in Wyoming was four gallons a week until October, 1943, when it was reduced to three gallons a week. It was cut to two gallons per week in March, 1944, and increased to three gallons per week in June, 1945.

There were A ration stickers for the minimum ration. There were also B and C gasoline stickers issued to persons showing special need, authorizing supplemental ration of gasoline.

Truckers were issued a T gasoline sticker that entitled them additional gas for the business. An illegal use of the stamps included giving ration stamps to filling station owners, who would then give additional gas to his friends.

On Jan. 7, 1943, a ban on non-essential "pleasure" driving was enacted, and in Sept. 1, 1943, it was revoked.

In May, 1942, everyone had to register for a book of sugar coupons. The upcoming sugar rationing was announced in January, 1942, and when the ration went into effect in May, all the sugar had been purchased with none available in the stores.

To correct this when registering for the ration books, the amount of sugar on hand had to be declared and was deducted from the rationing book.

In Nov. 29, 1942, coffee ration began. Every person over 15 was allowed one pound of coffee every five weeks. Coffee rationing was dropped after nine months when adequate supplies were found.

In Feb. 7, 1943, shoes were added to the ration list with three pairs of shoes per person per year and was reduced before the end of the war.

March, 1943, saw the issuance of War Ration Book 2. Red stamps were for meats, butter, margarine, edible fats and oils, cheese, canned milk and canned fish. Blue stamps were used for canned fruits and vegetables, fruit juices, soups, baby food, and for a short time dried fruits, peas and beans, and preserves.

March 1, 1944, red-and-blue plastic one-point tokens were introduced to supplement the supply of red and blue stamps and to facilitate change making.

Toward the end of the war, Wyoming meat counters were sometimes bare because much of the nation's meat was not flowing through normal channels, and conditions became worse in 1946.

Many people in Wyoming violated the OPA regulations when they had the opportunity, but the people of Wyoming did their part as did the ones who fought and gave their lives in winning the war.

❖

Women's Work:
Turn-Of-The Century
Businesswomen

by Ruth Lauritzen

Women in turn-of-the-century Green River had much to occupy their minds (and bodies) with rearing large families and keeping house in an era before drop-in daycare and vacuum cleaners. For some women, however, this was just a part of what they did. Whether by desire or necessity some women entered the then male-dominated world of commerce.

This was no easy proposition. According to a recent book *The Woman Entrepreneur* by Linda Pinson and JelTy Jinnett, for hundreds of years laws worked against a woman trying to own a business. "The efforts of early women entrepreneurs were hampered by laws which prevented them from entering into contracts, owning property, or bringing legal suits. Husbands could prevent their wives from opening bank accounts or starting businesses. A husband could claim all of a wife's wages in order to settle his debts." Fortunately for women in Wyoming many of these laws no longer applied. With statehood in 1890 came the right for women to vote and to own property.

In addition to legal roadblocks, at the time there were widely held beliefs about the physical and mental abilities of women. They were not regarded as having the intellectual capacity, temperament or even the physical strength required to deal with matters outside their traditional sphere of influence, the home. Some girls were even denied advanced education which would help them in business on these same grounds. Dr. Edward Clark, a retired member of the Harvard University medical faculty said in his 1873 book, Sex in Education; or, A Fair Chance for the Girls that the limited physical strength of the

In 1878, Martha Gravelle became a business-woman when her husband, George Gravelle, died. She continued to manage the drug store even after the death of her second husband, Henry Campbell, until her death in 1910. (Photo courtesy Sweetwater County Historical Museum)

young female body was not up to the biological strain of puberty and the mental rigors of study. He cited studies done on Vassar women which follow the hapless "Miss D", an eighteen year old student, who "..emerged from four years at Vassar a neuralgic and hysterical' invalid, her breasts and reproductive organs withered from excessive study and physical exercise...."

To the restrictive laws, doubts of physical and intellectual capabilities, and lack of appropriate education, add the popular Victorian belief of what was proper for a woman to do with her time and it is little wonder that the business community was not overloaded with females. However, a glance at business directories for Green River in the early 1900s indicates that there were women who had braved the opposition and stepped out into the business world.

Generally a woman would gain ownership of a business in one of two ways. She would start her own or, more commonly, inherit an existing enterprise from a deceased husband. Both situations occurred in turn-of-the-century Green River and the following stories of two women contain common threads of the experiences women were having all over the world.

The oft-widowed Martha Scott Baker Gravelle Campbell was thrust into the world of business by necessity. According to a family history in the Sweetwater County Historical Museum files, young Martha Scott came from her home in London, England to Omaha, Nebraska in the late 1860s where she met her fiance, William Baker. After their marriage they travelled to Bryan, a wild end-of-the-track town located about 20 miles west of Green River on the newly constructed Union Pacific Railroad. During their few years there Martha bore and buried two sons. When the switching point was moved to Green River in 1872 the Bakers followed the rest of the town in relocating there. In 1873 Martha gave birth to the first white baby born in Green River, Martha Rebecca Baker. She was expecting her next child when her husband drowned while fishing in the river. The widow bore her son and continued her life with two small children.

Tragedy struck again when a freak accident caused her infant son to drown in the same river that took his father's life. A popular picnic ground in Green River was an island in the river. Since no bridge existed the only access was to walk out on the railroad bridge and then climb down a ladder to the island. Martha was bringing her children along on a picnic with friends when she lost her balance, fell down through the rough logs of the bridge, dropping her baby into the river. A man nearby fishing attempted to retrieve the drowning child with his pole but was unsuccessful.

This man was George Gideon Gravelle, owner of a local apothecary shop. George and Martha were married in 1876 and to this union was born one child, George Gideon Gravelle, Jr. The marriage was not to be a long one as George Sr. succumbed to kidney disease in 1878, leaving Martha a widow once again.

During her brief marriage she had learned the business of running a drug store and she continued after the death of her husband. She remarried in 1881 to Henry Hudson Campbell, a carpenter working on bridge construction with the railroad. She changed the name of the business to Mrs. H.H. Campbell Drug Store and stayed in business through the birth of two children, Hattie Mary in 1882 and Madeline Blanch in 1885. Mr. Campbell apparently worked at his wife's store because according to the family history he fell dead there one morning in January 1894 while reaching for a bottle of patent medicine.

Martha continued to run her business until her death in 1910. In later years she was assisted by her son George Jr. who had received pharmacy training at the University of Wyoming. After her death George Jr. continued to operate the store as Gravelle Drug until 1915.

An example of the businesswoman who started her own enterprise can be found in Eleanor Eggs Gaensslen. At her death in 1956 she was the owner and manager of what was Green River's oldest continually operated business, the Gaensslen Shop. Eleanor R. Eggs was born in 1875 in St. Louis, Missouri to Charles and Carolina Eggs. Her parents, both German immigrants, moved the family to Green River in 1886. Eleanor's mother was a businesswoman in her own right as part-owner with her husband and manager of the Big Horn Hotel. The primary business for women in Green River one hundred years ago was the running of hotels and rooming houses. Business directories from the early 1900s show six such establishments under the proprietorship of women.

Eleanor was an accomplished musician and artist, travelling to Europe at age 13 to study music. The year 1900 found her continuing her studies in music at the University of Wyoming when she received a telegram from home requesting her presence for some unknown reason. Being a dutiful daughter she headed west on the train and upon her arrival in Green River found she had been appointed assistant to her uncle, Postmaster Bernhard Spinner. The Green River Post Office was a busy place in those days as the town was experiencing a mini-boom of sorts. Crews were engaged in some extensive rebuilding of the railroad grade up Peru Hill through Fish Cut west of town. Eleanor experienced a baptism by fire in the business of running a post office as indicated by an article about her in a 1954 issue of the *Green River Star*. "The intricacies of registered mail, special deliveries, money orders, and governmental accounting kept the young lady awake many a night until she mastered them."

She stayed with her job as assistant postmaster for two terms, all the while saving her money to start her dream business, a millinery shop. In 1906 her dream was realized when she bought her initial stock and, with one small display case, a mirror and a few pieces of furniture borrowed from home set up shop in what is now the Fred's Taxidermy Shop on Center Street. She also displayed her craft work and gave lessons in woodburning, china painting, and leather burning as well as piano.

Her marriage in 1908 to Emil A. Gaensslen resulted in a change of the name of her shop, but it continued to run. She eventually moved the business to the present site of Rose Floral on Flaming Gorge Way and ran the shop out of one side of the building and housed her increasing family in the other. She bore five children, three of whom survived to adulthood; Carl A. Gaensslen in 1910, Emil A. Gaensslen in 1913 and Eleanor C. Gaensslen Schofield in 1915.

These women and others like them laid the foundation for others to enter the world of business. Today women own fifty percent of retail businesses and seven percent of service businesses. Statistically women start about twice as many businesses as men and if present numbers continue will own about forty percent of all businesses by the year 2000. These are heady statistics which would no doubt astound Martha and Eleanor.

River Crossings, Ferries

by James W. June

At the major crossing of the Green River, ferries were operated for travelers to cross the river. These ferries were in use until the bridges were constructed across the river.

The first wagon bridge across the river was constructed in 1896 by the Town of Green River and Sweetwater County south of town. In 1910, the Big Island bridge was constructed across the river at Big Island by Sweetwater County.

In 1938, the CCC moved and constructed the "CCC Bridge" across the river at the Sweetwater-Lincoln County line.

Ferries were operated across the river up until the late 1950s between the town of Green River and the Wyoming-Utah state line, at which time the construction of Flaming Gorge reservoir began.

The mountain men operated the first ferries from 1842 to 1852. These early ferries consisted of six to ten dugout canoes tied together with a platform built on them to carry one or two wagons, goods and people across the river.

The livestock was usually tied to and swam across with the ferry. One of these dugout canoes was found along the river and is in the collection at the Sweetwater County Historical Museum.

The Mormons operated the ferries from 1853 to 1858. The Utah Territorial Legislature on Jan. 16, 1852, granted the ferry rights on the Green River to Thomas Moor for one year.

This gave the Utah Territory full right to control the ferries of the Green River. This caused hard feelings between the Mormons and the mountain men with the Mormons ignoring the squatters' rights of the mountain men.

The ferries were operated by various private individuals from 1858 until the 1950s.

The later ferries were built as flat-bottomed boats, with the sides about 3- to 4-feet high, and the ends were let down for loading and unloading. The ferry boats were usually 12-feet long by 7-

Peter Appel's ferry on the Green River near Green River City circa 1886. (Photo courtesy Sweetwater County Historical Museum)

feet wide, large enough to carry a wagon, or stock and supplies across the river.

The current of the river was used to move the ferry across the river either way by the use of the length of the block and tackle attached to the cable at both ends of the ferry boat.

The operation of the ferries was a very profitable business; not only for ferrying wagons, stock and people across the river, but by buying broken down stock at cheap rates and clothing which the travelers were glad to sell and selling new stock to the traveler.

The cost of the use of the ferry varied from year to year, from party to party, and occasion to occasion. The usual rates were from $4 to $8 per wagon and from 50 cents to $1 per head of livestock.

During the peak years of travel for the emigrant trails, lines of people waited for the ferry to cross the river, especially when the river was not fordable due to high waters.

The Green River was fordable during the late fall season. These concentrations were at times quite large on both sides of the river due to those waiting for the complete train to get across.

There may have been several trains waiting to cross. Emigrants sometimes waited two or three days to get across on the ferries.

On July 4, 1849, the height of the migration, there were three hundred wagons and their accompanying teams waiting to cross the river on the ferries.

The Green River Ferry No. 2 was located downstream from the Overland Stage Station near the town of Green River. This ferry operated from 1862 until 1896, when the first wagon bridge was built across the river.

From 1862 to 1868, Bill Hickman, one of Brigham Young's "Avenging Angels," operated this ferry and reaped a rich harvest of gold from the Overland pilgrims. A.J. Hammond operated the ferry from 1869 until 1880, at which time Pete Appel purchased the ferry and operated it until 1896.

The Green River ferries were a very important part of history and development of Sweetwater County.

❖

If Houses Could Speak!

by Marna Grubb

I would like to present the memoirs of a two-story home at 6 West 2nd North Street. Green River's history revolves around this home – a stately house that has kept its integrity throughout the years, even the inside is virtually unchanged. A tour of this home is like a step back in time.

This home had its beginning in 1888, when it was built for Edward Morris and his wife, Burtie.

Edward was born in Peru, Ill., Nov. 8, 1851. His family came to Wyoming in 1869, and settled at South Pass. His mother, Esther Hobart Morris, was instrumental in establishing Wyoming as the "Equality State."

On Dec. 10, 1869, Wyoming was the first government in the world granting women the right to vote. Esther Morris served as the first woman justice of the peace, holding this position for eight and one-half months during 1870, at South Pass City, Wyoming.

In front of Wyoming's Capitol building in Cheyenne stands a monument of Esther Hobart Morris. A replica of the statue stands in Statuary Hall at the nation's Capitol in Washington, D.C.

After leaving South Pass, Edward later moved to Green River where he served as county clerk for a number of years. Then Edward and his brother Robert managed the Morris Mercantile Company on Railroad Avenue.

After Wyoming became a state in 1890, Edward J. Morris was elected as Green River's first Mayor after Green River was incorporated under the laws of the State of Wyoming. There had been other mayors while Wyoming was still a territory.

Edward served as Mayor from 1891-1893, and 1896-1898. Edward's home was the house located at what is known now as 6 West 2nd North Street.

Elmer E. Peters and wife became the next owners of the home in 1905. Elmer was born in Hancock County, Ohio, April 4, 1861.

The Dickinson home at 6 West Second North in Green River. This home had been built by Edward Morris, Green River's Mayor in 1891 when Green River was incorporated under the State of Wyoming. Edward was the son of Esther Morris. (Photo courtesy Gwynn Dickinson)

In 1884, he moved to Omaha, Neb., and was employed for three years by the Union Pacific Railroad.

Elmer arrived in Green River on Dec. 31, 1887. He worked for the railroad as a carpenter until 1890. He began a lumber and contracting business in 1894. In 1913, he began the Peters Motor Company, the first garage in Green River. E.E. Peters also served on the city council.

From March 1896, until May 1896, he served as Mayor, filling the unexpired term of Mayor T.S. Taliaferro Jr., who had resigned to become an attorney.

In 1914, Charles L. Young Sr. and his wife Clara purchased the house from E.E. Peters. Charles and Clara had three children: Charlie Jr., Clara Young Jensen and Kenneth. Kenneth Young was the stepfather of Gwynn Dickinson, who currently resides at the home.

Charles L. Young was born April 4, 1868, in Elgin, Ill. At the age of 20, he came to Green River in the late 1880s. He served as

Sheriff from 1903 until 1904. He served as Mayor from 1915 to 1917. He also served many years as the town's night marshal. He passed away in May 1944 at the age of 76. Then after Clara died, the house sat empty for a while. Kenneth Young purchased the property from the estate and Gwynn Dickinson - present owner - inherited the home from her parent's estate.

Gwynn Dickinson has lived in the home for nearly 35 years. She grew up in Green River when it was a small town, probably 3,000 population.

"Everyone knew what everyone was doing," she remarked. When she was young, they played night games, hopscotch, jacks, croquet on the lawn and, of course, spent time swimming at the old, outdoor swimming pool.

"Christmas was great in Grandma's house," she reminisced, as she pointed to the window in the living room in front of which had stood the tree. "Grandpa Young lit candles on the tree Christmas morning for all to see when the sliding door (between the dining room and living room) was rolled back."

As a Girl Scout, Gwynn remembers going to the Chrisman house, after caroling, for cookies and cocoa. This is a fond memory of mine also. Mrs. Chrisman would have wind-up toys and her doll collection out for all to see.

Gwynn has three children - John was living in the Green River area, Pat in Cheyenne and Faith in Washington, D.C.

Gwynn is to be commended for keeping the historical values of this fine home intact. This house still stands proudly as everyone hurries by.

❖

Student Bloopers

by Bill Thompson

Okay folks, ...a change of pace... the season of negative campaigning is over... it is now part of our political history. For many, the charges and counter charges have left a bad taste. The candidates have had their personal and political history under scrutiny... studied under a bad light it seems.

In strolling through the Internet recently I ran across this view of history compiled by Richard Lederer at St. Paul's School. It is titled, "The World According to Student Bloopers."

This collection is almost as accurate as the view some of the candidates had about each other. The following then is mostly from Lederer's "Bloopers," but I have taken the liberty to add some more of my own. Enjoy!

One of the fringe benefits of being an English or History teacher is receiving the occasional jewel of a student blooper in an essay. I have pasted together the following "history" of the world from certifiably genuine student bloopers collected by teachers throughout the United States, from eighth grade through college level.

Read carefully, and you will learn a lot.

The inhabitants of Egypt were called mummies. They lived in the Sarah Dessert and traveled by Camelot. The climate of the Sarah is such that the inhabitants have to live elsewhere so certain areas of the dessert are cultivated by irritation.

The Egyptains built the Pyramids in the shape of a huge triangular cube. The Pyramids are a range of mountains between France and Spain.

The Bible is full of interesting caricatures. In the first book of the Bible, Guinesses, Adam and Eve were created from an apple tree. One of their children, Cain, asked "Am I my brother's son?" God asked Abraham to sacrifice Issac on Mount Montezuma. Jacob, son of Issac, stole his brother's birthmark.

Jacob was a partiarch who brought up his 12 sons to be par-tiarchs, but they did not take to it. One of Jacob's sons, Joseph, gave refuse to the Israelites.

Pharaoh forced the Hebrew slaves to make bread without straw. Moses led them to the Red Sea, where they made unleavened bread, which is bread made without any ingredients. Afterwards Moses went up on Mount Cyanide to get the 10 commandments.

David was a Hebrew king skilled at playing the liar. He fought with the Philatelists, a race of people who lived in Biblical times. Solomon, one of David's sons, had 500 wives and 500 porcupines.

Without the Greeks, we wouldn't have history. The Greeks invented three kinds of columns - Corinthian, Doric and Ironic. They also had myths. A myth is a female moth. One myth says that the mother of Achelles dipped him in the River Stynx until he became intolerable.

Achilles appears in "The Illiad," by Homer. Homer also wrote the "Oddity," in which Penolope was the last hardship that Ulysses endured on his journey. Actually, Homer was not written by Homer but by another man of that name.

Socrates was a famous Greek teacher who went around giving people advice. They killed him. Socrates died from an overdose of wedlock.

In the Olympic Games, Greeks ran races, jumped, hurled the biscuits and threw the java. The reward to the victor was a coral wreath. The government of Athen was democratic because the peo-ple took the law into their own hands.

There were no wars in Greece, as the mountains were so high that they couldn't climb over to see what their neighbors were doing. When they fought the Parisians, the Greeks were outnum-bered because the Persians had more men.

Eventually, the Ramons conquered the Geeks. History called people Romans because they never stayed in one place for very long. At Roman banquets, the guests wore garlic in their hair. Julius Caesar extinguished himself on the battlefields of Gaul. The Ides of March killed him because they thought he was going to be made king. Nero was a cruel tyrant who would torture his poor subjects by playing the fiddle to them.

Then came the Middle Ages. King Alfred conquered the Dames, King Arthur lived in the Age of Shivery, King Harold mus-tarded his troops before the Battle of Hastings, Joan of Arc was cannonized by George Bernard Shaw, and the victims of the Black Death grew boobs on their necks.

Finally, the Magna Carta provided that no free man should be hanged twice for the same offense.

In midevil times most of the people were alliterate. The greatest writer of the time was Chaucer, who wrote many poems and verse and also wrote literature. Another tale tells of William Tell, who shot an arrow through an apple while standing on his son's head.

The Renaissance was an age in which more individuals felt the value of their human being. Martin Luther was nailed to the church door at Wittenberg for selling papal indulgences. He died a horrible death, being excommunicated by a bull.

It was the painter Donatello's interest in the female nude that made him the father of Renaissance. It was an age of great inventions and discoveries. Gutenberg invented the Bible.

Sir Walter Raleigh is a historical figure because he invented cigarettes. Another important invention was the circulation of blood. Sir Francis Drake circumcised the world with a 100-foot clipper.

The government of England was a limited mockery. Henry VIII found walking difficult because he had an abbess on his knee. Queen Elizabeth was the "Virgin Queen." As a queen she was a success. When Elizabeth exposed herself before their troops, they all shouted "harrah." Then her navy went out and defeated the Spanish Armadillo.

The greatest writer of the Renaissance was William Shakespear. Shakespear never made much money and is famous only because of his plays. He lived in Windsor with his merry wives, writing tradegies, comedies and errors. In one of Shakespear's famous plays, Hamlet rations out his situation by relieving himself in a long soliloquy. In another, Lady Macbeth tries to convince Macbeth to kill the King by attacking his manhood.

Romeo and Juliet are an example of a heroic couplet. Writing at the same time as Shakespear was Miquel Cervantes. He wrote "Donkey Hote." The next great author was John Milton. Milton wrote "Paradise Lost." Then his wife dies and he wrote "Paradise Regained."

During the Renaissance America began. Christopher Columbus was a great navigator who discovered America while cursing about the Atlantic. His ships were called the Nina, The Pinta, and the Santa Fe. Later the Pilgrims crossed the Ocean, and that was called the Pilgrim's Progress.

When they landed at Plymouth Rock, they were greeted by Indians, who came down the hill rolling their hoops before them.

The Indian squabs carried porposies on their back. Many of the Indian heroes were killed, along with their cabooses, which proved very fatal to them.

The winter of 1620 was a hard one for the settlers. Many people died and many babies were born. Captain John Smith was responsible for all this.

One of the causes of the Revolutionary Wars was the English put tacks in their tea. Also, the colonists would send their parcels through the post without stamps. During the War, Red Coats and Paul Revere was throwing balls over stone walls. The dogs were barking and the peacocks crowing. Finally, the colonists won the War and no longer had to pay for taxis.

Delegates from the original thirteen states formed the Contented Congress. Thomas Jefferson, a Virgin, and Benjamin Franklin were two singers of the Declaration of Independence.

Franklin had gone to Boston carrying all his clothes in his pocket and a loaf of bread under each arm. He invented electricity by rubbing cats backwards and declared "a horse divided against itself cannot stand." Franklin died in 1790 and is still dead.

OUT OF THE MOUTHS OF BABES
(Gleaned, reputedly, from sixth-grade test answers)

Geography

The general direction of the Alps is straight up.

Most of the houses in France are made of plastor of Paris.

Manhattan Island was brought from the Indians for $24 and I don't suppose you could buy it now for $500.

History

Napoleon wanted an heir to the throne, but since Josephine was a baroness she could not bear children.

Queen Elizabeth was a fat woman. The demands of the Spanish ambassador she stoutly resisted.

The Civil War was caused by Lincoln signing the Emasculation Proclamation.

Science

Q. Why do we not raise silk worms in the U.S.? A: We get our silk from rayon. He is a larger animal and gives more silk.

The dinosaur became extinct after the flood because they were too big to get into the Ark.

Q: What happens when there is an eclipse of the sun? A: A great many people came out to look at it.

The four seasons are salt, pepper, mustard, and vinegar.

Physiology
Q: How does the blood circulate? A: It flows down one leg and up the other. The spinal column is a long bunch of bones. The head sits on top and you sit on the bottom.

The stomach is a bowl-shaped cavity containing the organs of indigestion.

To prevent head colds, use an agonizer to spray nose until it drops into your throat.

A person should take a bath once in the summer and not so often in the winter.

Language Arts
Definitions: Strategy - when you don't let the enemy know what you did with the amunition but keep on firing. Syntax - the money collected by the Catholic Church from sinners. Virgin forest - a forest in which the hands of man has never set foot.

Q: What kind of noun is trousers? A: An uncommon noun, because it is singular on the top and plural at the bottom.

Q: List three relative pronouns. A: Aunt, uncle, brother.

Miscellaneous
The correct way to find the key to a piece is to use a pitchfork. The men who followed Jesus about were called the twelve opposums.

As she is going to be married next month, she is busy getting her torso ready.

One of the main causes of dust is janitors. A Scout obeys all to whom obedience is due and respects all duly constipated authorities.

The triangle which has an angle of 135 degrees is called an absecne triangle.

That's all for now folks... But, "Stay tuned".

❖

Ah-Choo!!!: The Deadly Flu Epidemic of 1918-19

by Ruth Lauritzen

Before the seeming magic of antibiotics, common diseases could fell large swaths of the population. Such was the case during the Spanish influenza epidemic of 1918-19. World War I was just ending when the nation was struck with the virulent disease. Spanish influenza was much like the flu that currently makes its yearly appearance. It was characterized by congestion, fever and coughing, and very frequently would develop into pneumonia. According to Wyoming historian T.A. Larson the epidemic afflicted Wyoming from the autumn of 1918 to early the following year, killing a total of 780 persons statewide.

> Public meetings were banned; schools and churches were closed. In the belief that smoke might carry the disease, leaf burning was prohibited. In Cheyenne, stores that did not close were limited to five customers at one time for each twenty-five feet of store front. When show houses and churches reopened in January, people occupied only alternate seats. (History of Wyoming, T.A. Larson, p. 404)

Green River, while not as adversely effected as many other towns, did not escape the scourge. With the number of cases mounting daily the *Green River Star* published the following proclamation on September 11, 1918.

> Owing to several cases of Spanish Influenza being reported about town the school, theaters, and

all other public gatherings, including church services will be closed until further notice. Parents are requested to keep children off the streets.

J.W. Hawk, Mayor

The issue also carried a large article from the United States Public Health Service on Spanish influenza and the recipe for a preventative potion containing quinine and dilute sulfuric acid.

In spite of precautions the disease continued to run its course. The *Star* of September 18th reported three deaths from pneumonia and a number of townspeople stricken with the flu. The next week brought five more deaths and many others were added to the sick list.

Green River experienced some special problems because a major building boom resulted in many temporary residents living in town under crowded and substandard conditions. During the autumn of 1918 a great deal of construction was going on in Green River. A new potash plant was being installed across the river. The Union Pacific Railroad had purchased four blocks bordering the railroad tracks on the south side and was busy tearing down the structures in order to widen the yard and build new machine shops and car shops. The Christensen Construction Company was the contractor brought in from Utah to do the railroad jobs. The workers lived in various rooming houses and in "paper shacks" put up by the railroad.

According to Pearl Zimmerman, who as a girl of sixteen nursed several sick people in these insubstantial structures, the buildings were built from 1-inch by 12-inch boards with tar paper nailed over the outside. The railroad furnished coal to burn for warmth, but the residents "died like flies." In a 1989 oral history on file at the Sweetwater County Historical Museum she recalled caring for the seriously ill parents of a four year old boy. "They both died that night not knowing that the other one was gone and left that baby. So the grandmother had to come get the baby from Salt Lake."

Mrs. Zimmerman was asked by Dr. Charlotte Hawk to take care of a family of seven. The father and all of the children were down with the flu and the mother had collapsed from the exhaustion of nursing them. Young Pearl, a novice in the field of medical care, followed the advice of an earlier patient, a Mrs. Sams who was a trained nurse, and sponged all of her patients with warm water and alcohol every half hour. Even this simple act was not easily accomplished due to the fact that at the time alcohol was available only by prescription because of Prohibition.

She also stated that many died because they would not eat. "So I learned, the one thing that (you) could get flu people to eat, if you went at it right, was homemade tomato soup and crackers. So, the Green River Mercantile had to deliver canned milk and tomatoes and crackers down to that house."

After spending a long day with the family, working especially hard with the youngest child, she was informed of the results of her labors the next morning by Dr. Charlotte herself. "She asked me what I did to that baby. Well of course right quick I'm scared. She said, 'I wish I could get somebody to do what you did for that baby because he was out in the snow this morning in his pajamas'." The entire family survived.

Even though the *Star* continued to report weekly a grim toll of death and illness most churches were open again by the first of November. School reopened mid-November, although attendance was low at first. The five weeks lost to the epidemic were required to be made up by a shortened Christmas vacation, cancellation of spring vacation and an extra week of school in June. The December 12th issue of the *Star* contained the following announcement:

> Parents are urged to keep their children in school every-day if possible, so that at the close of the school year there will be as few tears as possible on account of their grades.

By January 1919 not only was the war with Germany over, but the war with Spanish influenza as well. Each week fewer cases were reported. Many had died, but many more had survived and the year of 1919 began as one full of bright promise. The town of Green River was in the midst of a great economic expansion fueled by the railroad, oil shale and potash development, and the addition of many new homes and businesses.

❖

Growing Up In Green River

by Marna Grubb

One Saturday in February of 1995, I called Mae Wright to inquire how she had been feeling and then asked her if I could interview her about her life.

Mae was in her early 80s and was not feeling well that day, but offered to see me the next day. In fact, it seemed to be something she wanted to do.

Mae Wright had always been a very private person and usually dido't discuss her life in much detail, but interesting tidbits escaped now and then. But that Sunday afternoon while I listened to her, she seemed to be enjoying herself as she relived and recounted memo-rable moments in her life.

Through the years, I had associated Mae with the Sweetwater County Historical Museum where she had worked for 17 years before retiring in 1985 at the age of 74. I also enjoyed Mae through the Sweetwater County Historical Society, of which we were both members.

Mae had joined the Society in 1961 - 34 years ago - and had served as secretary/treasurer of the group for 28 years. That alone is quite an accomplishment. The Historical Society was the driving force in starting a museum in Green River in 1967. Mae worked there as a volunteer, then was put on the payroll.

Donna Mae Preddy was born in Rock Springs March 2, 1911, to Albert Edward and Emily Preddy. Her father was working at the U.P. Coal Co. store. When Mae was one year old, the family moved to Diamondville, where her father managed Mountain Trading Co. store for seven years.

Mae's brother, Frank, was born Dec. 19, 1915, while the family lived in Diamondville.

In 1919, when Mae was eight, her family moved to Green River, living in a home on North Center Street. Her father managed the grocery department of the Green River Mercantile for 30 years.

Mae Preddy posed for this photo with her brother, Frank Preddy, while the family still lived in Diamondville, Wyoming. (Photo courtesy Evelyn Preddy Bucho)

Mae and her brother grew up in Green River. Her brother, Frank Preddy, married Evelyn Hermansen in 1937. Frank was part-owner and managed the Isis Theater for approximately 10 years and then was employed as a postal clerk for the Green River Post Office for many years until his retirement. Frank died at the early age of 53 in 1969.

Mae attended elementary school at the Masonic Hall and graduated from Lincoln High School with the class of 1928 as valedictorian.

Mae informed me that she had always enjoyed reading books. While growing up, she worked at the library after school in the evenings. Living close to the library, she said she read nearly everything they had.

In 1928, Mae was employed at the U.P. Power & Light Co. office in the Tomahawk Hotel building for approximately 17 years until her marriage to Emmett Wright in 1944. They bought their home at 25 East 3rd North.

Emmett Wright worked as a switchman for the Union Pacific Railroad in Green River and retired around 1965. They were the parents of two children - Lois Wright Brandner, who has followed in her mother's footsteps and is employed at the Sweetwater County Historical Museum, and Joanne Wright Holbert who lives in Rock Springs and is employed at City Auto Sales. Emmett died in 1972.

During her last years, Mae had a dear friend, Rodney Rollins, who was a faithful companion.

Mae was a member of the Union Congregational Church and most of her church work involved the children.

When asked of her responsibilities as a child, Mae remembered that she had to clean the silver on Saturdays. She added that "Mother wouldn't let me cook, so I learned from my husband after we were married."

She enjoyed growing up in Green River. She reminisced that "all the kids gathered and played games such as kick-the-can and ante-i-over" - I couldn't find anyone who knew how to spell this, but I played it also while I was growing up in Green River - which they played over at the county barn.

In the winter all gathered for sleigh riding on the Crosson Hill, followed by a chili party. She smiled as she said, "We had a lot of fun!"

Going back in our story, when four years old while living in Diamondville in 1914, Mae and her mother traveled to London on a ship to visit her grandparents.

"Grandmother wouldn't let me out of the house without white starched gloves and dress. They hired a nurse to take me to the park," she continued, "but the nurse would just sit and read to herself while I watched the children play."

Her eyes lit up when she talked about her grandfather. "He was wonderful," she said. "He had been a concert singer and would sing 'Asleep in the Deep' to me. The rafters would shake when he sang." They visited for about four weeks and then their visit was cut short.

World War I was starting so the British government escorted their ship halfway across the Atlantic since German U-boats had been sighted. She remembered seeing a whale one afternoon. "I remember walking down to the dining hall with two teachers who were taking care of me while mother was seasick," she said.

There were periods when they could not turn on their lights. Then the United States government escorted them the remainder of the way home.

When her father's parents had died, the children were spread around, so her father grew up in a private boarding school and trained in private merchandising. Her father was sent to Africa for eight years. He then returned to London where he met her mother, and traveled to Canada to visit two brothers.

Mae further explained, "Dad, his sister and husband wanted to come to the United States, so they got a map and while blindfolded, stuck a pin in the map to decide where to go - it was Rock Springs."

Her father worked in Rock Springs at the U.P. Coal Co. store a year, then sent for Emily, and they were married in Rock Springs. Emily had never cooked, had never seen coal or a coal range, so "Dad had neighbors teach her to cook. She was wonderful," she beamed.

Mae continued explaining that "Dad had asked for time off to marry and they wouldn't give it to him, so he quit his job." When Mae was a year old, they moved to Diamondville.

Mae's father retired in 1950 and her mother and father then moved to California. For 12 years, Mae and her girls traveled to California each summer for a visit.

After Mae's husband died, she and friend Eleanor Scritchfield did much traveling - several eastern trips.

In 1983, Mae and one of her cousins from Saskatchewan traveled to visit relatives in London. They stayed one week, then journeyed on to Germany and Switzerland.

In 1987, when her grandson Jon Brandner graduated from MIT, he and Mae took off for London, rented a car and drove all over Wales and England, stopping when they wished. "I had a wonderful time," she said. "It was a highlight of my life!"

Mae spoke fondly of her grandchildren. Dave and daughter Lois Brandner of Green River who have three children - Jon, Derek and Angela. Jon graduated from MIT with a bachelor of science degree in brain and cognitive sciences and lived in Marina Del Rey, Calif., where he was a financial systems consultant.

Mae said, "He flies all the time." Derek works for the Disney World Grand Hotel in Orlando, Fla. His degree was in hotel management. Angela graduated from the Colorado College of Art and

Design and was working for Michael Ricker Pewter and taking extra classes in Denver on computer design.

Gary and daughter Joanne Holbert have two children. Tami Holbert Love graduated from Weber State in Business Management, was married and was manager of Toy Liquidators in St. George, Utah. Her husband was taking radiology training. Her sister, Shauna Holbert, went to Florida where Derek Brandner was and she became assistant manager of Haircutters Beauty Salon.

At the end of the interview, Mae smiled contentedly and we agreed that she had had a good life.

Therefore, my "This is Your Life" rendition was offered as a birthday remembrance for Mae, as this article was published on her birthday - March 2, 1995. Mae died shortly after the article was printed in the *Green River Star.*

❖

Railroad Workers Demanded Protection of Their Daytime Sleep

by Marna Grubb

On Nov. 16, 1931, the Town of Green River, with a population of a little more than 3,000, deemed that "an emergency exists" and passed and approved Ordinance No. 175 which prohibits door-to-door selling.

William Evers was mayor at the time. Under this ordinance, a salesman must be "invited" into the home of a resident before he can knock on the door in an attempt to peddle his wares.

Night-shift railroaders and their wives had marched on the Town Council demanding that "something be done." Back in the depression days, thousands of Americans began moving from town to town and then house to house hoping to find someone to buy their wares, which would range from pots and pans to soaps, mag-azines, brushes, whatever.

Thus, the **Green River Ordinance** was drawn up by Attorney T.S. Taliaferro Jr. to "abate the nuisance" of house-to-house can-vassing in private homes.

In his Aug. 13, 1938, letter to W.A. Paxson, chief solicitor for the City of Washington, Ohio, T.S. Taliaferro Jr. stated that his second reason for drawing up the ordinance was "to prevent contagious diseases being carried by promiscuous peddlers, traveling in their automobiles from one community to another, which has been sustained as being both constitutional and desirable by the Supreme Court of Wyoming, the United States Circuit Court of Appeals, and by the Supreme Court of the United States."

When traveling in various cities and towns throughout the United States, one often sees a sign stating **GREEN RIVER**

ORDINANCE ENFORCED HERE. Thousands of towns and cities have requested a copy of the Green River Ordinance throughout the years, and it is still being enforced in Green River and various other towns and cities throughout the United States.

City police often receive calls from annoyed citizens when peddlers begin knocking on their doors.

Adrian Reynolds, a former editor of the *Green River Star,* discussed the ordinance in his **Chewin' the Fat** column saying, " ... the famed Green River Ordinance is not per se an anti-peddling ordinance... It is an anti-trespass ordinance that confirms the right of the householder to say just who comes into the home ... That is the reason that it holds up in the higher courts ... If you prohibited peddling in itself, I am afraid that the courts would say you are abridging the right to earn a living, or something of the sort .... "

As T.S. Taliaferro Jr. stated, "Some cities and towns have attempted to improve upon this ordinance, and in so doing have changed its character; so we find that the Town of Bel Air, Md., in attempting to enact the Green River Ordinance, added a provision that the ordinance should not apply to the merchants of Bel Air, or to the farmers corning into the town of Bel Air. Now, of course, this exception was just enough to make the ordinance unconstitutional, under the Constitution of Wyoming, and I presume under the Constitution of Maryland. See 192 Atlantic p. 417, Jewel Tea Co. v. Bel Air."

Taliaferro further stated, "In operation, the ordinance does not affect the merchants of the city, because they invariably have direct invitations to go to the residents occupied by those who deal with the local merchants."

The Fuller Brush Company sought to enjoin enforcement of the Ordinance by the Town of Green River, but the Fuller Brush Company's bill was dismissed by the Circuit Court of Appeals, Tenth Circuit. The Court held that "the Town has authority to declare and punish nuisances, that the practice of house-to-house selling is a nuisance, and that the ordinance was a reasonable exercise for police power and not in contravention of constitutional rights, or the commerce clause of the United States Constitution."

The Supreme Court of Wyoming upheld the conviction of a rep-resentative of Fuller Brush Company before the Police Judge of the Town of Green River, holding "the passage of the ordinance was a valid exercise of the police power of the municipality, and not in contravention of the Constitution and Statutes of the United States."

The Town Council at that time reported that "The above case

was taken on appeal to the Supreme Court of the United States, but on March 1, 1937, that court entered an order dismissing the appeal 'for want of a substantial federal question'."

So, the Green River Ordinance is still alive and well.

❖

42 Years of Law Enforcement with Chris Jessen

by Marna Grubb

Chris Jessen devoted 42 years of his life to law enforcement in Green River and Sweetwater County from 1921-1963.

He spent 10 years as undersheriff, one year as sheriff and 30 years as marshal or chief of police.

Jessen was appointed marshal in 1933 by Mayor William Evers and throughout the years, his duties included serving as day policeman, sexton of the cemetery, street commissioner, dog catcher, administering the town's sewer disposal system, and just whatever needed to be done.

"We worked 12 hours a day, seven days a week," he would say. He earned $140 per month as his starting salary.

Chief Jessen retired in November of 1963 and died in September of 1970 at the age of 78.

A former *Green River Star* editor, Adrian Reynolds, reported the following about Jessen in his *Chewin' the Fat* column in 1970:

> "Whether it was law enforcement work, helping families settle their differences, seeing that the town's sewage disposal worked, or that its streets were maintained, Chris Jessen, who died Thursday, took them all in the course of duty during his 30 years as chief of police, or marshal, of the town of Green River. Many a person still in town and many who now live away remember back to some helping act or word that aided them somewhere along the line... 'we always liked Chris' is an expression repeatedly heard. Chris broke into the law business at a time when understanding of a community and its people was highly necessary, as an

Chris Jessen, Green River's own law man. (Photo courtesy Marna Grubb)

> undersheriff during prohibition... and he came through it with trust on the part of the people... and to serve his people for three decades .... "

During his 10 years as undersheriff, Jessen's fondest case was the trial of Henry B. Morris for the murder of his housekeeper, Mrs. Anna Gabe, and her little girl.

The case gained national publicity and later reached the pages of *Real Detective* magazine.

Morris was charged with killing the woman and child in August 1925 then burying their bodies in the basement of his house in Rock Springs.

The bodies were found three years later after Matt Yovich moved into the house and dug up his water pipes.

The *Real Detective* story entitled "The Secret of the Basement Tomb," told that,

> "Sheriff Morton was bulked over a hole in the earthen floor of the cellar. Beside him, flashlight in hand, stooped Chris Jessen, his undersheriff. Big, powerful, typically western, Chris Jessen jerked his ten-gallon hat toward me in greeting."

The story later continues:

> "Big, mild-mannered and gentle, Chris Jessen,the undersheriff, was talking to Matt Yovich."

In May 1931, Sheriff Jessen received a letter from John Gale, System Chief Special Agent for the Union Pacific Railroad Company in Omaha, Nebraska, which read as follows:

> Dear Sheriff Jessen: On behalf of the Management and myself, I want to take this opportunity of thanking you for the prompt and efficient manner in which you and the men with you apprehended the two bandits, Russell Howarth and George Bachman, who held up passengers on Train #7, May 18-19, 1931. I appreciate this far more than the words in this letter can express. Will arrange to see you in the next few days. John A. Gale"

Jessen often commented on the routine knifings, shootings and brawls which were so much a part of early Wyoming life. He also vividly recounted the time when the old ferry across the Green River overturned and dumped himself, four other men and the sheriff's car into the swollen river.

All five climbed back onto the overturned ferry and rode it downstream safely. But a Green River man, an excellent swimmer, drowned the next day trying to bring up the car.

After reading of Chris Jessen in the October 20, 1960, the *Green River Star,* Lloyd C. Walker who had grown up in Green River and was a captain in the United States Air Force, wrote to Jessen from Bangor, Maine.

He said, "I am sure that there are many of us that have grown up in Green River under your thumb that feel as I do and certainly our parents feel the same. I join in with the comments made in the *Star* and add mine... To learn early in life that the law is to help us, to be a part of our every day life, is a lasting impression. .Just a sim-ple 'Thank You' for being the Chris Jessen I remember."

Christian Jessen was born in Omaha on October 15, 1891, the son of Peter and Mary Jessen. He came to Green River with his family at age three in 1894.

His father worked in the car department of the Union Pacific Railroad. For 75 years, he called Green River home, dying in September of 1970, at the age of 78.

He had three brothers, Henry, Albert and Otto, and one sister, Anna Jessen Lenhart.

Young Chris attended school in Green River in the old building located where the Masonic Temple now stands.

His first job involved stocking shelves at the Morris Mercantile at age 14. He then worked as a train call boy for the Union Pacific followed by driving the horse-drawn delivery wagon for the P.O. Christensen grocery store.

Later, he drove the power-driven delivery truck for the Green River Mercantile. He also worked for Leo Viox's meat market.

In 1917, during World War I, Jessen enlisted in the Third Wyoming Infantry, National Guard, and went overseas to France where he served as a drill sergeant.

Discharged in 1919, he returned to Green River and worked as a hostler for the Union Pacific handling engines in and around the roundhouse.

In 1921, Jessen was appointed undersheriff.

In May of 1924, the Rock Springs Miner reported the marriage of Esther Wiggen of Rock Springs to Chris Jessen of Green River.

The Rock Springs newspaper reported that:

"The groom is the undersheriff of Sweetwater County, and is one of the live wires of our neighboring town of Green River."

Chris and Esther had one child, Marna, and fine parents they were. This I know, for these are my parents!

War in the Pacific

by Bob Edwards

For Jim June, World War II began at the early age of 13.

In 1943 most Americans were unaware of the fact that the Japanese were using wind currents to send incendiary balloons across the Northwest portion of the United States. Jim describes the intent of these balloons as a means of destroying our natural resources.

Many of these bombs landed in Washington, Idaho and Oregon, setting fire to some of our large timber-producing forests. In addition to causing damage to our natural resources, the bombs were meant to serve as a sort of psychological warfare, by instilling fear in U.S. citizens.

During this time, Jim was employed by the Forest Service as a smoke jumper. The job of a smoke jumper was to parachute from planes to combat these forest fires before they could spread.

At the age of 15-1/2 Jim convinced his mother to allow him to enlist in the U.S. Navy and consequently he was sent to the Great Lakes area north of Chicago for basic training.

After completion of basic training, the Navy sent him to California where he trained as an underwater demolition expert. As a result of this training, he entered the war with the Navy CBs and was sent to the South Pacific.

Jim mentioned that he had served on Cipan and later, the island of Guam. His unit moved into Guam in advance of the Third Marine Corp, clearing obstacles for the incoming land craft and he remained on the island in preparation for the ultimate invasion of Japan.

Prior to what Jim thought would be the invasion of the mainland of Japan, the U.S. exploded bombs on Hiroshima and then Nagasaki.

When asked to comment on the necessity of this action, the devastation and aftermath of the explosion, Jim said, "I supported

Jim June, age 15.
(Photo courtesy
Mary Kay Bonomo)

these actions because ultimately it would save thousands of lives, both U.S. and Japanese.

"Also the Japanese had already demonstrated their beliefs in fighting to their death rather than to withdraw or retreat. I strongly believe that we did what was necessary to end the war."

Almost 50 years later, Jim could still recall, with clarity, his involvement in the "great war to end all wars."

The Green River Historic Preservation Commission

by Bill Thompson
(article originally published August 3, 1995)

The Beginning - In a memorandum dated May 10, 1990, Councilman Jim June informed Mayor Don Van Matre, Jr. that information from the Wyoming State Archives, Museums and Historical Department in Cheyenne stated that Federal and State funds were available for a historic preservation program in Green River. To qualify as a Certified Local Government (CLG) program, a town or county had to have completed: 1. an historic preservation ordinance enacted 2. a local historic preservation commission established 3. survey of cultural resources 4. a review of National Register nominations that pertain to the community 5. commission members must attend an historic preservation seminar each year.

Jim mentioned that it would take six months to fulfill the tasks and recommended that the city put an ordinance in place for certification and eligibility for historic preservation funding.

The "Ordinance creating a chapter in the Green River code of ordinances (90-14) entitled Historic Preservation Ordinance designed to recognize and protect the many sites of historical significance and unique architectural structures found within the city of Green River, Wyoming; to authorize the creation of a local Historic Preservation Commission with attendant duties and powers, to authorize a survey and inventory of significant culture resources and designation of the same," was passed and approved by the City on June 19, 1990. It was signed by Mayor Van Matre Jr. and attested by Norman C. Stark, City Clerk (and present Mayor of Green River).

The original members were; Jim June, Marna Grubb, Ruth Lauritzen, George DeLiguori and Sherry Espeland. Present mem-

Restoration of one of Green River's previous Town Hall buildings used from 1942 through 1954. (Photo courtesy Green River Historic Preservation Commission)

bers of the Commission are; Jim June, Marna Grubb, Ruth Lauritzen, Bob Edwards and Bill Thompson.

One of the objectives of the Commission is to make the general public aware of the history and historical sites in the Green River area. To meet this objective it was decided that historical articles in the *Green River Star* would be most effective. Keith Bray, Editor and Publisher of the *Green River Star,* gave full support to this idea. The column under the name ECHOES FROM THE BLUFFS was born November 1991. Articles are written on a rotating basis by each member and have appeared periodically from that date. The majority of them were researched and written by Commission Chairman Jim June.

Some Special Commission Projects have been:
National Register plaque for The Brewery Plaque
for the old cemetery (by the Library)
Self Guided Tour of Historic Green River brochure
Green River "Nature's Art Shop" brochure
Green River Mayors 1891-1995 brochure Various
bronze plaques around the city

A billboard advertising Green River (2.5 miles west of
town). This is funded for only a few more
months....$6,300 a year.

The Present - (From Mama's report to the City Administrator)
"We have done a reprint of our Self Guided Tour through funds
from the Joint Travel and Tourism Board.

Our Nature's Art Shop brochure has been very popular and all
copies were distributed. Many requests from the Chamber,
class reunions and school instructors brought about a reprint
request for this brochure. Also I requested a grant from the
Joint Travel & Tourism Board and was allotted $4,200 which
will provide 4,500 more copies.

Our current project is the restoration of the Old City Hall building which had been located at the site of the present Eagles building. We have been struggling with repairs due to damage from van-
dalism. Special tongue-and-groove lumber was ordered
from (Bates Lumber) Mountain View. This was used to repair the
damaged wood. We were informed that there would be no
charge for this lumber (a good-will gesture from owner Norm
Bates to the city of Green River).

Yet to be completed on this project are:
Final painting of the building. The primer coat has been
applied.
Cement sidewalk and steps to the door need to be poured.
Landscaping proposed- placement of large river rock,
possibly in a mortar base.
Two bronze plaques are being designed to be placed in
front of the building:
Photo and write-up on the Old City Hall building
Photo and write-up on the Old Outdoor Swimming Pool"

The photo shows the moving of the Old City Hall building
from the Parks yard to its present and permanent site near the old
swimming pool.

The Future - With these energetic people on the Commission,
being a member has been a bunch of learning and great fun! I look
forward with anticipation to our future projects and historical articles... What will they be?... What will they deal with?...
Suggestions anyone?

❖

Peace At Last:
The End of World War II

by Ruth Lauritzen

"Green River Rejoices War Ending" read the headline of the August 17, 1945 *Green River Star*. The surrender of Japan on August 14 meant the closing of the second front of the huge mili-tary clash that was World War II. After years of war and rumors of war what did peace mean to the people of Green River and how did they respond to it?

The first response of course was one of celebration and thanks-giving. According to the *Star* it was twelve minutes after the announcement was heard over the radio that the air was filled with the blasts of whistles from locomotives and the roundhouse, the peals of church bells and even the moans of the air raid siren mounted on the UP Social Hall. The cacophony continued for ten minutes as Green River shouted out its jubilation over the end of hostilities.

City officials requested and received the immediate closure of saloons and, according to the *Star*, "...those who would have cele-brated with bottled spirits roamed around the streets looking for something to do, but expressing their joy that the war had ended." The reason for this closure, which lasted through the next day, was probably to forestall a major party during which the business of the town would come to a standstill. The implied wisdom of this deci-sion was indicated by the report that there was practically no absen-teeism in the railroad offices, yards and shops the next day.

All retail stores were closed as were county, city and federal offices. Only churches were open and special services were held for, "...worshippers who chose to go to church to give thanks to the Almighty - and large numbers did that."

Once the celebration was over the extraordinary life of war-time was replaced once again by peace-time circumstances. During the war women took over some of the jobs vacated by men going to battle, particularly on the railroad where they worked in all departments performing functions from clerical work to track maintenance. The most obvious sign that the war was over was of course the return of the soldiers. Most of these war-time working women left their jobs with the return of the servicemen and this meant a major lifestyle change for both sexes.

For some peace would not mean a return of loved ones. Green River lost eight citizens to the conflict. The *Star* reports the posthumous award of the Air Medal and the Purple Heart to the widow of Sgt. Floyd C. Hoover, an aerial gunner who was lost in a bombing raid over Germany in 1943. Streets in the veteran's housing area of Green River were named in memory of these men; Hoover, T/Sgt. Ernest Pelser, Lt. H. Bert Jensen, Lt. Donovan Astle, Cpl. Howard L. Schultz, Pvt. Darell Barnhart, Pvt. John E. Logan, and Pfc. Robert James Bramwell.

Another sign of peace was the closure of the Green River Service Men's Center (USO). The center was maintained by various community groups such as the Homemakers Club as a place for visiting servicemen to read, write letters and play games while waiting for connecting trains. The USO was set up in a room in the Union Pacific Social Hall and was furnished with borrowed furniture. During its two year life the center served a registered 235 servicemen.

The end of the war meant an end to such inconveniences as gas rationing. Citizens celebrated this new period of plenty by filling their tanks for the first time since rationing began. Not only was more gasoline available, but the mandatory 35 mile per hour speed limit was lifted as well, making automobile transportation attractive and practical again. Car trips, so long an impossibility, were indulged in with gay abandon as reported by the *Star,* "...a large number of Rock Springs cars were evident in Green River as people from the coal city were out for a ride, just to feel the luxury of riding without fear of using up all of their gas ahead of time."

Public projects and activities on hold during the war were slated to begin again. Green River's annual rodeo resumed with " ... three days and nights of show .... ". Work on the Eden Valley project, already underway when war broke out, was scheduled to continue. This irrigation project was designed to increase the number of acres under cultivation in the Farson area.

Peace at last brought many changes to the residents of Green River, but the personal and local changes outlined above were minor in comparison to the major world social and political shifts brought about by the war itself. Though the celebrating citizens did not know it, they were poised on the brink of Cold War which would color the complexion of world politics for years to come. They were also witness to the opening salvo in the nuclear arms race which would become the abiding obsession of many of the world's armies for the next fifty years. These happy people were survivors of what some historians consider the watershed event of the twentieth century. Indeed, fifty years later as we commemorate the end of conflict, we can marvel at the changes that huge military clash has wrought.

❖

Reminiscing with Hugh Crouch: 91 and Going Strong

by Marna Grubb

In October of 1995, I spent an enjoyable afternoon visiting with Hugh Crouch, Sr. and learning of his life, some 91 years of it! Hugh and his wife, Elizabeth (Bess to her friends), devoted most of their lives to their family. They had eight children: Estelle of Denver, Arthur (deceased), Leonard of Green River, Hugh who lives at the family home west of Green River, LeRoy of Washington D.C., John who lives between Rock Springs and Green River, Robert of South Dakota, and Sara of Denver. They have 10 grandchildren and 7 great grandchildren.

Hugh W. Crouch Sr. was born in Butler, Mo. on April 16, 1904. His parents moved the family to Pittsburgh, Kan. in 1910 where he attended school. One of the games they played while growing up in Kansas was "shinny" where they would knock a can around with a stick while on ice skates. Hugh, accompanied with friends, left home three times between 1924 and 1926 looking for work. Many times they found themselves stranded without food or money. In 1926, on his way to Everett, Wash. to some people who had raised his mother, he had stopped in Utah and was working at a place called Strawberry. The parents of his best friend, Larry, lived in Dines, Wyo. (a mining town north of Rock Springs near Reliance), so they came to Dines and went hunting with Larry's father. Hugh definitely liked hunting and fishing, so he stayed until he finally got on with Colony Coal Company, where he worked for 28 years until the mine closed in 1954.

Hugh said that, if it hadn't been for the hunting and fishing, he wouldn't have wanted to stay in Wyoming at that time. There were no trees and no paved streets in Dines. It was strictly a mining camp of maybe 100 houses scattered on the hills. He had a sketch

The Crouches – Hugh Sr. and Bess in front of the family home west of Green River in 1984. (Photo courtesy Hugh Crouch, Sr.)

of the street on which he lived with the names of the families who lived there.

After Hugh had come to Dines, he met Elizabeth Frances Beane. Elizabeth was born in Platte City, Mo. on September 21, 1902. She had been valedictorian of her graduating class in St. Joseph and arrived in Wyoming in 1926, and Hugh must have decided right away that this was the girl for him, as they were married in 1926.

Times were tough in their early years at Dines. Most families were "in the same boat." They shared a lot. If someone got something hunting or fishing, then they shared it. Hunting became a way of survival. They enjoyed sage chicken hunting and cookouts. They became very close to the people in Dines. They were of many nationalities, but that didn't matter. Hugh played some baseball with Rock Springs and Dines fellows. They liked to play cards and go to the show when they could. The children went to grade school in Dines, then were bused to Reliance High School. Estelle was a cheer leader at Reliance High School. Estelle and Arthur graduated from Reliance High School. The other children graduated from Green River High School after the family moved just west of Green River in 1944. Hugh drove back and forth to work from Green River to Dines for 10 years until the mine closed in 1954.

When the family moved west of Green River, they found the town not to be as friendly as Dines. Of course, it takes a while to become acquainted whenever a person moves; but the more I research Green River's history I find it to have been rather "uppity." Rock Springs, mainly a community of coal miners, had many different nationalities, while Green River was a railroading com-munity and seemed to attract a different group of people. From an interview with Elizabeth Crouch done by David Kathka on April 14, 1975, I found to my amazement various incidents of discrimination. There was a cafe on main street in Green River that had a sign, "No Colored Trade Solicited." Also the Isis Theater had two rows in the back on the right side for blacks to sit. It took them a couple years before this was changed. When I was growing up in Green River and attending the Isis Theater, I had no idea this was happening. All I knew was that these people were my friends and classmates - and that's all that mattered.

Elizabeth Crouch further stated in her interview with David Kathka that "Everything has turned out real nice since. It has taken a while." Elizabeth was active in the Women's Auxiliary of the VFW for many years. Those of us who grew up in Green River learned to love and respect this family, as have many who have come in contact with them throughout the years. They have been good citizens of the community. The Crouches have a list in their photo album of "Good Samaritans (those who have helped us along the way)." It would be an honor to be on that list!

After the mine closed down, Hugh worked a couple years at the railroad and Joe Desmond's Plumbing, before he began work at the Court House as Custodian. He worked there from 1956 to 1973 with helpers such as John Manning, Rocky and Fred.

During the Dines and Reliance reunion on July 15, 1995, Hugh was a tour guide speaker for the bus tours of the mines. "There's nothing left at Dines now," he said. "There are no houses, just dirt and sagebrush."

I asked Hugh what was his secret for a long life. He laughed, he said he didn't think he had a secret; although he said he never smoked or chewed. He said he got some black lung while in the mine, but it doesn't seem to bother him. Then he said that he and his three buddies (Charles Menapace, Bill Lakko and Dante

Piaia) liked to go to the mountains, Pinedale and Boulder, and would walk 15 to 20 miles. He chuckled as he said, "We called ourselves the mountain men." They went backpacking every summer for 20 years. All that walking must have been another secret for his long life, plus he just came from "good stock." His mother was a beautiful lady and lived to 105 years and Elizabeth's mother lived to 100 years.

In closing, Hugh volunteered the fact that "Wyoming is one of the finest places to live anywhere - don't know of any better." He said he had traveled all over, to Mexico, California, and elsewhere, and there was no finer place. I have to agree!

❖

Snowball Warfare, or How to Have a Proper Victorian Snowball Fight

by Ruth Lauritzen

Who doesn't remember as a child the excitement of the first snow of the winter? As the first flakes began to fall everyone in the school room rushed to the window in spite of the teachers oft-repeated admonishments of "Sit down, you've all seen snow before." Yes, we had all seen it before, but this was the first snow we had seen in a long time.

Oh, the things you can do with snow! These wonderful activities have been around as long as kids and snow have coexisted. These snow games are passed from generation to generation with parents and older siblings teaching the younger crowd the proper methods for snowball fights, making snowmen and forts and making a proper snow angel. Writer and founder of the Boy Scouts of America, Daniel C. Beard made sure that the Victorian concept of a proper snowball battle was preserved in his book, *The American Boy's Handy Book,* first published in 1882. In fact, he devotes a full chapter to the activity.

One cannot have a battle without an objective, the capture of the snow fort. He describes the construction of the fort in great detail from the rolling of the large snowballs to shaping of the slanting exterior walls with spades. He suggests leaving a large pile of snow in the middle of the fort to support the flag pole and to use as back-up ammunition in the case of an emergency. Once the fort is complete the attackers have to be outfitted with shields made from the heads of barrels and sleds made from the barrel staves for carrying their ammunition.

With all of these preparations made, war may begin in earnest. For those modern "snow warriors" interested in doing things the classic way, Beard's ground rules, presented in his own 19th century prose, follow.

Two commanders, or captains, must be elected. If the forces engaged be very large, each captain may appoint one or two assistants, or lieutenants. These officers, after being elected and appointed, are to give all orders, and should be promptly obeyed by their respective commands. The captains decide, by lot the choice of position.

In choosing sides, the captain who is commander of the fort has first choice, then the two captains name a boy, alternately, until two-thirds of the boys have been chosen. The defenders of the fort then retire to their stronghold leaving the boys unchosen to join the attacking army, it being supposed that one-third behind fortification are equal to two-thirds outside.

Only the attacking party is allowed shields and ammunition sleds.

At least thirty yards from the fort a camp must be established by the outsiders or attacking army, and stakes driven at the four corners to locate the camp. Imaginary lines from stake to stake mark its limits.

Each party will have its national colors, in addition to which the attacking party has a battle-flag which it carries with it in the assault.

The defenders of the fort must see to it that all damages to the fortifications are promptly repaired.

Any soldier from the fort who shall be carried off within the limits of the camp becomes a prisoner of war, and cannot leave the camp until rescued by his own comrades.

Any one of the attacking force pulled into the fort becomes a prisoner of war, and must remain in the fort until it is captured.

Prisoners of war cannot be made to fight against their own side, but they may be employed in making snowballs or repairing damages to fortifications.

Any deserter recaptured must suffer the penalty of having his face washed with snow, and being made to work with the prisoners of war.

When the outsiders, or attacking army, can replace the enemy's colors with their battle-flag, the fort is captured and the battle is won by the attacking party; all fighting must then immediately cease.

But if, in a sally, or, by any means, the soldiers of the fort can take the colors of the opposite party from the camp and bring them inside their fortification, they have not only successfully defended their fort, but have defeated the attacking army; and this ends the battle, with double honors to the brave defenders.

No water-soaked or icy snowballs are allowed. No honorable boy uses them, and any one caught in the ungentlemanly act of throwing such "soakers" should be forever ruled out of the game.

No blows are allowed to be struck by the hand, or by anything but the regulation snowball, and, of course, no kicking is permitted.

Following these simple rules of engagement a civilized snowball fight can be enjoyed by all.

❖

Jaycees Park:
The Jaycees' Legacy

by Bill Thompson

A popular song of yesteryear asks, "Where have all the young men gone? ... " This plaintive question could be applied to the former Green River Junior Chamber of Commerce.

The Green River Junior Chamber of Commerce began its thirty-some years of existence in the middle 1950s. Alton Hermansen, a charter member, smiled fondly as he recalled some of the early days of the organization. (When doesn't Alton smile?)

"We started the group with the idea of helping the town with a variety of activities and to have a fun time too." The national objective of the Junior Chamber was to encourage young men from the age of 21 to 35 to participate in civic activities and to ultimately become involved in business and become members of the Chamber of Commerce in their chosen municipalities. "We concentrated mostly on the civic activities since Green River was a much smaller town and the business opportunities were somewhat limited." Alton recalled ... "but gosh we had fun!" In a Museum Christmas exhibit there was a picture of Junior Commerce member Alton with Santa Claus as participants in one of the club's early projects.

By 1961 when I arrived in Green River as a brand-new teacher (best professional move I ever made) it was taken for granted that all young men would join the club...and then later when they became "Exhausted Roosters" (reaching the age of 36) they would join the Green River Lions Club ... another civic organization concentrating on eyesight conservation. At that time

time the Lions were more laid back in their activities because the youthful Jaycees were expected to be involved in the more "vigorous" projects in the community. This takes nothing away from the Green River Lions Club which focused on different worthwhile objectives. In the 1960s the national organization changed the name from Junior Chamber of Commerce to the "Jaycees" for brevity's sake.

The Christmas decorations for the city were put up every season by the Jaycees. The city paid for the decorations and added to them as needed...in one case while I was placing some reindeer on the Sheriff's lawn across from the old courthouse ... an exuberant Jaycee jumped from the steps onto my back. In the process of removing him by flipping him through the air, a reindeer was "slightly" damaged. One year, a new Jaycee quickly learned that when electrical cords for the lights are repaired, two bare wires are not to be taped together. .. another time a Jaycee lost his grip from the TV boom truck and fell off in the railroad underpass .. .it was a testament to youthful driving skills that the close-following Jaycee cars were able to avoid such a moving (rolling) object. He was skinned up some though.

Christmas tree sales were a money making project for the Jaycees. With permission from the city, the trees were sold from the Island Pavilion. Jaycees Al Carollo and Dick Schuck decided to expand the sales territory. At that time the main highway came through town. There were no twin tunnels. They stopped all the through traffic on main street. .. and sold trees to those who wished to continue on their way. Trees were tied to the tops of cars, on the radiators of trucks ... any place handy. Traffic was backed up to the edge of town for a time, but Christmas trees got sold ....

The Jaycees sponsored Turkey Shoots at the old Kanda Rifle Range, ran raffles and developed other money-making projects. These were done with the idea of sponsoring and aiding areas that needed help in the community. There were scholarships, Boys and Girls State sponsorships, help to the needy, banquets, dances and so on. Many of these events were broadcast throughout the community by Jaycees riding in the back of pickups and using loudspeakers.

Two outstanding Jaycee projects were the Sabin Polio vaccination for Sweetwater County residents . . . and the Green River Jaycees Park.

In the early 1960s, with help from our two local pharmacists and doctors, School District #2, and the local papers, the Jaycees held an oral inoculation clinic for all residents of Sweetwater

Sign at Jaycees Park on Astle Avenue in Green River. (Photo courtesy Bill Thompson)

County. The high school auditorium was busy that day as sugar cubes laced with Sabin Polio vaccine were distributed free to those who came from all parts of the county.

In 1964 Jerry Vanbuskirk, a high school teacher and active Jaycee, proposed that since Green River had no real top-notch ball-park for the youngsters, we should build one. We did.

The city donated a portion of land next to the Game and Fish building, Mountain Fuel donated pipe, Peter Kewitt and some of their personnel (D. Kelley, J. Guindon, and "Squeaks" Garlick) donated and ran earth-moving machinery; the High School metal shop classes helped build the bleachers. The Jaycees were the mules, and welders, and all-around "go-fers". When contacted at Minatare, Nebraska, where he is now Superintendent of Schools, Jerry said that although he won the Wyoming Outstanding Jaycee Project Award that year, "it could never have been done without all the help we had...wow!"

The Green River Jaycees Park was turned over to the city and was put to immediate use from that time up to the present. A later generation of Jaycees provided a scoreboard for the field.

So, at no cost to the County, the residents had the opportunity to protect themselves from the dreaded disease of polio.

So, at no cost to the City of Green River, the municipality obtained an award-winning park ... thanks to the young men of the Green River Jaycees.

By the middle of the 1980s dwindling membership took its toll. The Green River Jaycees were no more and the scoreboard had disappeared.

If present city plans for the Greenbelt and Stratton-Myers Park are followed, the Jaycee Park will be no more. It will be replaced by a paved parking lot for the Greenbelt. .. this will remove the last physical reminder that the Green River Jaycees existed. I am opposed to the loss of this park, of course.

I am convinced that every municipality, for its own good, needs an active Jaycees chapter and most certainly Green River does. Their youthful energy focused on community and human service is sorely missed by this "Exhausted Rooster."

❖

Couple Meshes
Diverse Cultures

by Marna Grubb

Armando and Trudel Lopez have become known to Green River residents as the connoisseurs of fine Mexican and German foods; although, this also has led to confusion.

When they managed Trudel's Restaurant'e in the Old Post Office building, customers were amazed that a Mexican restaurant also would offer German food. Of course, after becoming acquainted with Trudel and Armando, it all becomes quite natural.

Trudel's Restaurant'e was located in Green River's Old Post Office building. (Photo courtesy Armando and Trudel Lopez)

The summer of 1995 they were at the Rolling Green Country Club and in 1996 in business at Trudel's Gasthaus in Mansface Plaza for evening dining.

In 1993, Trudel was employed part time by the City of Green River to maintain shrub and flower beds at City Hall and Centennial Park and to pick up trash in these areas. Her supervisor, Parks Supervisor Dave Waterhouse, submitted a letter of recommendation for Trudel and, in December of 1995, Trudel was honored as the City's outstanding part-time employee, and very deserving she was.

In his nomination letter, Dave Waterhouse said, "Through her motivation and attention to detail, Trudel has accomplished more than we ever expected, and we have received many compliments about her work from residents and visitors alike. Her performance also has done a great deal to improve the image of the city, particularly for those just passing through town on Flaming Gorge Way."

He further reported that, "She did an outstanding job of maintaining these areas. Once she had them under control, she asked to take on more responsibility and now plants and maintains all the flower beds in the city." Trudel planted 1,500 tulip and daffodil bulbs throughout the city making a colorful spring!

Trudel and Armando were married in 1962 while Armando was stationed in Pirmasens, Germany, with the U.S. Army. Armando met Trudel while she was working for Americans at an NCO Club in 1961.

"I knew immediately that this was the girl for me," Armando recounted. He later journeyed with his friend to her sister's house to fix "Red's" (Trudel's) stereo and this blossomed into a lasting relationship.

Armando, born in Carrizo Springs, Texas, and raised in Sabinal, Texas, had quite a military career. His military service includes World War II and the Korean War. His unit was the 313th Combat Engineers of the 88th Infantry Division, attached to the 5th Army. He served in North Africa and Italy, and then in Germany, from January 1961 to February 1964, with the Army Signal Corp. as a Sergeant.

Armando came from a large family of seven brothers and four sisters. He had many chores since his family had a butcher shop, a restaurant, grocery store, bakery, service station and barber shop. One of his favorite memories as a boy was when he would take out his little red wagon to sell breakfast items such as eggs, tomatoes, cheese, sweet breads and tortillas.

The Lopezes in Germany, 1961. (Photo courtesy Armando and Trudel Lopez)

At holidays and Easter, Armando has fond memories of family get-togethers. The big attraction was the big pot of tamales made by his mother, grandmothers and aunts.

On Christmas Eve, his family would cut a Christmas tree and, before dinner, the tree was trimmed with oranges, apples and real candles. Since it was a big family, each received something they could use, such as an item of clothing.

As a young boy, Armando's favorite sports were baseball and basketball. He enjoyed swimming in the Sabinal River. The older boys would teach the young ones to swim in their favorite swimming hole.

"The best part was the care shown for the young ones by the older boys," he said.

His father was very strict and "disciplined with great love." He has fond memories of going to school and appreciated the education, but mostly he enjoyed his schoolmates - his good friends. He said sadly that he lost many of his friends while they were in the service during World War II.

Across the Atlantic, Trudel was born in Nussfdorf Pfalz, Palantine, Germany, the oldest of three children, her mother still lives in Landau (population 65,000). Her father's father was a Frenchman.

Trudel has a sister in San Diego - 30 years in the United States - and a brother in Stuttgart, Germany, the location of the Mercedes home office. Her father did wallpapering and interior wall finishing and rode a bicycle to and from work. As a hobby, he had a small vineyard and made his own wine.

She learned to cook when eight years old and always enjoyed cooking. She and her sister shared one homemade doll. Life was difficult. They learned how to knit, embroider and crochet when about five years of age. She said they were disciplined by "spanking nicely," but "never abused." They enjoyed outings to the park or zoo for ice cream.

"Christmas was very magic and very secretive," she mused. "Trees were put up on Christmas Eve and seemed to appear magically to children along with gifts. Real candles were used on the trees." Her fond memories include backpacking three or four miles into the forest for a picnic on Sundays. There was much singing. Also they would walk three or four miles one way to collect blueberries. In the fall, they would gather chestnuts.

Between 1942 and 1944, half of the school had become a hospital for wounded soldiers. In 1944, when she was 11 years old, they moved to the Bavarian Alps and stayed to mid-1945 to get away from the firing lines.

At the end of the war, American troops had moved into Bavaria and located heavy equipment. She remarked, "If it had not been for the Marshall Plan after the war, many more people would have died of starvation." After settlement and occupation by the Allies, her area was occupied by the French.

As stated previously, Armando and Trudel were married in 1962 and have two children, Pedro Lopez and Ursula Lopez, both born in Germany. They moved from Germany to the United States in February of 1967.

They lived five years in Georgia, three years in Nevada, then moved to Green River in April 1974. Armando had been trained as a vehicle mechanic while in the Army, so he was employed as a vehicle mechanic in Georgia and Nevada.

Ursula graduated from high school in Sparks, Nevada. Pedro graduated from Green River High School in 1981. Ursula and Pedro both graduated from the University of Wyoming, Pedro with a bachelor of science degree in computer science and mathematics and Ursula with a bachelor of science degree in business.

Pedro was a high school mathematics instructor in Hugo, Colo. Ursula was assisting with the family business.

❖

Taking Wing:
The History of Aviation in
Sweetwater County

by Ruth Lauritzen

In the years following World War I the imagination of the American public was fired by tales of the exploits of a new type of American soldier, the flying ace. The Great War, as World War I was called, was one of the first major conflicts using airplanes in the fighting. The tales of the infamous Baron Manfred von Richthofen, alias "The Red Baron"; Edward V. Rickenbacker, an American ace and other daring aviators contributed to the public fascination with flight.

It was also the era of the great civilian aviators. Charles A. Lindbergh made his famous non-stop solo flight across the Atlantic in 1927, and the first female aviator of note, Amelia Earhart, rose to prominence. She received much attention during a stop at the Rock Springs airport in 1932 on a transcontinental flight in a gyroplane, a forerunner to the helicopter.

Several local residents caught the flying fever. Rudy Stefoin, John Gosar and Leonard Hay owned and flew planes. Early pilot Curly Powell also ran a flight charter service.

The air race became a popular activity. The first to come through this area was in 1919 in celebration of the first anniversary of Armistice Day. The seven week long event included a flight from the Atlantic Ocean to the Pacific and back again with check points along the way. A portion of Hutton Heights in Green River was cleared as a temporary landing field for the flyers. The local Boy Scout troop volunteered to guard the planes from souvenir hunters during their stop.

During the 1920s an entertainment event known as a "flying circus" began to appear in Sweetwater County. Groups doing aeri-

A bi-plane takes off from the rough Green River airfield on Hutton Heights around 1919. Note the Hutton home and the smokestacks from the potash plant in the back-ground. (Photo courtesy Sweetwater County Historical Museum)

al stunt shows would put on a free performance and then charge for rides in their airplanes.

It was at this time that the practice of carrying mail by air came to the Unites States. Many of the early airmail pilots were former military pilots flying planes also left over from the war. In 1920 the U.S. Airmail Service got its start in the east and by 1924 transcontinental service had begun.

The chosen route followed the Union Pacific railroad. The pilots of the early planes had very few instruments for navigation and those they had were often not reliable. For this reason they often followed "the iron compass", flying low enough to keep the rails in sight.

Rock Springs was a terminal on the transcontinental airmail route. Through the efforts of John Hay Sr. and the Rock Springs business community a landing field was bladed out of a sagebrush flat four miles north of town on the site of the present county fair-grounds. One hangar was built on the site and airmail service began with Rock Springs as one of a string of airfields, primary and emergency, across the United States.

In the beginning the mail was flown only during the daylight hours and good weather. This was due in part to the type of plane used. The D.R. 4 was an open cockpit biplane with a wooden body and propeller, and wings of canvas stretched over a frame stabilized with wires. Rock Springs was the overnight stop between Cheyenne and Salt Lake City with the pilots staying at the Park Hotel.

In order to improve service in 1928 the decision was made to go to night flying. The landing fields were lit and guidance beacons were installed along the route.

Night flying proved both safe and successful, but by 1930 the government decided to get out of the airmail business and contracted the work out to a private company. The first company, Boeing Aircraft, and those companies that followed also ran passenger and freight service to the Rock Springs airport. The government mail contracts paid the bills while other services provided the profit. It was during the early '30s that the first metal planes came to Rock Springs and the "rag-wings" disappeared.

It soon became apparent that a new airport was needed. The short runway length was not suitable for the new larger and faster planes. Also, the federal government was attempting to upgrade the national air transportation network in response to the growing threat of world war.

Thus during the late '30s the site of the present airport was chosen and construction began on a new facility. Once the new airport was completed the old facility was abandoned, ending an exciting and novel era in aviation.

❖

Graduation

by Bill Thompson

Bill Thompson interviews himself at retirement from the Green River school system in 1996. (Photo courtesy Green River High School Photo Lab)

Q: "So, you are packing it in and retiring finally?"
A: I prefer to use the word "graduate" since it is more accurate in this case. After all, how many seniors are "retiring" from high school this month? None. They are moving on, planning new adventures and so it is with this "senior".

Q: How long have you been associated with School District No. 2?

A: I came here on assignment as a student teacher to Mrs. Fraum in 1961 - 35 years. She was one of the great teachers in this district and I learned a bunch from her. After all these years, I think about her at least once a week. Quite a role model. She was one among the many that I was to learn from in the high school faculty. After a couple of weeks of student teaching, Principal Vern Newman asked if I would be interested in a job (contingent upon graduation). It was to be a new position, a split assignment of English/Social Studies.

Q: Why that combination?

A: The high school population was growing slowly and there was a need for a part-time assignment in English and also in Social Studies (plus one class to be 8th grade Social Studies).

Q: By today's standards, what was unusual about Lincoln High School in 1961?

A: The 7th and 8th grades were housed in the same building.

Q: The town's population was around 3,500 to 3,800 at that time, wasn't it?

A: Somewhere in there. The number of students that have been in my classes then up to the present totals out to about that same figure.

Q: Can you remember every one of them?

A: Can you? I was looking through one of the high school annuals the other day. One page opened to a class of juniors I had. There were two future state legislators, one county commissioner, two city council members, one school and city attorney, one general and a school board member. That was one page, mind you.

In 1970 our population was 4,200. By 1980 we had exploded to 12,800. This growth put tremendous pressure on the city, the school, the county, the state. As you knew, things changed. I was fortunate to get here soon enough to experience some of the "old Green River" and its people. I fell in love with this place, basically because of the quality of the people, their zest for living and their welcoming attitude both in the town and in the school. A few of those "originals" are still around and still contributing too. Thank heaven.

The new Monroe Junior High in the early 1960s relieved student pressure in the high school for a time. As school population grew the administration experimented with different solutions. So, in my public school career I can state accurately that I have been a teacher in a junior high, a four-year high school, a three-year high school and a four-year high school and never left town to do so.

Q: Public school career?

A: Yes. I have taught college classes for Western Wyoming and was an adjunct instructor for the University of Wyoming also.

Q: Talk about the three-year high school.

A: Well, a reason given was that it was to relieve class size and population pressure in the high school. A notable effect though was that the maturity level of the new sophomores seemed comparable to the maturity level of the "old" freshmen. I felt that, by the students remaining an additional year in the grades, stimulus for social maturation was lacking to some degree. Later when we shifted back to the four-year high school again we found ourselves with two classes at freshman level social maturation, the freshmen and the sophomores. It took awhile but it smoothed out over the years.

Q: Then you are opposed to a...

A: I am in favor of a four-year high school.

Q: And the middle school concept of today as opposed to the "old" junior high?

A: Our teachers in the middle schools are of the highest quality and highly dedicated to their students' development.

Q: That's all you're going to say about that concept?

A: Yes.

Q: Give some examples of how times have changed here.

A: As a new teacher, I was hired at one of the highest base pay schools in the entire state. I was told that the first two years of pay were very good and that after two years I would get an excellent written recommendation to another district of my choice. I noticed that pay raises drastically dropped beginning the third year. I learned that there were three teachers working past the age of 65 on a year-to-year contract until they would reach the age of 70. What dedication! Later one told me they were doing so because it was difficult to retire and live on $40 a month. Two things to note here - one is that the school board showed understanding and compas-sion for those sweet ladies and I admired those members for that. The second thing to note is that the students and faculty benefitted from the additional years the brilliant, vibrant teachers stayed in this district. Me most of all I think - I followed those energetic ladies around like a little puppy. For I knew I hardly knew anything compared to them and they were willing to help the new kid on the block. Hell, I get misty-eyed thinking about it.

Q: Me too. What were their names?

A: Helen Haynes, English; Hazel Fraum, Social Studies; Helen Taylor, Art. When they retired in 1965 there was a total of 134 teaching years amongst them!

Another example of changed times is that when I looked for a place to rent then, I learned that only one teacher in the district owned his own home. A few years later one teacher applied for and got a loan for low-income housing. His teaching salary met the federal guidelines at that time.

A lot of our early elk hunting trips were made up of pooled equipment from among the young faculty. No one had all the stuff - one had a pickup, another a tent, one most of the cooking equipment, and so on.

I developed and introduced three new classes into the high school (Sociology, Wyoming & the West and Military History of the United States) for the total cost of $347. Try that amount today for just one class! But my most economical contribution to the high school curriculum was when the foreign language teacher told me of his troubles in getting a needed class in Latin. The powers to be had told him that if there were books it could be done, but there was no money budgeted for books. I mentioned this dilemma to a fellow Lions Club member in another town. When we went to that town for a regional Lions Club meeting we met this fellow member at a service station. He loaded several cases of Latin language books into the trunk of my car - they were in very good condition, but the school in which he worked had gotten a new edition to replace them. These were brought back here and were used for our new class in Latin - funny though, no questions were ever asked by the principal about how the books were obtained. The foreign language teacher and I didn't push it either. Want to try it today? Don't answer.

Once in class a young student kept turning around and talking to her friend in the desk behind her. She heard a "thunk!" and upon turning back around to face the front she saw my pocket knife vibrating between her hands which were resting on the wooden desk top. She stopped talking...screamed some though. Her name was Sandy Spence...now known as Mrs. Rudy Gunter.

Another example, a custodian would not empty my classroom wastebasket, and after a week or so it was overflowing. Students were aware of this. One day in class I mentioned my chagrin and tossed a lighted match over my shoulder into the basket and kept on teaching. Soon, the students stopped paying attention to me and began watching the wastebasket. Finally, Bob Archuleta hesitatingly interrupted me (you didn't do that either in those days) to inform me the basket was on fire. I walked over, picked it up, opened the classroom door and invited my class to follow me out into the hall to help me dance. Knowing that I was part Indian (Native American - another change) the boys came out in the hall where we proceeded to whoop and holler while dancing around the fire. The custodian came running with the fire extinguisher, but my dancing kept getting in his way and he could not reach the fire which eventually burned out. I picked up the now empty metal wastebasket with my handkerchief and carried it back to its accustomed place and resumed class. It never overflowed with excess paper again. Want to try some of that stuff now?

Q: No thanks. There would be a SWAT team in place and several helicopters circling.

A: Well then I won't tell you about the time a certain teacher pointed a pistol in class to encourage a reluctant student to study. Nor give you the name of the student who began to get passing grades.

Q: Good.

A: But his initials are Merle Brown. Ask him for details if you want. And by the way, why did you choose me for the subject of your article this time? Sort of smacks of narcissistic egotism doesn't it?

Q: Not at all. It represents an example of **Tales from the Educational Triassic.**

Q: You have told your students that you teach and lecture on about three different wave lengths at the same time, and that they are to recognize the silly and obvious first level for what it is. But then they are to find and understand the messages in the two higher frequencies as well. You have done that in this interview too, haven't you?

A: Yes.

❖

"A Strange Night Had Come":
The Solar Eclipse of 1918

by Ruth Lauritzen

Major astronomical happenings almost always gather an audience of interested observers. The solar eclipse of June 1918 created particular excitement in Sweetwater County because much of the southern part of the county was in the zone of totality, the area where a full eclipse could be viewed.

Scientists ready their instruments to observe the eclipse at the Yerkes Observatory viewing station north of Green River in 1918. (Photo courtesy Sweetwater County Historical Museum)

Green River became the headquarters for observational activity by four different institutions: the University of Chicago Yerkes Observatory from Williams Bay, Wisconsin; the Solar Observatory from the Carnegie Institution in Mt. Wilson, California; and two Salt Lake City schools, All Hallow's College and the University of Utah.

The town was selected as the observation site by these groups because of its clear skies. Scientists knew that even slight cloud cover would prevent the effective viewing, study and photographing of the eclipse. Therefore much effort was put into finding an observation point with the best possible chance of clear skies. For five years prior to the eclipse daily weather observations were made in towns in the zone of totality. Local resident William Hutton reported the Green River weather and, once the town was selected, served as a local contact.

Members of the largest expedition, the Yerkes party, arrived in Green River in early May. This group was led by E.E. Barnard, Professor of Practical Astronomy at the University of Chicago. He reached Green River on May 4th along with several assistants and the carpenter and superintendent of construction, H.M. Foote. The advance party was to secure accommodations, choose an observation point and to begin construction of the necessary buildings. The remainder of the crew, including E.B. Frost, Professor of Astrophysics and director of the Observatory, arrived later in the month.

The chosen site for the Yerkes observatory was located between Castle Rock and Teapot and Coffeepot Rocks, north of town. The Yerkes crew put in place a shop, a storeroom and observation tower to house the equipment which included two telescopes measuring sixty-one and eighteen feet, as well as spectroscopes and other instruments for examining and photographing the corona, the field of light surrounding the sun which is only visible during a total eclipse. The other two observatories were located in approximately the same area.

There was much interest in the town about the impending eclipse. Professor Barnard gave a lecture entitled *The Total Eclipse of the Sun.* Barnard illustrated his lecture with lantern slides of other total eclipses and the instruments used to view and photograph them. The "magic lantern" was an early optical device which used an oil lamp to project enlarged images from glass slides. According to the *Green River Star,* the address "...was attended by a large audience, which received much enlightenment upon the subject."

When the great day finally arrived all interested parties anxiously viewed the sky, watching the accumulating clouds in the early afternoon. Fortunately as totality approached the clouds thinned enough to provide a reasonable view of the phenomenon.

At exactly 4:16 p.m. on June 8, 1918 the moon began to cover the face of the sun. While the scientists were photographing and analyzing the event, spectators were busy viewing what the *Green River Star* describes as "... the most marvelous and never-to-be-forgotten spectacle .... The corona shines out in all its glory, a soft pearly radiance, and in the place where the sun was; but just now the moon is seen projected as a black globe on the bright background. Rose-colored flames, the solar prominences, appear to project from the edge of the moon..... As suddenly as the light went out, a jet of light broke out and a hubbub of voices announced the end of the phenomenon that for the spectator will never be forgotten."

The scientists were unable to do some of their planned obser-vations due to the light cloud cover, but some new information was gleaned. Professor Barnard discovered a new star which the Green River Star reported as the brightest body of this kind discovered since 1901.

Scientific discoveries aside, for most of the citizens of Green River the 1918 eclipse was a happening of great excitement, a period of time when world renown experts made the town a center of astronomical study and most memorably, a once-in-a-lifetime opportunity to view the rare phenomenon of a total eclipse of the sun.

❖

Trip Down Memory Lane with Irene Kalivas

by Marna Grubb

The name Kalivas is a name which has gathered much respect in Green River throughout the years.

I recently visited with Irene Kalivas and shared her memorable moments from a recent trip to Greece with four of her grandchildren - Stephanie and Andrew for graduation presents and Philip and Amy who will be graduating in 1998. Irene informed that her husband John (now deceased) always said that the grandchildren should be taken to Greece to visit the country from which their

Irene Kalivas, age 5 (Photo courtesy Irene Kalivas)

great grandparents had come. I'm sure this will be remembered as the trip of a lifetime for all involved.

The trip, July 1-14, 1996 began when they flew to Athens and then on to the Kalamala Logga island where the parents of Irene's husband, John, were raised, then back to Athens and onto Chios island where Irene was raised, then back to Athens and home.

Irene shared pictures of their trip. One showed the beautiful island of Chios, which is located on the Aegean Sea. While there they visited a monastery. In Athens they visited the famous Acropolis, the Parthenon, Socrates' grave and the Delphi Museum. Of course, no trip would be complete without shopping; and a good time was had by the grandchildren at the Flea Markets.

Irene (Bekiarellis) Kalivas, a charming person, was born in Gary, Indiana to Aristidis and Anna (Morivick) Bekiarellis. In 1929, when she was five years old, Irene's father took her to Greece to visit his parents, her grandparents, and she returned to the United States in 1946, shortly after the end of World War II.

"Those were hard times during the war while the Germans occupied Greece," she said, and further stated that these were times she would rather forget. Irene worked in the steel mills at Gary, Indiana when she returned to the United States.

In 1947, Irene came to Green River to visit her uncle and met John at a party. John had been born in Green River to James and Efthirnia (Mandros) Kalivas. In 1949, Irene returned to Green River, and John and Irene were married. They have three children: James and wife Richi, Peter and wife Carol, and Aristidis and wife Marlene, plus eight grandchildren and three great grandchildren. Irene has a half brother living in Hobart, Indiana. Her half sister died 10 years ago.

John Kalivas was working for the Union Pacific Railroad when they married. Later he was self-employed with his brothers, Steve and George, managing The Independent Store. Eventually, the store was managed by John, wife Irene and three sons. In 1973 John became employed at Allied Chemical west of Green River. He worked there until his retirement in 1984.

The Independent Store was located on the comer of 2nd South and Center Streets where Brady's Auto Body is currently located. The upstairs was called The Tin Castle, which were sleeping rooms rented to railroaders. The crew callers would come by to call the railroaders back to duty when needed. These ladies were officially called "call girls" and were respectable women from throughout the community who were employed by the Union Pacific Railroad to call crews.

The Independent Store. (Photo courtesy Sweetwater County Historical Society)

While growing up in Greece, Irene was very fond of her grandparents. She now enjoys visiting with cousins in Athens. While growing up in Greece, she had cats and a goat for pets. Christmas and Easter were religious holidays and were observed as such. They didn't exchange gifts for Christmas. They would give money as a present for New Years. Christmas dinner usually consisted of chicken and many other fine Greek foods and pastries.

All of Irene's years of schooling were in Greece, so she forgot the English language until she returned to America in 1946. The games they had played in Greece were jump rope and marbles, but mainly they made their own entertainment.

Irene isn't found to be idle these days. She is a volunteer at the Sweetwater County Memorial Hospital, a member of the Golden Hour Senior Citizens and assists with their monthly public breakfasts, donates her services to the Soup Kitchen in Rock Springs, and does a beautiful job of crocheting.

I enjoy this lady very much. She plays a great game of pinochle, plus her Greek cookies, koulouria, are super and one of my favorites. In fact, I received a big plate of these when I completed this interview. Yum!

Ward v. Race Horse – 1896: Could Wyoming's Game Law Supersede a Federal Treaty?

by Bill Thompson

Almost one-half of Wyoming is owned by the state and the federal government. Such land was classified as "unoccupied" during the treaty-making period of the 1860s.

On July 3, 1868, at Fort Bridger, Utah Territory (22 days later it would come into the boundaries of Wyoming Territory) a treaty created the Wind River Reservation for the Eastern Shoshones in Wyoming.

Undersigned by Chief Washakie of the Shoshones and by Chief Targhee of the Bannock tribe (Targhee National Forest) it permitted the Shoshones to "admit amongst them other friendly tribes" (Bannocks). Article IV gave the Indians the "right to hunt on the unoccupied lands of the United States."

Traveling from Green River in any direction one soon is surrounded by "unoccupied" land. But one sees no Bannocks or Eastern Shoshones legally hunting year-round as guaranteed by that 1868 Federal Treaty.

This longer-than-usual article for *Echoes* will use historical background information from Utah, Wyoming and Idaho leading up to the case of Ward v. Race Horse - 1896 which has a direct impact on your and my Wyoming hunting rights.

The history of the Bannock Indian is interspersed with incidents of conflict and warfare. The nation never numbered more than several thousand. Described as a tall, strong-bodied people, they were lighter complexioned than the Shoshones with whom they lived and hunted. Only their small numbers kept the Bannocks from a reputation comparable to that of the Sioux or Blackfeet, their hereditary enemies.

The Bannocks supplemented their numbers by coercing other tribes to join them in fighting the whites. In sporadic raids of horse stealing, wagon burning and scalp lifting, they struck and fled in scattered bands. In 1858 they attacked the Mormon missionary post at Fort Lemhi in the Salmon River Country.

Brigham Young had kindly accepted the Indians as brethren. In explaining their surprise attack, the Bannocks claimed that the Mormons had shown partiality to the Nez Perce in trading ammunition and horses.

The Bannocks further stated that since the Great Father (President Buchanan) had sent Johnson's army in 1857 to punish the Mormons, the Bannocks would not be punished by the U.S. Troops, and they weren't. They continued to make attacks on white travelers and settlers.

This all-out threat of the Bannocks was stopped, however. Their lesson was administered by troops comprising two California Volunteer regiments, infantry and cavalry, stationed at Fort Douglas near Salt Lake. These were joined later by an attachment of Nevada Volunteers, both placed under the command of Brig. General Patrick E. Connor.

The Indians were encamped in a deep ravine about a mile from Bear River near the Mormon settlement of Franklin, Idaho. The Indians had a clear field of fire with a treeless plain to the front. Two avenues of escape were the mouth of the ravine to the river, and the head of the ravine near the low hill.

Knowing that the Indians would be alerted and might flee at sight of such a large body of troops, Connor started his infantry on the night march of Jan. 22, 1863, and his cavalry two days later. On the 29th, the cavalry moved in advance, swimming their horses across the ice-packed river. The hostiles had prepared a natural fortification of intertwined thick willows and had dug steps for firing positions. The women, children and old men remained in teepees at the bottom of the ravine.

At approach of the troops a war chief rode out from the ravine, gesticulating with a lance on which hung a scalp.

The warriors shouted obscenities in the language of their civilized, pale-faced enemies, "Fours right... fours left... Come on you bluecoat sons of a B...!" As soon as the troopers were in range, the Indians began their fire.

The battle lasted more than four hours. In a frontal attack, strengthened by detachments flanking the ravine the troopers routed the Indians into attempting to escape from avenues turned into death traps. Many warriors did escape by fleeing into the hills or plunging into the river.

The number of Indians killed including women and children varied in reports from 224 to nearly 400. Soldier casualties were listed as 23 dead, 44 wounded, 79 disabled by frostbite. Had it not been for the kindness of several Mormon settlers who searched the next day for survivors left on the battleground, many more Indian women and children would have perished from hunger and freezing.

For after the battle Connor's forces destroyed the teepees and captured their horses and food supplies. Although from Connor's report he "left a small quantity of wheat." In the Battle of Bear River where the Shoshones greatly outnumbered the Bannocks, Patrick E. Connor distinguished himself as the General who whipped the Bannock. Never again did the Bannock exert such fighting spirit. Even the Bannock War of 1878 was pale in comparison. The author's Bannock great-grandmother was a babe in arms at the Battle of Bear River.

After the Bear River Battle it became clear that while the Sioux and Cheyenne had been reimbursed for many years, the Bannock and Shoshone tribes had never received substantial annuities of any kind. Subsequently the 1860s evolved into the treaty-making period between the U.S. Government and various western tribes.

It was Article IV of the Fort Bridger Treaty of 1868 that caused controversy and bloodshed among the white settlers in Wyoming and the Bannock Indians of Idaho. It took 27 years of growing animosity to get the situation settled in the courts.

The Bannocks continued to hunt in Wyoming especially in the Jackson Hole country. Against the bitter protest of settlers, the Indians recalled their "promised right" to hunt as mentioned in the treaty.

Often the Bannocks hunted off the reservation because of dire hunger. They were grimly disappointed at Fort Hall, Idaho, when told that their promised allotments were being shipped instead to the Eastern Shoshones in Wyoming to where they must travel if they wished to receive the Bannock's share.

Wyoming's first Territorial Legislative Assembly in 1869 had enacted game laws for the protection of the game and fish of the Territory. But the Fort Hall Indians continued to hunt off their reservation, with or without the agent's permission. This emboldened Washakie's Wyoming Shoshones to do likewise. The controversial question gained more bitterness from repetition: Did the Indians have or have not the right to hunt on unoccupied lands?

After Wyoming gained statehood (July 10, 1890) officials believed the question was answered in the passage of other state's hunting and fishing laws which set up "closed seasons" but made no provision at all for the Indians. They reasoned that despite the U.S. Government treaties, the state of Wyoming was vested with sovereign power to make and enforce its own laws whose terms should be applied to law-breaking Indians as well as to whites.

But in 1893 high-ranking officials were involved in complaints against the Indians hunting. Governor Osborne complained to the Commissioner of Indian Affairs and the Secretary of the Interior presenting them with a signed petition from the Uinta County settlers. They "prayed for relief from depredations of roving Indians." In September of 1894, Fremont County officials complained to Governor Osborne about "insulting behavior of Fort Washakie Indians and their refusal to submit to arrest."

Vociferous among the complaints were those from Marysville, Wyo., (first post office in Jackson Hole and now the town of Jackson). In 1895 the new Governor, William Richards, wired Marysville officials "to enforce the laws of Wyoming; to put the Indians out of Jackson Hole." On June 7, 1895 Constable William Manning and his deputies started out on the first of several expeditions to search for Indian trespassers and to arrest all violators of Wyoming's game laws. Most of the Indians caught with game were Bannocks. Some paid the fines, others did not and would not submit to arrest ... even when threatened that U.S. soldiers would be sent after them.

Eight Bannocks were arrested on July 4, 1895. Six were fined with costs totaling around $1,400. Unable to pay, they were held in jail... until the guard was relaxed and the Indians "escaped." Knowing how this incident outraged the settlers, Manning determined that sterner measures would be taken when he left with 26 deputies on July 10. Fifty-five miles from Marysville in Hoback Canyon, they surrounded an encampment of Bannocks comprising nine braves, 13 squaws and five papooses. Ordering each brave between two deputies and the squaws and children to the rear of the line, Manning started the march to Marysville. He told the Indians that they would be shot or hung there. The Indians went passively until reaching a thicket of aspen. The Whites began loading their rifles and the squaws began to wail, the braves made a break for the timber. The deputies opened fire, killing one, wounding six and maiming the other so badly he was left for dead. The rest escaped including the squaws with the exception of two papooses who were jostled from their mother's arms. One of these babies was later found and cared for by Mrs. Martin Nelson for a year and then was returned to his mother. Later in adulthood he fought for the U.S. in WWI. The other baby was never found.

Now that the controversial '68 Treaty provisions had caused such a tragic climax, officials began a search for a Fort Hall Bannock who would willingly come to Wyoming to "contest" this Treaty and submit to a court decision. In procedure he would be arrested for killing game out of season. Then an application of a Writ of Habeas Corpus for his release would be brought by the U.S. District Attorney for Wyoming. But, it was emphasized, the decision would have to be forever accepted not only by this Bannock contestant but by the entire Bannock-Shoshone tribes.

The Bannock was Po-ha-ve, known to the Whites as Chief Race Horse. He and another tribesman left Fort Hall for Wyoming. In Uinta County they killed seven elk. Race Horse was arrested and taken into custody. The case came to trial November 21, 1895, before the Honorable John A. Riner's Circuit Court at Cheyenne. His decision stunned the whites. The laws of Wyoming were invalid against the treaty rights of the Indians! The decision affirmed their right to hunt on the unoccupied public lands of Wyoming in and out of season. Race Horse was dismissed from custody.

Seemingly to forget that the decision was to be the final word on this Treaty, Governor Richards urged an appeal. On May 25, 1896, the United States Supreme Court reversed the decision deciding in favor of the state of Wyoming.

In a remarkable legalese display of, "what's mine is mine, and what's yours is mine!" Justice White (ironic last name isn't it?) in delivering his opinion stated; "The power of a state to control and regulate the taking of game cannot be questioned... when in 1868 the Treaty was framed the progress of the white settlements westward had hardly... reached the confines of the place selected for the Indian reservation... according to the Act admitting Wyoming on July 10, 1890, 'Wyoming is hereby declared to be a State of the United States of America and is hereby declared to be admitted into the Union on an equal footing with the original States in all respects whatsoever' ... The act which admitted Wyoming made no reservation whatever in favor of the Indians."

The case, Ward v. Race Horse (#841) settled the matter. Persuaded to return from Fort Hall and to give himself up, Race Horse was remanded to the custody of the Uinta County Sheriff who released him on a $500 bond. On Sept. 7, 1896 before the

District Court, Race Horse was solemnly instructed by the Judge that the Indians could be imprisoned for their crime of hunting contrary to Wyoming laws. He was permitted to return to his reservation where he lived out the rest of his days with honor. He is buried at the tribal cemetery at Fort Hall.

So there you have it folks. A State Law of Wyoming superseded a Federal Treaty! According to the United States Constitution that sort of thing cannot be done... oh yeah?

Point of Interest (maybe); listed as a hostile Bannock for leaving the Fort Hall Reservation to go hunting and trapping was Pam Pig-e-mena, my Great-Great-Grandfather. He was at the Bear River Battle also.

Basic information for this article was obtained from historical research and published work from Edith M. Thompson, Wyoming Award-Winning Author.

❖

Hoffmanns

by Marie Finney

I met Kurt and Margaret Hoffmann in 1994. They were a quiet, pleasant couple that I had come to know and respect. They, like many of the emigrants that made the arduous journey to America and the West, came filled with hopes and dreams of starting a new and bountiful life.

Kurt was born July 17, 1906, in Liatkawe, Germany to Rudolf and Ida Haenel Hoffmann. Margaret was born to Gustau and Hedwig Luka Schirbel, in Breslau, Germany, on March 4, 1908. Both graduated from school at the age of 14, which was usual for all German children. Kurt's mother managed to pay for him to continue his schooling another two years. As was the custom, no matter what the job, one had to serve an apprenticeship. Kurt followed in his father's footsteps to become a butcher and sausage maker. Kurt served three years working from 4:30 a.m. to dark, seven days a week. He received no pay, only room and board. Margaret wanted to be a seamstress; however, there were no positions available so the job placement center recommended she become a bookkeeper/stenographer. She worked for seven years for the same employer until she left to join Kurt in America.

Kurt and Margaret recalled that the first time they saw each other was in passing on a train. They did not speak to each other at that time but Kurt did wave to Margaret as she departed. A few moments later they saw each other again. Kurt started flirting with her now and before they knew it they were taking long walks and talking.

Inflation was bad in Germany during the 1920s. At his mother's persuasion, Kurt decided to come to America. On the eve of their engagement Kurt boarded the train to join his mother and stepfather in America. Little did these two young people know that it would be another three and one half years before they would hold each other in their arms. They wrote to each other, but it took weeks for mail to cross the ocean.

After his arrival in Wyoming, Kurt landed a job with the Rock Springs Butchering Company, a local slaughter house. Even though he made what he thought was good wages, Kurt became discontented. He sought his dreams elsewhere, which led him to Milwaukee, Wis., in a sausage kitchen practicing his trade. At this time Kurt sent for Margaret to join him.

Like all young brides-to-be Margaret dreamed of walking down the aisle on her father's arm, but it was not to be. Kurt had earned only enough to purchase a one-way ticket for Margaret. As she boarded the train, she kissed her family farewell to begin a long journey to America and an unknown future.

Margaret arrived in New York Harbor on March 11, 1930. She traveled by train the next day to Milwaukee. Upon arriving in Chicago where she had to change trains, she had a pleasant surprise. Kurt came to meet her so they traveled the rest of the journey together. Kurt and Margaret were married in Milwaukee on March 19, 1930, by a German minister as Margaret could not speak English. Margaret jokingly tells her friends that she had to get married. After the shock wears off she proceeds to tell that it was because her visa stated she was only permitted to enter America to get married. Six weeks after they were married, Kurt and Margaret moved to Rock Springs. This was only the first of many moves.

It was not until 1935 that the Hoffmanns finally settled down in Green River. They purchased the "Yellow Front" Store on Railroad Avenue and opened up for business on April 1, 1935. Green River had a population of less than 3000 people at the time and Railroad Avenue was the business district. Green River was starting to boom again and soon some of the stores started to move up to the upper street, which was then US Highway 30, now Flaming Gorge Way. That was when they bought the old E.E. Peters Lumber Company Building, in 1937. It was a dilapidated two-story building on the corner, but had three small apartments beside it which rented for $25 a month. So there was some income. When it came time to remodel, a local contractor, Charley Johnson, approached them to do the work. Kurt and Charley worked out the arrangements and in time the Hoffmann's had a new grocery store, Highway Market, with living quarters and eventually seven cabins for tourists.

Kurt became a U.S. citizen Sept. 8, 1939. Although Margaret applied for citizenship shortly thereafter, no citizenship was given during the war years. Finally, Margaret became a U.S. citizen on March 13, 1946.

They were doing well with the store and they seemed to have a bright future. Then March 29, 1940, Kurt and Margaret were blessed with the arrival of their first child, Mark. Now their lives felt more complete. Kurt closed the store in 1942, due to the possibility of being drafted into the war and the fact that it would have been impossible for Margaret to handle the store alone. Jan. 11, 1944, Kurt and Margaret were again blessed with the birth of their daughter, Kay Ann. They were happy and their children were a delight.

The Hoffmanns continued to rent the apartments and cabins, which were known as the Highway Lodge until 1955. In 1956, the name was changed to the Hoffmann's Motel and operated until they sold it in 1973.

After selling the motel, the Hoffmann's set up housekeeping in Jamestown on property they had bought back in 1945.

Kurt established a sign shop in the basement and spent several years making all sorts of signs.

After retirement, Kurt and Margaret spent their time working in their yard, as well as writing a book of memories for their children and grandchildren.

❖

Green River Winter

by Bill Duncan

We waited breathlessly at the foot of Castle Rock. School age kids, young adults, parents with toddlers, all eyes were on the little man at the bottom of the hill.

Actually, he was standing in the middle of Highway 30, the transcontinental road that ran from coast to coast. The bundled black form was waiting for a break in the truck and car traffic to stop everything and give the sledders a chance.

Steam puffs from each anxious sledder mixed with the fog from the coal-burning engines to form a haze over the Green River of the early 1940s.

I stood clutching my new, wooden sled with red, metal runners. This would be my solo trip down the hill. The policeman raised his arms holding his palms out to stop semis with PIE printed on the side, older cars with thermometers atop their radiators, and sleeker new models. Talk on the hill died in anticipation. As the thin, silvery whistle tone came to us, the more experienced sledders, the high school guys, took a running start down the hill.

It was slow at first past the high school, but by the time I passed Mortimer's green, brick garbage burner, the cold January air stung my eyes and burned my throat. A little bump on the road, then we whizzed past the tidy houses on each side of the street. I drug my feet a little to slow down as I crossed the Lincoln Highway. The big guys who had started first were already on their way back up the hill for another run. Other people had stopped by the big hedge where the road turned toward the river. Everyone stopped here because the fastest part of the trip was over. It was really foolish to sled as far as the underpass, the going was too slow.

Another popular, winter gathering place was a pond by the river west of town. I was too little to go by myself and didn't have ice skates, but my mom and dad often took me on cold winter after-

Ice skating below the Palisades west of Green River. (Photo courtesy Sweetwater County Historical Museum)

noons. Many Green River folks walked to the foot of the Palisades to enjoy skating, sliding and warming around the bonfire there. The park nestled between a river oxbow and the sheer cliffs. Huge cottonwoods ringed the pond and lined the river banks. Parents pulled their kids on sleds or in boxes. Some figure skaters carved graceful figure-eights in the ice. Palisades Park was the winter social center and a place to sip hot chocolate, schnapps and show off. A place to see and be seen.

Highway construction changed the river's course and filled in the pond. Trees were felled and brush cleared. Skaters braved other parts of the river because ponds that froze smoothly were scarce. After the outdoor swimming pool was razed and filled in on the town side of the bridge going to Expedition Island, that site served as a skating area for a few years. The Recreation Center has sometimes flooded a cement multi-use area for ice skating. Most skating now is the roller blade variety that happens in the summer on sidewalks and streets.

Green River's hills often provided sledding for young people. Kids who lived in the Paxton-Webb addition made many bumpy rides down "Tank Hill" in the '60s. The hill wasn't very steep. It was strewn with rocks and brush. But it was close to home and mothers could keep an eye on their children easily.

Several generations of Green River kids entertained themselves on the steeper hills in Mormon Canyon northwest of town. These rocky slopes claimed many broken bones and skinned limbs when youngsters reclaimed hoods of old cars, pulled them up the side hills and tried to ride them to the road at the bottom of the hill. The last time this was really popular was in the mid-70s.

About this time plastic saucers, plastic rugs and plastic sleds replaced the cardboard and steel runners of the past. Sure, cars still pulled kids' sleds tied to rear bumpers on city streets, but the town's growth was paving a lot of the good hills and housing blocked other runways. Jensen Street didn't connect with Bramwell for awhile and a couple of short runs bit the dust when Clark and Jensen were paved.

As the city's population moved south and east, nice runs were widely used around Hitching Post and Upland Way. Kids lined up on hills behind the Rec. Center and a block east, but housing developments and new High School construction have taken those away. The southwest hills around Knotty Pine and Easy Street never got the same sledding traffic as some of the other hills did. Installation of the water tanks took some of the fun from there.

Like most everything else, technology has changed Green River's winter activities. Snow machines and ATV's go faster, farther and provide lots of thrills. Ice skating mostly happens indoors. Both kids and grownups compete in basketball and volleyball leagues and tournaments. World-class commercial ski areas are just a few hours drive away. Cross country skiing has become a popular family activity.

I'm not sure any of this can match the thrill I enjoyed as I looked down at the bundled traffic cop, clutched my Snow Racer, checked my snowshoe buckles and waited for the sound of the silver whistle.

❖

Tuning In: The Arrival of Television in Green River

by Ruth Lauritzen

Almost exactly forty years ago the 20th century miracle of television came to Green River. Although television broadcasts were available out of Salt Lake City in the early 1950s, no one in Green River had television service. The town's distance from the nearest broadcast point and the rugged terrain in between made getting a television signal impossible.

For this reason what is known now as "cable TV" came early to Sweetwater County. In 1955 Albert Carollo of Rock Springs made application to the Wyoming Public Service Commission (PSC) to supply television service to Rock Springs and Green River. He quickly gained some competition from a Kemmerer group headed by Fred Steinhour. The Steinhour group had brought TV to Kemmerer very recently and were looking to expand their market into Sweetwater County. Both of these entities sought to supply TV signal through coaxial cable.

Another possible avenue of service was proposed by E.J. Vehar of the American Electric Company of Green River, which just happened to sell television sets. He proposed the establishment of a community antennae which would be funded by voluntary subscriptions. To be located high above the town, this antenna would collect and rebroadcast television signals down into the Green River valley where it would be received in homes by use of an aer-ial antenna. In short, it would be a community supported means of bringing in "free" TV to Green River. This plan was discarded when the two cable companies began proposing their services.

The Carollo and Steinhour groups applied to the PSC in November of 1955 for a certificate of public necessity to supply community TV service. According to the *Green River Star* the town of Green River favored neither applicant over the other, but simply wanted to bring TV service to Green River as soon as possible. There was concern on the part of the citizens that service be offered to Green River at the same time it became available in Rock Springs.

Another point of fairness was brought up by the Green River City Council in January 1956 when they requested that the signals available for Green River be tested before the PSC granted the certificate to either company. "Declared in the meeting, by all concerned, was that tests at Rock Springs would not determine the quality of television which would be received at sites near Green River." *(Green River Star,* Jan. 6, 1956). Picture testing had been done on a site on White Mountain which had determined the clarity of the available picture in Rock Springs, but no testing had been done on potential sites for Green River reception. Tests on the White Mountain site were deemed acceptable to the representatives only after they received assurances that if good reception was not found in the potential Green River reception sites that signals would be brought in by coaxial cable from the White Mountain site.

After lengthy hearings Albert Carollo received the permit to service both towns in April 1956. Construction was slated to begin immediately on the reception towers and a distribution system. Carollo was quoted in the *Green River Star* of May 3, 1956,

> "I am gratified to have received the PSC certificate to serve the two towns...and I also express my gratitude to the people of the two towns for their fair attitude towards the applications considered by the PSC. I want to assure them that the dirt will really fly in our effort to complete a satisfactory community TV system for the area. We are getting to work right now."

Construction proceeded throughout the summer and, according to newspaper articles, good progress was being made. The reception antenna was completed and a pole line installed to town. However, things were not moving fast enough for some Green River residents. In a late October editorial a new movement was discussed,

> Last week, a group of railroad employes (sic) who have been studying televisions decided to try something about getting TV into town. To ascer-

tain the interest of our townspeople, they ran a "blind" advertisement in the *STAR*, asking if people were interested in their proposition. By noon, 80 had returned the coupon in the advertisement, two petitions were voluntarily circulated, and this office had diverted several dozen telephone calls to the men who were originators of the idea.

The immediate response is significant. Green River people want TV the quickest possible way. They want it badly, and they are impatient waiting for the installation of the community TV system now under construction. The men installing the system say they cannot bring wires into town until service poles are cleared to proper clearances of other utility wires. But the people of Green River are at the point they will not wait if they can have other means of receiving TV, despite the large amount of money being spent on community TV.

The fact that television arrived officially in Rock Springs in mid-November and no specific arrival date for Green River had been announced fueled the movement. The newspaper reported the establishment of the Green River TV Experimental Co-op and announced plans to revive the plans of E.J. Vehar to provide for aerial transmission of TV into town. Donations of $15 per household were sought and quickly received along with much donated labor. Within weeks television service was available in Green River. On Tuesday, November 27, 1956 the first channel was successfully received.

Green River went television crazy. Five dealers were selling TV s in town including American Electric Company, Yates Furniture, Bill's TV and Service, Davis Furniture and Jeffries Furniture. An estimated 200 TVs were sold during the first ten days of service. The TV log began to be printed in the newspaper as did advertisements for TV sales and repair. It is interesting to note that at this time the Little Theater Company which had successfully been presenting three plays a season to a substantial audience announced that they would be making refunds on season tickets. They reported being, "unable to find the persons who had time to devote in preparing a production." *(Star,* May 5, 1957). Whether this is a reflection on the social change TV brought to Green River, or simply a coincidence cannot be determined, but the juxtaposition of these two events is interesting.

Cable television finally came to Green River under the Carollo company in the fall of 1958. The television co-op continued to provide service, but as it was funded by subscriptions with no formalized or truly efficient means of collection, only lasted until 1969, a total of 15 years. By this time most citizens subscribed to the cable service which had more available channels and more reliable service. Use of the system ended in 1969 and the next year the community antenna was demolished.

❖

Heart Mountain

by Lori Woodward, youth representative

After Pearl Harbor was bombed by the Japanese Dec. 7, 1941, a mini-crisis erupted in a few of the western states of the United States.

Right after the infamous bombing of Pearl Harbor, West Coast panic spread, along with fear and anger at the Japanese. Many people took their anger out on the Japanese-Americans.

Although they were legal residents of the United States and most were loyal to the United States, many people thought something needed to be done about these "potentially harmful and dangerous aliens."

The bombing fueled rumors, many stemming from racial prejudice, about a plan of Japanese-Americans who planned to sabotage the United States war effort. This led President Franklin Roosevelt to sign Executive Order 9066 on Feb. 19, 1942. This order forced all Japanese-Americans, regardless of their citizenship or loyalty to the United States, to evacuate the West Coast.

Racial tension was extreme during this period of time. Although many people were glad to see President Roosevelt sign this order, for some it wasn't enough. A number of people wanted to see harsher treatment of the Japanese-Americans.

Along with the people who wanted to see harsher treatment of the Japanese, there were those who were against relocating the Japanese-American population. This was not for the interest of the Japanese-Americans who were being moved from their homes in California and other West Coast states, but for their own personal interests.

Many Wyoming residents just didn't want the Japanese population to be in Wyoming instead of the West Coast.

By Aug. 9, 1942, the relocation camp at Heart Mountain would be receiving and would be ready to house an estimated 10,000

Japanese-American evacuees. A Sept. 6, 1942 article from the Billings Gazette states, "Three months ago only rabbits and rattlesnakes inhabited these flats under the white cap of Heart Mountain. Today they are the home of a population that rapidly is nearing 10,000 people, and may grow in the next few weeks or months to 13,000."

Edith Sunada, a resident of Green River who was living here during this time, talks of her visit to Heart Mountain during the war. She was with her family, which included her brother who was a soldier for the U.S. Army. They were refused service in a Cody restaurant, even with her brother in his soldier's uniform.

Prejudice was at a high level in the towns of Cody and Powell because these were the nearest towns to the Heart Mountain relocation camp. Even a United States soldier in his uniform and his family were refused service simply because of race.

As the war went on, few people changed their opinions regarding the relocated Japanese-Americans. Feelings were very strong amongst the Japanese-Americans returning home to their native states after the war was over.

After the relocation camp had officially closed on Nov. 15, 1945, the relocated Japanese-Americans were neither forced to stay or to leave Park County. Heart Mountain is a large part of Wyoming's history. It affected not only the residents in Park County, but residents all over the state of Wyoming.

The Covered Wagon

by Marna Grubb

Why is there a Covered Wagon Exit west of Green River across from the golf course exit? Was this to an area for covered wagons? According to Jane Seppie, daughter of Frank and Tess Wozniak who were the last owners of the supper club known as the Covered Wagon, this exit was designated as such by the Wyoming Highway Department at the request of her mother for an entrance to their business. Before the exit was constructed, the Covered Wagon burned to the ground as reported in the *Green River Star* on Oct. 25, 1962, but the construction of the exit approximately four miles west of Green River continued as planned.

Dee and Elaine Slaughter, owners of the Covered Wagon west of Green River from December of 1952 to June 1961. (Photo courtesy Dee and Elaine Slaughter)

The Wozniaks had purchased the Covered Wagon 16 months prior from Dee and Elaine Slaughter. The *Green River Star* of Oct. 25, 1962 reported that it was "completely destroyed by flames of an undetermined origin." A brick chimney was all that remained. A bell belonging to the Lions Club and reported to have been from the old steamboat, the Comet, used on the Green in 1908, could not be found after the fire. Jane Seppie explained that the cause of the fire was probably due to faulty wiring which was in the process of being replaced.

Originally, the building had been built by Jim Maher in circa 1936 for "Sweetwater" Martha Selakovich. After a short time she moved to Great Falls, Mont., and operated a night club there. Then the building was owned by Elizabeth and Henry Rizzi, later Frances Hazen, and in Dec. of 1952 it was purchased by Dee and Elaine Slaughter who were residents of Rock Springs at the time. They were told they would never "make a go of it" since the people in Green River didn't know them, but things went well. In 1953 Dee and Elaine moved to an apartment at the Covered Wagon and remained there with a "thriving business" until they sold to the Wozniaks on June 1, 1961.

The Green River community had accepted Dee and Elaine Slaughter with open arms, and Rock Springs came also, so it brought the two communities together. Before television, people would often venture out to just socialize. FMC was doing its first major expansion in 1952 and 1953 and, with the influx of new employees, the Covered Wagon became an increasingly popular place for meetings and for business and family dining. Regular meetings of the Lions Club, the Chamber of Commerce, and the Jaycees were held at the Covered Wagon as these groups were very active with many enthusiastic members. The Covered Wagon also hosted special dinner meetings for the VFW, the Womens Club and various other organizations, plus wedding receptions. It was a stopping place for Governor Milward Simpson, Congressman Keith Thomson, Senator Lester Hunt and various other politicians as they traveled the state. Its clean, friendly atmosphere attracted many. The nickelodeon was always playing songs such as "Salty Dog Rag," "Cotton Eye Joe," "Personality," and "Memories Are Made of This," six songs for a quarter, and people would dance or just enjoy. Sometimes there would be a live band. A piano located in the orchestra pit in the front area was sometimes played by Bill Heatherington and Bill McCurtain, resulting in sing-a-longs. Another time, the famous violinist Rubinoff had been in the area performing and a luncheon for him was held at the Covered Wagon,

Covered Wagon west of Green River as it looked after purchase by Frank and Tess Wozniak in 1961. (Photo courtesy Marna Grubb)

which resulted in an informal performance by his pianist and himself at the violin.

Elaine did the majority of the cooking and quoted their prices as "a half-chicken dinner served in a basket $1.75, fried shrimp $1.50, club steak $1.75, and a large T-bone $3.50." The sizzling steaks were served on a sizzler. The dinners also included tomato juice, salad, French fries, homemade muffins and honey. I, myself, remember many fun times at the Covered Wagon and especially enjoyed the delicious homemade muffins served with honey.

Dee Slaughter was the friendly bartender who greeted everyone as they entered the door. He always bought an after-dinner drink for everyone. The children were served a "Shirley Temple" or a "Roy Rogers."

As I reminisced with Dee and Elaine about the Covered Wagon, it became quite apparent that we were talking about people, not the building. It was the owners who attracted the customers, and it was the customers who made it such a success. Fond memories of many fine people were exchanged.

After selling the Covered Wagon, Dee was employed at Stauffer Chemical as a shipping supervisor, from where he retired on Jan. 1, 1983. Elaine was employed at School District No. 2 as the Junior High receptionist-secretary and retired on June 1, 1984.

Dee and Elaine still reside in Green River, as do their two sons, Brad and Robb, and their families. They have enjoyed golfing for many years at Rolling Green Country Club, as have their two sons. For the past nine years, Dee has been a volunteer driving the refreshments cart at Rolling Green for the Thursday morning ladies' day golf, which I hear is much appreciated!

❖

Town Provides For Its Senior Citizens

by Marie Finney

After World War II, our country became increasingly aware of the problems and needs of its older people. By 1960, every state had one or more official units to deal with the overall field of aging. Congress had bills introduced to help the states initiate or expand programs for older people. The first White House Conference on Aging in 1961 was attended by 10 delegates from Wyoming and became an important milestone in the field of aging.

President John Kennedy, in Feb. 1963, challenged Congress to pass, "... a...program of assistance to state and local agencies and voluntary organizations for planning and developing services; for research, demonstration, and training projects leading to new or improved programs to aid older people..." The Older Americans Act (OAA) of 1965 as enacted, with bipartisan support and signed into law July 1965 by President Lyndon B. Johnson, at the same time he signed the much-debated, long-awaited Medicare Act.

On Jan. 25, 1971, a small, informal gathering was held for anyone interested in discussing the possibilities of a Senior Center in Green River. The get-together took place in the basement of the old Episcopal Church located at 72 W. Second North at 2 o'clock. Fifteen senior citizens participated. Green River's latest census showed a preliminary figure of 4606 population with approximately 230 being senior citizens. During the months to follow this small group set to the task of writing its first OAA grant request, or application, which was submitted April 22, 1971.

They received the Notification of the Grant Awarded under Title II of the Older Americans Act on May 20, 1971. The Green River Senior Citizens Center held its formal opening June 10, 1971, although they were currently holding activities every Monday,

The first senior citizens activities took place in the basement of the old St. John's Episcopal Church. (Photo courtesy Sweetwater County Historical Society)

Wednesday and Friday afternoon in the Episcopal Church basement. In 1976, the center started serving lunches one day a week, prepared by the staff, using many of their own utensils.

Jan. 1, 1978, the center was moved to its present location at 115 E. Flaming Gorge Way, the former Tomahawk Drugstore which was purchased and remodeled by the county. With more room and better facilities, a cook was hired and meals were increased to three times per week. Other services were added or expanded. During July 1981, 139 participants were served. During the year over 400 different people were served, out of an estimated 600 senior citizens in Green River. The 1990s senior population rose to more than 900 with the center providing services to more than 600 different people.

June 10, 1996, the center celebrated its 25th Anniversary. In the 25 years that the Golden Hour Senior Center has operated, it has provided and expanded a variety of services to the senior citizens in our community. The Center is open Monday through Friday from 8 a.m. to 4:30 p.m. except holidays. Noon meals are served daily. Hot meals are delivered to homebound people by volunteers.

The Senior Center since 1978 has been in the old Tomahawk Drug Store building on Flaming Gorge Way. (Photo courtesy Marna Grubb)

Special diet needs are met through networking with Castle Rock Convalescent Center. Preventive Health Clinics are offered routinely each month with health education programs scheduled throughout the year. Various programs are available daily. For additional information about services, you are invited to come by the Senior Center at 115 E. Flaming Gorge Way or call 872-3223.

The vision for the Golden Hour Senior Center is one which will continue to meet the needs of the senior citizens in our community for generations to come.

The dream is to have a new and larger facility in which our seniors may gather and one in which all of the community members are welcome.

❖

Making the Rounds

by Bill Duncan

"Fill 'er up with regular, Mr. Duncan?"

The man was already wiping the Plymouth sedan's windows with his soft, red rag. We had just pulled up to the Sinclair station on Green River's main street, a couple of blocks up the hill from the new underpass.

I was really excited to be able to go with my dad to Farson this early spring day. We planned to go see the Smails at the shearing shed near the Wells, visit Andy Arnott at the hotel and stop at a few of the farms in Eden Valley.

I sat up real tall to try to see out the window. There was a black sticker with a white "A" in the lower corner of the windshield. It

Theresa, W.D. Billy Duncan and W.L. Bill Duncan.
(Photo courtesy W.D. Duncan)

regulated how much gas we could get. The back side of the sticker asked us to drive at 35 miles per hour to save both gas and tires because there was a war on.

Dad went into the station to pay money and rationing stamps for the gas. I traced the pattern of the Mayflower in full sail on the dash of our Plymouth. It matched the hood ornament above the shiny, chrome grill.

As we pulled out of the station, I noticed the cement pillar on the opposite corner. It was painted with red, white and blue stripes at the top and had a medallion of Lincoln just under the stripes. Dad said it was to commemorate the Lincoln Highway.

I looked out the side window as we went down the street past the red brick Congregational Church, another gas station, Moedl's drug store, Piggly Wiggly grocery and the Merc.

Soon we were across the alkali flats and into the small canyon east of town. In no time at all, we were following the rail road tracks, past the Log Inn, the Purple Sage Club and into Rock Springs. We hardly slowed as we came into town across the bridge, past a drive-in with a root beer barrel on top, and Howard's where many Greyhound buses parked.

We took a turn under the Rock Springs Coal arch, went past a tipple and headed for the Wells.

The road twisted and dipped enough to tickle my tummy. Dad told me a story about a car that had tried to ford a dip and had been washed away by a flash flood. He pointed out herds of antelope, mountains and prairie dogs, but he wasn't quick enough.

"I have to go Dad, real bad." "Come on Billy, can't you wait till we get to the shearing sheds?"

"No, now!" The sight of the shelter sheds and their outhouses always triggered the same response in my body.

We pulled into the road carved out of the brush and grass. Several shelters lined the road to Farson and Dad knew he would have to do a better job distracting me, or he'd be asked to stop at each one. Dad said that people used them during the blizzards that blew up with little warning and could stop travel for days.

Hundreds of sheep were penned around the weathered buildings. A few cars and pickups were mixed with horses and wagons. A gas pump with a tall glass on top sat in front of the house across the road. A young man dressed in khakis was pulling the side lever back and forth, pumping amber gasoline into the top. As we pulled near the house, an older man dressed in blue bib overalls came over to the car and began to talk to my dad. He asked about my Scottish grandparents, talked wool and prices, and invited us over to watch the shearing operation.

I followed Dad inside. Sheep were everywhere. The shears buzzed and wool seemed to roll off the bellies and sides of the sheep. Talk seemed to be about how much better and more dangerous the electric shears were than the manual clippers. We laughed at the funny-looking, white, newly-shorn ewes as they bleated on their way back to the pens.

I got to pull some of the greasy, smelly fleeces down the wooden walk to the tall, wooden frame. A rough burlap bag hung so it could be filled with fleeces. I was too small to throw the fleeces into the bag, but I knew I had "worked" from the grease on my hands and the way my clothes smelled.

Back in the Plymouth after a milk and oatmeal cookie snack, we talked about the big tree planting project in Eden Valley. Cliff Sims, who ran the University Experiment Farm, and Dad had worked to bring in small cottonwoods and many other varieties to have the homesteaders plant as windbreaks. I was disappointed to see little twigs sticking out of the ground because I had pictured tall giants swaying in the wind. We drove past new homes and raw fields carved from sage prairie.

The brick hotel stuck up like a monument on the plain. Early green highlighted a small stream and a couple of dusty roads crossed in front of it. Andy Arnott was a spry Scot with an engaging personality.

We joined him and his wife around a table filled with thick, meat sandwiches on homemade bread. I was fascinated with the combination locks of the mail boxes in the post office part of the store.

Conversation centered around my grandparents, friends around Lander, relatives and the farming situation in Eden Valley. I went out and played with their Collie until it was time to leave.

On the way home we stopped at the experimental farm. Cliff Sims took us on a walking tour to show us some of his experiments with tree varieties and grass plots. His son Duane took me to see some of the baby lambs and chicks they kept. Before we left Mother Annie served tea, with lots of milk and sugar, and baked potato scones, covered with sour, homemade orange marmalade. I wanted to stay longer and play, but Dad said we were expected to be home in time for supper.

I lasted through the short drive down the lane and out to the main road. By the time Dad had shifted through to high, I had put my head on Dad's lap and fallen asleep.

Fred and Betty Oliver: Fred's Taxidermy

(Originally published April 3, 1997)

by Bill Thompson

The sign on the door of Fred's Taxidermy now reads, "Thank God were (sic) closed." Through the years when I took our variety of moose, elk, antelope and buffalo to Fred's for mounting the sign read, "Sorry were (sic) open." To the uninitiated this sign was their introduction to the dry humor of the owners Fred and Betty Oliver. Fred, Betty and their children, Charlotte and Judy, arrived in Green River from Missouri in July of 1971 during the "Boom." "You can imagine how we felt at first, leaving all the

Fred and Betty Oliver. (Photo courtesy Bill Thompson)

*Fred's
Taxidermy.
(Photo courtesy
Bill Thompson)*

trees and greenery," Betty says. "There were no houses to rent, so we stayed at Tex's Trailer Park." After a time they purchased a larger trailer. In September of 1972 they "hung out a shingle" for their taxidermy business. It was on 37 N. 1st East which was between Nick the Barber and Edith's Beauty Shop. "At the time Fred was the only licensed taxidermist in the county."

In 1975 they bought the home and buildings on 61 North Center which became Fred's Taxidermy. The present address is now 55 N. Center (home) and 77 N. Center for the business buildings. These addresses are the site of Green River's **first City Hall.**

Three single-story wooden buildings **built in Bryan** in 1868-9 were moved to this location in 1872. Through 1891-1908 one of the buildings was rented by Mrs. H.H. Campbell for $10 to the town for a Council meeting place. In 1909 a millinery business was started by Mrs. E.A. Gaensslen in the building next to the Campbell house. The United States Post Office next occupied this building in 1910. In the late 1930s the north building held the Williams Sheet Metal Works. For a time the Higginson Transfer Co. sold coal from there. By 1953 the Yates Furniture Store and home was at this location.

Late one night, a sound woke Fred and Betty. A section of their glass storefront had been broken by a rock. After several such incidents (rocks, beer bottles, etc.) they remodeled the store and paneled much of the front. The double doors were covered.

In the 1950s a small warehouse from the **Green River Brewery** was moved across the alley and attached to the store. Later, while doing remodeling, Fred and Betty found various "antiques." In the wall were two types of labels in mint condition from the Brewery. They read, "Green River Since 1872" and "Wyoming Brewed Beer." Found also were several metal crates for 24 bottles of brew with the company label embossed on the side. Fred brought one in from where it was serving as a temporary back step. "Really shouldn't be doing that I suppose," he said with a twinkle. They led me to a SO-gallon crock which he and Betty had found in its original crate. It was used for years in their business. Next Fred displayed what he thinks may have been one of the **first elevators** in the county. Betty also pointed out several sections of the floor and a desk which were made from the **original bowling alley** lanes.

Years ago, former County Commissioner and one of Green River's **original citizens, George Stephens** (see "A Sister Remembers," *Green River Star,* Wed., April 30, 1980) related the following to Fred and Betty. In the 1950s George and some friends were out in the desert on Union Pacific land when they came across a deserted rock building containing dynamite. When notified about this, the UP asked George to dispose of the dynamite and this unknown building. Which he did. Jimmy Yates asked George for some of the building's stones. Jimmy then built the **present rock wall** around the residence from that mystery building.

Fred's Taxidermy is noted for high quality work. A moose head on the wall done in 1974 looks like this year's job. A cute little duck in the showcase has been a patron favorite and conversation piece for years (1970). There have been an assortment of "freak" heads, but a **3 antlered elk** might be the most unusual. "It is a 6 inch by 4 inch by 2 inch," Betty says with a smile, knowing that I would be confused. I was. Presently, the head is on display at Crueljack's. A young man, John LeFaivre, worked for them. He became as close as a son. Once when he had mounted his own antelope (on his own time) he complained that, "Something is just not right!" After adjusting, checking and measuring, it seemed wrong yet. After a time they noticed that the antelope head had an all-white face. One of John's favorite questions to customers was, "With or without ears?" It was John's humorous way of facing a tedious job. **Ears are the hardest part to skin.** This fine young man's untimely death saddened all of us.

Fred says that in all the years of skinning he was never cut or hurt. Although he does mention that he concentrates "very hard" when working. "Then Betty, walking like an Indian, comes up behind and says something and, Oh My Gosh! ...scares the heck out of me as I whirl around with my knife!" Betty tilts her head and looks at Fred.

As part-time taxidermists increased in this area, it became difficult to maintain a full-time business in taxidermy. "A game warden told me that there were some 15 or 16 part-timers in the county," Fred says. So now these historic buildings and home are up for sale. And when sold, **Fred's Taxidermy will close.** Fred and Betty will continue working in the store until then. The city of Green River will lose more than a business. Fred and Betty plan to retire in the Pinedale area occupied with other endeavors. The invitation to come visit will be out to their friends. There are many.

Leaving the Olivers, I see their sign on the door, "Thank God were (sic) closed" but in my imagination I see a sign that could be placed there by the city of Green River which says, "Sorry you're closed, Thank God you came!"

❖

Cowboy Poetry

by Marie Finney

Cowboy poetry. Two words that seem to go together like a cat and a mouse. To this city girl "cowboy" conjures up the image of a rough outdoors man, riding horses, breaking broncos, branding and moving cattle, spending long days and lonely nights on the open range. "Poetry," on the other hand, calls up the image of the classics of Longfellow, Frost and Browning with their rhythmic, metered verses of beauty, love and adventure. To my great surprise, I learned that cowboy poetry had been around for a long time.

Cowboys of yesteryear had to draw on their own resources for amusement and entertainment. They passed the long hours entertaining each other with stories, poems and songs for as long as they've built campfires. Their poetry and song reflected their working lives. It recorded the difficulties, tragedies and even the humor of their daily routine on the range.

Contrary to most beliefs, many of the cowboys were literate and had some education before coming out west to capture their way of life in verse. It was common practice to set their verse to popular songs, which accounts for the estimate that three-quarters of the original cowboy songs began as verses composed by working cowboys. Much of their verse is lyrically descriptive, evoking places, people or events that have slipped into the past. Much of it contains humor, mixing everyday cowboy common sense and dialect with abstract philosophical issues.

Today, hundreds of cowboy (and cowgirl) poets gather throughout the West to recite old favorites and to present new material. Sweetwater County hosts a Cowboy Poet and Music Festival annually at the County Events Complex. It is held the second weekend in May. If you are interested in the event, contact Gregory Gaylor at the Community Fine Arts Center in Rock Springs.

This new fan of cowboy poetry has had the privilege to know a couple of Green Riverites that have the gift of verse. John Hofeldt

(1919-1996) was a local rancher, and Robert Larimore, who still puts his pen to paper for various occasions.

Bob was born in Bladen, Nebraska in 1927, the youngest of seven. His family moved to Green River in 1933. He told me that he had always dreamed of riding a horse. As a child in school he looked forward to the days when a local sheep herder allowed him to ride his horses. Bob would do any kind of work if it enabled him to ride a horse.

Over the years, he worked for the railroad, and finally for Stauffer Chemical. Yet every moment of spare time he spent riding, roping and branding. He explained that the most enjoyable time was spent chasing the wild horse herds in the area.

Bob started writing his verse as a joke, to make light of someone's mistake. He always wrote in red and signed his work, "the Phantom." Everyone called the writer, "the Red Pencil." No one knew the author until a friend retired and Bob wrote a poem in his honor. Bob writes for birthdays, weddings, memorials, retirements and just for fun.

Bob retired from Stauffer in 1986, but still does what he loves best: riding horses and chasing cows. He has had one of his poems, "A Season" published in "The Sound of Poetry", by the National Library of Poetry.

He shared with me one of his unpublished works about a hair-raising event that happened in 1953.

THE FIRST AND THE LAST

I left the T Quarter Circle one beautiful, sunny day,
Was breaking this colt to ride, what I could teach him along
    the way.
Worked on teaching him to rein, to turn with a leg cue;
To go into a speed run, away just like a bird flew.
I thought of books I'd read, things cowboys did with a rope;
Roping cougars, bears and even a buff, bringing them home on
    a lope.
What's that ahead of that big bush? A big, golden eagle on the
    ground;
Hissing, screaming, spreading his wings, glaring at me with
    a frown.
Here was something I guess, that had never been done;
If I could pull this off, it sure would be lots of fun!
I undone the old seagrass, poked a hole in the end of it;
Made myself a mighty cast, around his neck - it really fit.

With a scream from a nightmare dream he came, he sure was
    broke to lead;
It was way past time to go, on me this eagle would fee-a.
Ole Duke took off like a shot, he never spun a wheel;
We dunked ale eagle in the dirt, all he ever saw was our heel.
With a great sigh I turned to look, to see if we made the cut;
There was the eagle, his mouth agape, about to bite my butt!
You better do something old horse, to make that eagle slow; A
ha! He was slipping in yellow, that poor, scared horse had
    let go.
Well, I turned loose of the rope, dodged around a great, big tree
Poor eagle hung up on the trunk, that's the last he saw of me!
We stopped our great retreat after a mile or so,
Went back to get my rope, sure was happy it was found.
As I saw it laying there, was happier no eagle was around. I've
done some crazy things, in the dim, distant past;
But this was really nutty, and this first was certainly the last!

Crossing the Green

by Bill Duncan

(This is the third story in a trilogy of Bill Duncan's childhood memories around Green River in the late '30s and early '40s.)

I was really excited as I crawled into the front seat of our black Plymouth. We were headed south to visit Mrs. Holmes' ranch along the Green River. Whenever she visited us, she always gave me a treat. Sometimes candy, sometimes a trinket - but always some-thing. I looked forward to my first visit and seeing her cows and horses for myself.

We went down through the new underpass and past the big roundhouse. I bounced up and down, straining to see the black engines spouting tall, white plumes. I always tried to wave at the engineers, sitting at the engine windows and spot the cabooses at the end of the train.

I was on Mom's lap as we crossed the single-lane bridge to the other side of the river. We talked about how green the water was and how low the river was. Dad said a person could almost wade across without getting his feet wet.

We wound up the gravel road to the top of the hill south of town. As always, we looked for antelope, magpies and hawks. I tried to see everything that was pointed out to me. If I did, then it was time for the counting exercise. How many? Let's count them.

Mom had brought a bag of cherries for a snack. "Eat them one at a time now, I don't want you to choke," she said. I tried to keep the sweet juice from running down my chin, and I was careful to put the seeds into the small bag she'd brought along. I really wanted to spit the pits out the open car window like Dad, but I wasn't allowed. They tasted so good that I had to be told to slow down several times.

In no time at all, we turned onto the rutted, steep, windy ranch road. I was a little scared as branches swept the side of the car and the wheels swerved in and out of the deep ruts. Finally, the road leveled, and I could see the chokecherry and currant bushes and big cottonwood trees that lined the river. Across the broad river was a man perched on a horse-drawn rake, putting hay into long rows.

Dad muttered something under his breath as we stopped on the riverbank. Both the cable-driven ferry and the little hand car on the top cable were on the far bank. The cable car was to be left on the opposite bank from the ferry, so that a person could use it to get the ferry if needed. Dad considered the possibility of wading the river to bring the ferry back to our side. He took off his shoes and rolled up his trousers above his knees.

He didn't wade very far. "Hey, this is really shallow!" Instead of going on across, he began to go up and down the bank. I think the river rocks hurt his feet, because he soon returned to the shore. I, of course, wanted to join him, but Mom had zillions of reasons why I couldn't. I didn't see her taking her shoes off either.

"I think we can drive across," Dad said enthusiastically. Mom wasn't so sure. "Wagons have forded here for years." Mom said something about "just because the Plymouth had a boat ornament on the hood was no sign it could float."

I was frightened as the car nosed down the bank into the Green. All I could see as I looked out the window from Mom's lap was water. It was up higher than the running boards. I managed to sneak several cherries at one time. Mother's attention was focused on the rising water, too.

We reached the middle of the river and relaxed a little. Dad began to sing a little song. Mom protected the bag of cherries. I was worried about what to do with a mouth full of seeds.

Suddenly, the car lurched over to our side. The front wheel sank and water began to creep in under the door right under my feet. I screamed. The car stopped. I thought we were going to sink and drown. Dad's song turned to another under-the-breath oath. Mother began a mini-lecture about his judgment - or lack of it. I clung to her with both hands and both feet. I was crying.

We all got out to survey the damage and figure out what to do. I was still sobbing. Mom had her shoes and anklets off and her pant legs rolled up. I clung tightly, fearing she might drop me into the water over my head. Dad was already striding toward the opposite shore, shoes held high. Mr. Holmes was unhitching his team to come help us. The Plymouth's front wheel had disappeared in a river hole.

Soon, the team pulled the car to shore near the ferry and under the cable car. Dad was drying out car parts under the hood. Emma

Holmes, dressed in a blue work shirt, Levis and an old slouch hat, was headed our way with cookies. It would take many cuddles and cookies to put me back in good spirits.

Our return trip across the river was uneventful. The car was mounted securely on the ferry and I was inside the car, hunkered down, not peeking out the window. I didn't relax until we were back on the road to town....

...And it took me a long time before I ever ate cherries again!

❖

Historical Minutes

by Bill Duncan
prepared for KUGR Radio during
Flaming Gorge Days, June 23-28, 1997

REMEMBERING THE OLD SOUTH SIDE
Green River's colorful history is filled with names that stir the imagination. Cat Eye Willis and the Owl's Club. Ruby Larue ... and Little Bit. The Oxford Club ... the Dew Drop Inn ... The Old Green House. The Blue Front Cafe... Polka Rose and Dorothy Weddington. The Silver Slipper .... All of these people and places were south of Green River's railroad yards. Men who wanted to party, gamble, or spend time in the company of women came to the south side. Cat Willis's Owl's Club was a bright green brick build-ing located about where the ABR business is now. Cat was the acknowledged leader of this part of the community. The Owl's Club catered to anyone looking for the illegal and immoral. Prohibition didn't slow down this area of town either. The Oxford Club, most lately a laundromat, also had a reputation for being able to provide anything needed by men out on the town. Rose, Dorothy, Ruby and others managed as many as 30 "working girls" during this time. Fortunes were made and lost in blackjack, poker and the popular Greek game Barboot. Whiskey was never in short supply. Old timers might be surprised at the changes. The south side, once home of the town's vice dens, is a quiet residential area with a variety of businesses lining the main street. And yes, all of the businesses are legitimate.

EVERS FIELD In just a few days Evers Park will host a flea market, 3 on 3 basketball, band concerts, and a lot of Flaming Gorge Days activities. Before World War II, Evers Field was the center of summer activities, too. It was the home of Green River's semi-pro baseball team, sponsored by Union Pacific. This team was made up of locals and recruited men who boarded the train on

Saturdays and Sundays to play teams like Superior, Reliance, Rawlins and Hanna. When the Ogden team came to town, the dark green stands were packed with rabid fans. In later years Green River's American Legion baseball team played their games at Evers. The field was laid out much as it is now, so it was possible for a power hitter to get one into the outdoor swimming pool - over the fence. But times change. The UP no longer sponsored semi-pro teams. Evers Field fell into some disrepair and was torn down. Now, bats crack all over town, day and night. Youth are involved in baseball, soccer, and football. But adults now spend most of their time coaching. And those who can will be shooting hoops, not running out hits at Evers this summer.

LEGEND OF THE GR

Traditionally, one of the jobs of GRHS's freshman class was to whitewash the GR on Mansface hill in the southwest part of town. The GR was a collection of flat rocks loosely piled into shape and refinished each fall during homecoming activities. Time and visits from neighboring vandals to the east gave the GR a more bedraggled look each year. Finally, the high school shop classes, under the direction of Dick Schuck, built forms and poured the cement. A bright, white GR graced Mansface. Since the original rocks were just in the way, they were randomly thrown down hill. The graduating class that year gathered the white stones and arranged them for their graduating year. Soon the stones magically took on any year of a class that took the time to rearrange them. Not long ago, 76 was the number. Just now 97 is there. With alumni back to remember Lincoln High School, who can tell what years will be remembered this summer. Perhaps the biggest question is how long can the original rocks last?

LOOKING FOR A PLACE TO EAT?

The shiny, chrome building on Green River's West end is a throw-back to the '50s era when diners were popular. But where did Green River folks really eat in earlier years? Railroaders ate at "the Beanery" which occupied the west side of the depot. Other popular cafes along the railroad included The Teton, which burned down a few years ago and was replaced by the Embers. The Y-Bing, across the street to the east, and the Wyoming Cafe, later the Coffee Cup, also catered to workingmen's appetites. The Wyoming burned down too. Its site is the vacant lot next to the Ponderosa. One of the most popular places was the Sugar-Bowl. A teen gathering spot for a couple of decades, kids could munch a burger and sip a malt there. Located about where the First Security Bank parking lot is now, the Sugar Bowl boasted a big juke box, teen food and teen talk. It was THE place in town to see and be seen. As cars gave kids mobility, an A & W drive-in on the West end of town, now the Finer Edge, and the Burger-A-GO-GO on the East end gave young people a place to roost while "dragging main." Can you imagine eating out without pizza, tacos, burritos or ribs? Times and tastes have changed, and so have Green River's restaurants.

EVOLUTION OF GREEN RIVER'S GROCERY STORES

Like most towns along the Union Pacific, Green River's business district was once clustered along both sides of the rails. Grocery stores served their own neighborhoods and residents ran charge accounts. The Independent Store, owned for a time by John and Irene Kalivas, served the South Side of town until the mid-60s and specialized in Greek foods. Steve Nitse ran the Up-To-Date Store in the same part of town. Over on the north side the Green River Merc sold groceries and housed a meat market. At one time a Piggly Wiggly grocery store was also part of the Merc's complex. Across the street OP Skaggs grocery was one of the first to have a parking lot. This grocery, now site of the Ace Hardware, was owned and operated for many years by Dell White. Joe and Olga Gosar had a modern store serving the east end of town. As Green River grew south of the river, The Hilltop Grocery, now the Window and Door Store, met neighborhood needs. The Handy Store, a block and a half South of Lincoln School, served mostly students on their way to Lincoln High and Jefferson Elementary. With the trona boom Mr. D's Supermarket, later bought by City Market, and Smith's Supermarket spelled the end of the neighborhood grocery. Convenience stores with gas stations may fill some of the void, but family-run groceries with their individual charge accounts are long gone.

EARLY SOCIAL GATHERING PLACES

Early Green Riverites chose various sites along the river for picnics, social get-togethers, and what was then called "sparking". A rope ladder from the railroad bridge provided access to a secluded island for families and young people early in town history. High water and channel dredging did away with this island. Palisade Park a mile or so west of town gave citizens a place to picnic, skate in winter, and enjoy the tall cottonwood trees along the river. Road construction took this park away and the county area a couple of miles up river. As young people had more access to cars, the greasewood flat across the river, soon to be the home of the water treatment plant, was a popular place to park. South Hill, the area just west of the Recreation Center, was a fine place to show a girl the town's panorama at night. Today, Green River has several well-developed picnic areas and walking areas. Young people socialize in store parking lots or find seclusion on the surrounding hills or along the river.

JUMPING OFF INTO THE UNKNOWN

On May 29, 1869, Major John Wesley Powell began the last great exploration of unknown territory in the continental United States. Powell was a civil war veteran with a profound interest in botany, geology, and biology. His party embarked on the Green River near Expedition Island. Ten men manned four awkward wooden boats not really suited for the long trip or the white water rapids to follow. Early accidents robbed the group of equipment and provisions. The explorers made their way down the Green past Flaming Gorge, which they named, to the confluence with the Colorado and into Grand Canyon. Three men who left the party at Grand Canyon were killed by Indians. Powell and five others completed the first exploration on August 30. In 1871, Powell made another trip down the Green with more suitable equipment and provisions. Powell was appointed Director of the US Geological Survey and worked to preserve Western lands. Today, Expedition Island is a National Historic site, serves as a community park, and contains a pictorial history of river exploration along the Green.

THE DIAMOND HOAX

In 1871 Philip Arnold and John Slack, two miners with an eye for quick profit, purchased about $30,000 worth of diamonds, rubies, emeralds, sapphires, and other precious stones in Europe. They salted those stones in an area southeast of Rock Springs. Exactly where is in dispute. Arnold and Slack persuaded some rich and famous people to help form a mining company. Horace Greeley, Civil War General George McClellan, and Europe's Baron Rothchild were early investors. Diamond fever was fed by newspaper articles telling of the "find." Fortunately, Clarence King, a government surveyor, became suspicious. He was familiar with the area and in the fall of 1872, he located the supposed gem field. King found a cut diamond, curious locations for stones and improbable combinations of gems. The surveyor exposed the fraud to the nation. Some folks lost money, others suffered embarrassment at their gullibility, and the new territory of Wyoming received some dubious notoriety. But maybe, some of those stones are still there.

BRYAN

When Union Pacific officials were unable to dictate land sales in Green River as the railroad came through in 1868, they abandoned the town and moved the division point 12 miles west along the Black's Fork. The new town, called Bryan, thrived briefly as Green River City became a ghost town. Bryan's canvas and log shacks housed as many as 5000 residents at its peak. Like other rail towns the rowdy lifestyle included 24 hour saloons, gambling dens, and other pleasure houses designed to separate workers from their money. Federal troops moved with the railhead to protect rail construction crews from Indian attacks, keep peace because there was no organized government, and give the Union Pacific their way in land deals. Captain Arthur McArthur, father of the famous General Douglas McArthur, was charged with keeping the peace at Bryan. Four years later the Black's Fork had run dry and the railroad was forced to move back to Green River. Today, only a garbage dump about a mile and a half north of 1-80 remains to remind us of riproaring Bryan.

COXEY'S ARMY

The panic of 1893 was a major economic recession that caused mass unemployment throughout the United States. General Jacob S. Coxey from Ohio called for the government to institute public works programs to provide jobs for the unemployed, a radical idea for that time. Many members of his supporters, called Coxey's Army, commandeered trains in the West and passed through Wyoming in April and May, 1894, on their way to Washington. Some Wyoming towns gave them provisions rather than have them overrun the communities in search of food. United States Marshall Joseph Rankin and many deputies arrested fifteen leaders while recapturing a train in Green River. 130 men were put up in the Green River armory for the night. The next day, four companies of troops from Fort Russell near Cheyenne took charge of the Coxeyites and escorted them back to Idaho. The fifteen leaders were sentenced to four and five month jail sentences in Cheyenne. Other members of Coxey's Army were jailed in Evanston.

❖

From Ruts To Roads: The Development of Major Transportation Routes

by Ruth Lauritzen

Traditionally the best roads were the most travelled. The route followed by Sweetwater County's busiest road, Interstate 80, was no exception. Long before the four lane concrete ribbon stretched across the county its approximate path was a trail used by the Native Americans. As Anglo Americans moved west they also began to use it. First came the mountain men who showed it to government explorers who in turn, literally, put it on the map.

In his 1849-50 survey Captain Howard Stansbury, led by Jim Bridger, explored and mapped the route across southern Wyoming. Stansbury's expedition was one of those mounted by the U.S. government to find the best route for the planned transcontinental railroad. Two important mountain passes were verified on this trip, Bridger Pass in Carbon County and Cheyenne Pass in Laramie County. These discoveries provided a new westward trail to compete with the great emigrant highway through South Pass.

This alternate route became increasingly important as the Indian Wars on the northern plains began to heat up in the early 1860s. Travel on the northern trail became hazardous and traffic moved to the southern route, soon known as the Overland Trail. It was used extensively by emigrants, freighters and Ben Holladay's stage line, the Central Overland Express. The trail crossed the Green River at the confluence of the Bitter Creek, near the horse corrals, and the stage station was located roughly where the Game and Fish building is on Astle Avenue.

After several years of delay, primarily caused by the Civil War, the transcontinental railroad pushed through the county in 1868. It followed in large part the route explored by Stansbury. The railroad handled much of the traffic, both freight and passenger, which had formerly been on the westward wagon trails. The rails could carry one quickly and comfortably to nearby Rock Springs, or on to more distant destinations. Until the advent of the automobile the railroad remained the undisputed long distance transportation king of Sweetwater County and most of the nation.

However, as more people acquired automobiles and came to rely on the flexibility and independence they provided, there came a demand for better roads to drive them on. By 1912 there was talk of an improved transcontinental highway and a national group was formed to promote the idea. After much investigation a variation on the old reliable Overland Trail route was chosen as the best and shortest way and the completed roadway was called the Lincoln Highway in honor of Abraham Lincoln.

Originally "improved" meant roads had a gravel surface, but by the 1920s most were asphalt or oil treated. In 1917 the Wyoming Highway Department was created and as one of its first official actions designated principle highways in the state. One of these was the Lincoln Highway.

The Lincoln Highway came right through the town of Green River, going over the railroad tracks at the Elizabeth Street (1st East) crossing. It crossed the river on the Old Wagon Bridge, (located just upstream of the current highway bridge), and continued west through Telephone Canyon.

The Lincoln Highway and the increasing use of automobiles in general had an effect on Green River. Gas stations and garages became a part of the business community and hotels and motels began to sprout up to serve the traveling community. Two large hotels, the Tomahawk (comer of 1st East and Flaming Gorge) and the Stanley (comer of Railroad and 1st West) were built in 1919 and 1921 respectively. Numerous gas stations and repair shops also appeared along Flaming Gorge Way to serve highway sojourners.

Highway construction and improvement moved to the federal level when in 1944 Congress passed the Federal Aid Highway Act, creating the Interstate System. Construction on the Wyoming stretch of Interstate 80 began near Wamsutter in 1956 and was not completed until 1969. A notable feat in the construction was accomplished near Green River when in 1966 twin tunnels were punched through solid stone under Castle Rock.

Good routes, once established, often remained the best way of getting from place to place. The early Indian trail across Sweetwater County proved to be just that as shown by its later history as a wagon and stage trail, railroad route, improved road and finally a federal interstate highway.

Mollie Yowell

by Marna Grubb

It seems no matter how bad things are, many times something good comes from it. As the result of World War II and the Korean War, the United States became the home to many brides of returning servicemen. Green River became richer with the arrival of Mollie Yowell after her marriage to Donald (Duke) Yowell in England while he was serving as a sergeant in the United States Air Force.

Mollie was born in Swindon, Wilts, England, one of three daughters of Harry and Lillian Axton, and was nine years of age when war broke out. Many parents feared for the safety of their children. Mollie's family had relatives living in Canada; therefore, Mollie and her older sister Cynthia were invited to live with them in Canada until the war was over. This they were intending to do until one day they heard that a ship on its way to Canada with a number of children had been sunk. Needless to say, her parents decided they probably would be safer at home with their baby sister Lillian.

Children were being evacuated from the London area and many of them were brought to Swindon in double-deck busses. Children were deposited at various houses where space was available. Mollie's family already had a houseful, but she remembers feeling so sad for the children having to leave their homes and their loved ones.

Around 1940-41, Mollie recalls having air-raid practice at school. A hooter (siren) was used as a warning. They also had practice to determine how long it would take for each child to get home. If it took too long, a home would need to be provided closer to school for the duration of that air raid. Mollie grew into a teenager during the war, going from 9 to 15 years of age.

Swindon was a major repair point for the railroad and is 80 to 85 miles southwest of London. Mollie remembers being very fright-ened when hearing waves of German bombers flying over. Her Dad could tell the difference between Allied bombers and German bombers by

Duke and Mollie Yowell at their 1953 wedding in England. (Photo courtesy of Duke and Mollie Yowell)

the sound of their engines. Fire reflecting in the sky from a nearby town told them that tonight was not their time.

Many had air-raid shelters in their back yards, but they had a table shelter made of steel in their home under which the family would huddle when the warnings would sound. It also served as a dining room table. Blackout drapes or shutters were used to darken the rooms. No street lights were used during the war. Mollie remembers being frightened to go out at night because it was so dark.

Swindon was bombed several times, but only by stray planes. One time a bomb dropped about a block from their home killing eight people. The big windows in the back of Mollie's house blew in and the windows in the front of the house, where "Mum" had been standing, blew out, although she was not injured since the glass was blowing out. Her father would ride to work on a bicycle since there was a shortage of petrol for cars. He hurried back home when he heard the bomb had fallen on Groundwell Road, where they lived, and Mollie tearfully revealed that he was relieved to find that no one was injured. On one occasion, German fighter planes flew down and strafed the town with machine gun fire.

Mollie also has many fond memories of England. She enjoyed being able to go to the seaside within a short distance. They would swim, build sand castles, have picnics and collect sea shells. At Christmas, the family would all gather at 1:00 p.m. for a turkey or chicken dinner followed with Christmas pudding. At 5:00 p.m. they would have high tea with cake and jelly.

Mollie met Donald (Duke) Yowell in 1952 at a picnic while he was stationed in England. Mollie worked as a British rail clerk. They were married on May 30, 1953 in Christ's Church in Swindon. They moved into a tiny trailer - like a camping trailer. Duke would ride a bicycle to the base. When they were married in 1953, ration books were still being used in England. Rationing had been quite severe. The meat supply was so scarce that they began selling whale meat. Fish was not rationed. The popular saying was, "Two ounces per person per week...perhaps!"

They moved to the United States in September 1954 and Duke was discharged from the Air Force. He returned to his job with the Union Pacific Railroad Company in Green River and retired in 1991 as Car Distributor after 43 years of service. Mollie was a sales clerk at Brooks Ladies' Apparel in Green River for many years, and then three years at the Diet Center.

They are both active in the community with the Sweetwater County Historical Society, the Museum Foundation Board, St. John's Episcopal Church, the Masons, Eastern Star and with the Shriners and Daughters of the Nile. They enjoy golfing in the summer and bowling in the winter.

Mollie and Duke have two sons, Michael of Omaha, Nebraska and Daniel of Green River.

❖

The More Things Change...

by Bill Thompson

(Written especially for those who came to
Green River after the 1960s)

It has been said that, "The more things change, the more they remain the same." Well for the fun of it let's remember that statement and go back to the early 1960s and look a little bit at Green River and see what you think.

Basically the town (approx. 4,000 pop.) was on the north side of the river. The Lincoln High School football games were played in the afternoon. There was no KUGR radio station to broadcast the games. But there was linotype coverage from the *Green River Star* located at 162 N. 3rd East. There were no Twin Tunnels. The highway came through town on 1st North (named Flaming Gorge Way later). There were no Flaming Gorge or Fontenelle dams completed yet. There was no Recreation Center or the Western Wyoming College Annex. Garbage could be burned in your 55-gallon cans in the alley. By a previous city council decision there were no major grocery stores allowed to locate here (Bye Bye Safeway, hello Rock Springs). A new county courthouse was being contemplated to replace the old (1876) one on Main Street. The Carnegie Library was housed in what later became the County Court building. Where did they put the new Green River County Library? It was completed in 1980 and built over an old graveyard at 30 N. 1st E. Some graves were found and reburied. City repair crews digging in the area periodically unearth remains (Steven King where are you?). The taverns closed at midnight on Saturday and remained closed until Monday.

The Union Pacific Railroad with its towering smoke stack and the world's largest roundhouse was the School District's main tax base. Some 400 employees worked in the machine shop and yard. The railroad underpass was the only town access to either side. .. unless one headed west on Highway 30 past the Covered Wagon for a few miles and turned south from the LaBarge overpass. This road is still in use. After several miles it fed into Highway 530 south of Green River. This route was used when the underpass became blocked with water or ice or sometimes by a car or truck mishap. Turning northward (left) one could then come back into the south side of town.

The old highway passed within a few yards of the airport dirt runway and the relay and microwave towers. A quick right turn past them would take you down through what is now our state award winning landfill (no burning). A few hundred yards further down, if in season, you might see a shotgun armed Chukar hunter walking the rock formations.

Turning west off old Highway 530 a short way out of Green River would take you to the pet cemetery. This was an unofficial burial ground for the deceased pets of Green River residents. The new highway route obliterated this of course (Steven King where are you?).

In the Salt Creek Oil Field (Midwest, Wyoming) where I grew up, any loud explosive noise would startle and even terrify us. There were pumping wells, pipelines and oil storage tanks seemingly everywhere. Our folks made us very aware of the danger of an unguarded spark or flame. My first few nights here in Green River would find me sitting straight up in bed with eyes as large as saucers... the Union Pacific engineers were coupling the trains....

I enjoyed walking the short distance to work at Lincoln High School. I had rented a room from the Andersons on West 1st North and later a little apartment from the Roy Camerons across the alley. The rent was $50 which included water. They did not charge for the summer months when I was gone. I would cross West 2nd North and look for the cheerful squirrels who browsed the treeways westward from Postmaster Harold Mortimer's house. But sometime in the 1970s they were gone. Hazel Frahm, an extraordinary Social Studies teacher and my mentor, would also walk to Lincoln High School from her apartment. She used "The Path" as it was called then. It is the street at the base of Castle Rock, West 2nd N.

Entering the high school I would go into the main office to get my mail, announcements, etc. There I would give Peanuts a pat or two in passing as he sprawled on the floor by the counter. This gentle dog, friend to all, belonged to Ruth Ann and Alton Hermansen who were employed at the high school. He was a school fixture. Once a vacationing friend of the Hermansens sent a card to him. The only address was, "Peanuts, Green River, Wyoming." It was delivered promptly to Ruth Ann and Alton...and Peanuts.

At the present location of the yarn and craft shop, Simple Elegance, was the Red Feather Gardens tavern. One weekend I needed some cash. So I grabbed a counter check (a counter check?) and filled it out for $10. That amount would take care of my Saturday night entertainment expenses and leave enough for my Sunday breakfast at the Teton Cafe where the Embers is now located. The proprietor Pete Nomis cashed it and gave me a five dollar silver certificate (paper) and five silver dollars. I went on my way.

A couple of weeks later while balancing my checkbook from a monthly teaching income of less than $400, I noticed an odd colored check. It was for the other bank in town for which I had no account. I had filled out the wrong counter check! Bewildered I turned it over and saw that it had gone to that bank which had stamped it and then transferred the check over to my bank which had honored it!

I got no inquiring phone calls from either institution. No sheriff (George Nimmo) arrived at my door, no fines, no penitentiary time. They knew me (and everybody else in town) and without fan-fare carried on with their business. I'm sorry that the check has disappeared through the years. What a collector's item it would be!

So remembering that incident in the 1960s, it should be understandable why I would grit my teeth in the 1990s when asked politely by a local teller, "Do you have an account with us sir?" Yes I understood that cashing out-of-town checks for playing music is more closely scrutinized...but, do I have an account "sir"?!!!#*#

As I look at our football field I recall the times I legally hunted rabbits there. And driving past our water storage tank I see the ghosts of antelope herds and a coyote or two running through the state streets of present day Ward 3. It was rare to see deer in town then. But it is no ghost herd that browses the greenery in major parts of our city today.

Well I'm happy to say that, although the squirrels are gone from West 2nd North, grey ones have been seen cavorting several blocks to the east; and recently, across town, a brown one was spotted inspecting garage tops along with a buddy.

I am happy to say that former students of mine now working at the bank recognize me. Knowing that I have an account there, they cash those out-of-town checks without a qualm. Yea!

So maybe the more things change, some things sorta stay the same. In the 1960s it didn't take very long for me to fall in love with Green River and its residents who made a young newcomer feel welcome. I realized what a fortunate choice I had made in selecting my new home town. What warm creative people! I came to stay. After 36 years here I (may) have changed somewhat, as has the town. But some things remain the same, especially my feelings for Green River and its citizens.

❖

The Green River

by Marie Finney

As one walks along the Green Belt, your attention is drawn to the river. Its steady flow seems tranquil and almost mesmerizing. You can see fishermen along the bank patiently waiting for that big catch. In the summer, children wade out into its cool, refreshing water. Rafters enjoy the calm, quiet scenery and wildlife as they float down the river's winding route. Today, as in days gone by, the Green River holds a lure of mystery and the call of adventure. Many have answered the "call of the river."

In 1825, William Ashley, trapper and fur trader with seven other men looking to make their fortunes floated the Green River in bull boats. These boats were nothing more than buffalo hides stretched over wooden frames. Later, these trappers and mountain men used dugout canoes made from cottonwood logs. In 1849, William Manly was in a hurry to reach the California gold fields. His impatience made him leave the safety of the overland trail to travel the Green River. He lost his boat over Ashley Falls and, ending up in Salt Lake City, Utah, decided that it was wise to again join a wagon train to California.

We all have heard the stories of the Powell expeditions in 1869 and 1871. John Wesley Powell, a Civil War veteran, set out from the city of Green River to map the river and plot its fall. He and his crew had to deal with many difficulties and obstacles in their two expeditions. Then in 1890, Nathaniel (Than) Galloway, a sometimes trapper and prospector from Vernal, Utah revolutionized river travel. His flat-bottomed boats were designed so that he faced downstream and could see where he was going. This technique of boating is still used today.

The Green River was also used in practical ways. For nearly 100 years from 1868 until 1941, the river was used to supply ties, which supported hundreds of miles of UP track. The ties were cut, shaped and stock-piled on the tributaries of the upper Green. Then

The Sunbeam, 1908 stern-wheeler launch used for excursions at the Island Park. (Photo courtesy Sweetwater County Historical Museum)

in mid-June, with the spring runoff, the ties were floated down Horse Creek, Fontenelle, LaBarge, New Fork and Piney creeks to the Green River. About 4,000 ties made this trip each year.

In 1937, Haldane "Buzz" Holstrom, built his own Galloway-style river boat and was the first to float the Green and Colorado solo. The following year, Holstrom, with his friend Amos Burg, made the trip together. Burg with his new inflatable rubber raft named "Charlie," didn't know at the time, that the raft would prove the way of the future.

In 1938, a French trio, Bernard DeColmont, his young bride Genevieve, and their friend Antoine DeSeyne, set out to travel the Green and Colorado rivers. Genevieve was the first woman to run her own boat and float the falls. Although she was on her honeymoon, she did her share of the work and was the best of the three boaters. She never damaged or flipped her boat in the rapids. In 1940, Norm Nevills and A.K. Reynolds with Mike Hallacy and G.G. Larson built cataract boats and started Reynolds-Hallacy River Expeditions.

In 1980, J.P. Moerke, Frank Briggs, M.C. Peterson and C.W. Johnson were owners of the amusement park on the island. They purchased the "Sunbeam" and the "Teddy R.," gasoline propelled stern wheelers, for pleasure excursions on the Green River. In 1911, the Kolb brothers, who were photographers, brought the new invention - a movie camera - and were the first to take moving pictures of the river and its canyons. Then in 1909, Julius Stone with Than Galloway, C.C. Sharp, Seymour Dubendorff and Raymond Cogswell made the fastest descent of the Green and Colorado rivers and their canyons at the time. It took them only two months to reach Needles, California.

These adventures are only a few of the many that answered the "call of the river." In our local library, you can check out several books about river travel on the Green and Colorado rivers. One in particular is, *If We Had A Boat*, written by Roy Webb. This book highlights Green River explorers, adventurers and runners.

If you walk through the Island Park, be sure to read the sign posts erected by the Green River Parks and Recreation Department for information about the river.

❖

Things I Learned
I Don't Need Anymore

by Bill Duncan

I lay under the Christmas tree squinting my eyes to make the colors fuzzy. The popcorn and cranberry garlands blended in with the construction paper stars, garlands of metal tinsel and red and white striped candy canes. Some of the colored lights had a metal reflector behind them. We had other lights that sported paper shades with designs or Christmas figures. The little shades spun around on their lights. Each shade was mounted on the light with a cone that had a pin in the small end. This pin supported the shade that was spun by the heat from the lamp. I needed all the dexterity and patience an eight-year-old could muster to make sure the colored bulb was exactly straight up on its branch so the shade would spin on its pin.

Christmas light strings were built so if one bulb burned out, the whole string went out. With a lot of patience, I became pretty good at figuring out which colored bulb in the string had burned out. I had to start at one end with a fresh light and try every bulb. It was really rewarding when I hit the right one and the entire string glowed brightly. But if two bulbs were burned out in the same string at the same time, I could spend hours (in eight-year-old time) trying to find the culprit. Of course, this gave me an excuse to check out the presents piled under the tree and maybe sneak a lick at one of the candy canes.

When I think of the time, patience and skills it took to string cranberries and popcorn, cut out intricate construction paper designs and arrange the lighting just right, I wonder about the skills everyone learned as second nature. I can wrap gifts a bit better today because I use double stick tape, pre-made bows and curling ribbon, but I still have trouble with "drugstore" corners on the ends of packages and picking that tan tape off the roll and getting it just right on packages. I marvel at the time people took to make so many decorations. Maybe it was because we had the time to learn how to cut, paste and craft.

Both of my Grandpas could sharpen their own straight razor on the leather strap hanging next to the wash basin. Even Barbasol and Burma Shave, the creams in a tube that replaced the soap cup and brush, have been replaced by the electric buzz. Tooth powder needed that little wrist flick to jump onto the brush. Plastic tubes have removed a lot of the toothpaste squeezing controversy that metal tubes caused. It really doesn't matter who squeezes from where now.

When I think of all the hours I spent in school making circles and jagged up and down waves with a metal nib shoved in a wooden holder, I shudder. My greatest skill was making designs with the inkwell's saturated cork top. I was just getting the hang of filling a fountain pen with the little lever on the side when teachers decided it was OK to turn in school papers written in ball point.

A lot of finely honed skills are stored in the attic, gathering dust with other relics made useless by new technology. Remember the particular wrist twist it took to remove a paper cover from a milk bottle? What about the concentration it took to pour just the cream at the top of the bottle into a pitcher? And the right fingernail pick it took to pry the paper pull tab from the inside cap? I loved the satisfying hiss I received when I had put the pop bottle into the opener on the side of the cooler and pushed down with just the right force. Another "good" hiss was hooking the "church key" on the side of the can and flicking the wrist to make that triangular hole.

How many hours did you spend learning how to use a slide rule? Probably about as many as you spent learning to do research from library cards. I know that I spent hours in typing class learning how to erase carbon copies without a smear. Many of us conditioned ourselves to throw the manual carriage return at the bell sound. What a transition we all had to make when the carriage didn't move any more and the little Selectric ball bobbed, spun and whizzed back and forth. Once that little trick was mastered, it didn't seem a very big step to be able to move a cursor all around the computer screen. And how many word processing systems have you had to learn?

Our communication skills continued to change. We no longer have to know how to ring up an operator with the lever on the side of the box or dial with a rotating system. Modern phones have taken away the need for remembering Aunt Harriet's number. What a disaster it is if a static shock zaps the memory or mobile ability of today's phone! Faxes, modems and wireless transmission mean that skills needed in this area will continue to change. I won't even touch on things like programming VCRs, watches and other digital toys. It's enough to say that my grandchildren can do this much better than I can. They tend to lose patience with me while they are trying to teach me video games, just as I lose patience trying to learn.

Skills associated with cars are constantly being added and dropped. I learned the fine art of advancing the throttle and retarding the spark on my Grandpa's 1929 Dodge. I also needed to learn how to read the thermometer way out on the radiator cap to see if the engine was overheating. I wasn't very old when I learned to crank open the bottom of the windshield so we could cool off without getting too many bugs in our teeth. But I really never mastered the skill of driving with vacuum-driven windshield wipers. It took a real pro to see out while the car was headed uphill. What a flurry the wipers made when the driver eased off the gas pedal.

We've all had to learn to fill gas tanks ourselves because the attendants, their red wiping rags and their "check your oil, sir?" at every fill, are gone. Did they really recommend changing oil every thousand miles? Ranks of the mechanics who could raise the hood, listen and tell you your car's trouble are thinning fast. Those who know how to hook their computer to your car's computer are multiplying even faster.

As a kid in Green River, I could light and stoke a coal fire. Now, I just turn the thermostat until the gas kicks on and try to remember when I last changed the filter. I know I won't need to know how to tuck my thumb under while cranking a car, or where to find a bottle opener. It's much easier to change my Christmas tree bulbs. But instead of counting the things I used to be able to do that I don't need to know any more, I'll face the new challenges. It's much more fun to learn new skills than it is to lament about the old ones.

Change...
And All That Garbage

by Ruth Lauritzen

The recent controversy surrounding the institution of the new garbage disposal system in Green River just goes to prove the old adage, "The more things change, the more they stay the same." In order to illustrate this point, let us travel back in time some twenty-seven years to visit Green River on the cusp of another moment of flux in the ongoing quest to get rid of the garbage.

In 1970 garbage disposal was a two-fold system. Most of the daily refuse was accumulated in fifty gallon drums on business and residential properties where it was then set afire. The remains of these fires, ashes and unburned items, were picked up at irregular intervals by city crews and taken to the town dump located south of the Monroe Avenue area. Residents could also haul material to the dump. All trash deposited at the dump was then burned.

This method of trash disposal had worked for many years but as the decade of the 1970s dawned its inadequacies became more apparent to Mayor Richard "Dick" Schuck who began to spearhead an effort to revise the town's method of handling garbage. As Schuck saw it, the program had several major drawbacks. First, burning in curbside barrels was an unsightly and unpleasant way to dispose of trash. In an interview on file at the Sweetwater County Historical Museum Schuck commented, "I always said probably the best recipe for the garbage can was Sears catalogs and fish heads. Neither one burned very well and so on a hot summer evening when you decided to have your windows open, why the odor was not too neat."

Secondly, the United States as a whole was becoming more concerned about land, air and water pollution and the current trash disposal practices of Green River did not fall into new accepted

A Green River home with the ubiquitous fifty-gallon ash can on the far right. (Photo courtesy Sweetwater County Historical Museum)

guidelines. As both councilman (1964-68) and mayor (1969-71) Schuck had become involved with WAM, the Wyoming Association of Municipalities. For this group of local government leaders impending anti-pollution legislation and regulation was a very hot topic. Schuck said, "... the writing was on the wall. It was just a matter of time until everybody was going to have to provide a sanitary landfill. ... "

Finally, according to a March 1, 1970 article in the *Green River Star,* the current system was not economically feasible. A report done by Maintenance Superintendent Day Evans showed that the town garbage disposal costs exceeded the income from the program. For these reasons the city council began to revise the garbage ordinance of the City of Green River during the summer of 1970.

One of the first steps was accomplished in July when the city dump south of Monroe Avenue was closed and a new landfill was opened in the current location in a canyon south of town. In the new landfill no burning or scavenging was allowed and the garbage was to be covered over daily. Many residents expressed concern about this new way of handling garbage. In spite of assurances by city leaders that proper precautions were being taken, there were worries about flash floods running through the landfill causing ground water pollution.

The controversy continued to grow as a new garbage ordinance was drafted in October. It called for a ban on all trash burning in town and specified proper containers for trash to be stored in between regular pick ups. It also provided for an increase in garbage collection fees. According to the October 15th issue of the *Green River Star*, this latter provision, which would increase the quarterly fee from $4.50 to $9.00, especially incited public wrath.

The same article chronicles the considerable discussion at a public meeting on the ban on burning in town. "One side could see no harm in continuing present practices, with the cars being declared a greater violator, while the other side said, 'keep your smoke and sparks out of my window'."

Hopes of having the new ordinance in place by the beginning of 1971 dimmed as opposition to the plan increased. By December a petition bearing roughly 900 signatures of persons opposing the new ordinance was presented to the council. Final action was delayed pending a large public hearing to be held in January. This meeting was held in the auditorium of the Lincoln High School in order to provide room for the anticipated large turnout. The meeting, according to the January 14, 1971 issue of the *Star*, "...showed continued heavy opposition with speakers attacking the proposed ordinance on the same grounds it had been previously opposed - rate increases, opposition to 'no burn', alleged hardship on citizens, among others."

In response to the meeting the issue was tabled for further study and a revised plan was presented in February. The new ordinance included the "no burn" policy and the use of covered containers of a limited size. Changes included abandoning the requirement for a special paper liner and a smaller increase in fees, from $9.00 per quarter to $7.50 per quarter. The garbage ordinance was passed in late March and most provisions went into effect in April. A sign of this change was an advertisement by Yates Furniture and Appliance on April 28th, "We Now Have Garbage Cans. 30-Gal Galvanized Metal. Available At The Regular Price of $5.79."

Fallout from this controversial change was predictable. Dick Schuck lost by a landslide in the election that fall. He was defeated by R.K. "Rosie" Lake with a vote of 938 to 267. In retrospect Schuck said, "...if I had wanted to be a career politician I probably wouldn't have taken that attitude because I know my term as mayor was probably short lived once I started this feud."

Oddly enough, the issue which caused so much uproar and bad feeling in the town also was responsible for Green River receiving accolades. Late in 1971 it was announced that the Green River systern for the collection and disposal of solid wastes was declared the model system for the State of Wyoming. The garbage collection and disposal ordinance and the solid waste management budget were included in the Wyoming Solid Waste Management Plan.

Change, while rarely easy, is a part of life. It affects all aspects of our existence. Perhaps citizens of Green River should take a few moments, maybe those spent rolling their new garbage can out to the curb, to consider change... and all that garbage.

❖

Trona Industry Beginning

by Marna Grubb

When I graduated from Green River High School in 1950 (seems like only yesterday!), I was employed by the Westvaco Chlorine Products Company. In the fall of 1948, Westvaco had merged into the Food, Machinery and Chemical Corporation with corporate offices in California, giving the Green River project the greater financial resources it needed. It was a new industry in the area having its beginnings at the Westvaco site in 1946/47.

I was transported approximately 23 miles to work each day at Westvaco in a small Zanetti stretch bus which gave many exciting rides throughout the years. Many fond memories come to mind when discussing the "good ole days," even though the office was in a small, wooden building with one bathroom with a hook on the door, which was shared by men and ladies. The men complained about the women "camping" in the restroom, since it seemed to take longer as we also combed our hair and freshened our makeup. Water was furnished from tank cars brought in on the railroad spur.

There was one mine shaft, compared to eight today, used for transporting the miners and also for hoisting the trona ore to the surface from approximately 1600 feet underground. We had to crank the telephone to place calls through the Green River telephone office. I remember stuffing rags around the windows to keep the snow from piling up on my desk. But it was the wonderful people that made each day so enjoyable.

Of course, we did all our reports and letters on typewriters; there was no such thing as computers. Minutes of meetings and correspondence were taken in shorthand as there were no recording machines. Carbon copies were made of letters done on letterhead. Corrections had to be erased on each copy, with the last copy looking quite pale.

Copies of reports were run on **ditto** machines. The **ditto** masters had a soft, purple backing which could be corrected by scrap-

Westvaco Office Staff members in 1951, left to right, are John Anderson, Margaret Montgomery, Nettie Roosa, Marna Grubb, and Tula Kourbelas. (Photo courtesy Marna Grubb)

ing the back of the sheet with a razor and then typing over it. Purple scrapings would get all over the typewriter, get on our hands and many times, decorated our faces. If many changes or additions had to be made, it was necessary to retype the entire document. What big strides have been made in the office settings with the coming of computers, tape recorders and copy machines!

Pat (Evers) Sadler was the first secretary hired at the site; then Margaret Montgomery was employed as an accountant. Nettie Roosa and I were later employed as secretaries and I replaced Nettie as the Manager's secretary when she left Westvaco to work for the Union Pacific Railroad.

I became secretary to the first five resident managers - Carm Romano, Norris (Mac) McDougal, Robert Bondurant, Edgar Stout and Robert Love. When I was employed, Robert Love was assistant mine superintendent. Gil Gaylord was mine superintendent. Larry Marshall and Charlie Johnston were mine engineers. Edelle Pirtle also was working in the mining department. John Jacobucci was a chemical engineer and had been a Green River contact for the venture. John Anderson was office manager; Tony Pivik was lab analyst and Allen McCue was Production Superintendent.

Maintenance Foreman (and later Mine Maintenance Superintendent) Jack Wilson was employed in 1946 and lived on site until 1952, when he moved into Green River. While living on site, he was available at all times to perform maintenance duties. His home was directly behind the office building and also housed his wife, Keenie and their three children, Jacky, Jimmy and Shirley Jean. I enjoyed seeing the children and they would knock on my office window for candy after learning we had a free-will box of candy in my bottom file drawer. This didn't last very long as Mom soon became wise and forbid them to come near the office.

There was no air conditioning in the office; therefore, the doors and windows were wide open in the summer for air. This led to a visitor now and then. The Wilson's dog would wander through periodically and put his cold, wet nose on my elbow while I was typing. The cat gave us a start one day when it jumped through the payroll window and across Margaret Montgomery's desk.

By 1953, No. 2 shaft was completed, the plant had been expanded and we moved into a new brick office building. We were all spread out and many new employees were employed. We had Sharon Rhodes as a receptionist with a "modern" switchboard equipped with plug-in cords and a head set.

We had a multilith machine which made nice looking reports. I would take a photo of the mine or plant and make them into the company Christmas cards. We began an employee newsletter. Times were good. It was so enjoyable to be involved with the many fine people involved with the beginning of such an interesting and valuable process.

FMC Wyoming Corporation, as it is now known, was the first producer of natural soda ash from Green River's trona deposits. Four other producers have since entered the area. Throughout the years, trona has been mined much like coal.

The trona in this area was created by an ancient body of water which has become known as Lake Gosiute. In the course of geologic time, the lake shrunk. With the loss of outflows, highly alkaline (salt brine) began to evaporate depositing the beds of trona. The trona beds now define the bottom of Lake Gosiute, with the center about 20 miles west of Green River. The beds were reported to be from 4 to 10 feet thick and located from 400 to 3500 feet beneath the surface. It was reported that this corner of Wyoming contains the world's largest bed of trona. Trona is processed into soda ash which is shipped throughout the United States and now overseas. Principal users include the glass industry, soap/detergent industry, non-ferrous metal refining, chemical manufacturing and water treatment.

Try to picture our community without the trona industry. All of the producers have been such an asset to Green River by providing a solid economic base, a job market, the beautiful Trona Bridge and a wealth of talented people. **HATS OFF TO THE TRONA INDUSTRY!**

❖

Ironies

by Bill Thompson

By request, here are some historical ironies and questions modified from presentations I have given. Some situations may be known by you and are not entirely brand new. But in most cases they represent original thought. The given format is designed to stimulate thought and questions. Some of these are "hooks" that I used from time to time in my high school and college classes in order to snare student interest. These question/statements can cause discussion in a variety of subjects. Some are items that people mistakenly think they "know". None are falsehoods, but sometimes the sentence structure is designed to give a different perspective of the historical facts. If you violently disagree, hold on, check it out and take it from there. Have fun!

Isn't it ironic, strange, sad, weird, interesting (take your choice):

- that Protestant America was "discovered" by a Roman Catholic?
- that ten years after the "discovery" there was not an American Indian left alive on the island?
- that although the majority of the colonies in America were founded due to religious intolerance in Europe, those colonies were EXTREMELY intolerant of a different religion other than their own?
- that the colony of Maryland which had a Catholic Governor was the one that allowed Freedom of Religion?
- that the Protestant and Freethinker founders of the Constitution of the U.S. patterned the Electoral College (to choose a President) after the College of Cardinals' procedure to choose a Pope?
- that the Reverend Weems had to lie about George Washington and the Cherry Tree incident in order to illustrate how nice it is

to tell the truth?
- that Abraham Lincoln's Emancipation Proclamation freed not a single slave?
- that the man who made the "Inalienable Rights of Life, Liberty and Pursuit of Happiness" famous in the Declaration of Independence owned slaves until the day he died?
- that in the war between the states in regard to the South, the "Industrial North" was also the "Agricultural North"?
- that George Washington was unanimously elected president of the U.S. by an electorate of which approximately only one out of seven was allowed to vote?
- that King George III of England (Revolutionary War) spoke German and not English?
- that George Washington was a traitor to his country?
- that George Washington lost more battles in his career than he ever won?
- that the old Soviet Union's border was less than eight miles from the U.S.?
- that Reno, Nevada, is farther west than Los Angeles, California?
- that the Atlantic opening of the Panama Canal is farther west than the Pacific opening?
- that Washington, D.C. is not "back east" but rather "down south"?
- that if the early explorers and cartographers would have done their job properly, the Missouri would be known as the longest river system in the U.S.?
- that Jan. 1st through March 24th was the year 1752?
- that the only Indian credited with defeating the U.S. Army, the Great Sioux Chief Red Cloud, was arrested near Casper for killing game out of season and for not being a resident of Wyoming? (After being fined and most of his goods confiscated he was escorted to the city limits, kicked in the butt and told never to return.)
- that Sweetwater County's major river is the Green and that the Sweetwater River is not in the county?
- that Green River is the County Seat of Sweetwater County but much more than a handful of county offices is located fifteen miles away?
- that a phone call to Rock Springs from Green River is charged as long distance while one to Granger is charged as local?
- that although Wyoming was the first state in the Union to give women the right to vote, it was the women of the state of Utah who voted first?

- that the Lewis and Clark Expedition never entered Wyoming? (But that's okay since Zeb Pike never climbed the peak named for him either.)
- that Jim Bridger, who could not read or write, and known as a notorious liar, has more places and things named for him in Wyoming than any other man? (The honorable Chief Washakie is in second place for names.)
- that the pronghorn antelope found in such abundance in Wyoming is the only known animal that sheds its horns?
- that most people believe that John Kennedy was the youngest president of the United States rather than Teddy Roosevelt?
- that people who know that buffalo (bison) will face into a storm and that cattle will drift with it are not at all concerned with knowing how cattelo or beefalo will react in a Wyoming blizzard? (sideways?)
- that in United States history books, the majority of battles the white man won over the Indians are called "Victories" while the battles where the Indian did all right are called "Massacres". (Ever hear of the Custer Victory? I have.)
- that if immigration means to come into an area and that emigration means to leave, who left Emigration Canyon in Utah and why are people still there?
- that the Union Pacific and the Central Pacific Railroads were not joined at Promontory Point, Utah? (Be careful on this one, there are some history books that erroneously state this as fact).

And as a final item for you card players:

- that in the Wyoming Revised Statutes 1931, Section 32-912 - anyone playing "three card monte" on railroad or passenger trains in this state shall be fined not more than $100 and imprisoned in the county jail not less than 10 days nor more than 90 days?
- the conductor or any person in charge of the train is to arrest and deliver such players to any civil office within this state. (I wonder if a legislator on his way to a session in Cheyenne lost his donkey playing a card shark and the above statute was the angry result?)

Radio's Changing Ear

by Bill Duncan

I crawled up on the chair and stretched to reach the micro-phone. My Mom lifted my younger brother, Tom, up on the chair beside me. She told us both to hold on tightly to the back of the chair and walked over to the studio piano. At her nod and intro chord, we both began to sing, "Ridin' Down the Canyon."

Mother had entered us in a weekly talent contest sponsored by Hurst Dairy on the local radio station, KVRS. Listeners sent in paper bottle tops with their favorite contestant's name written on the back. The winner was the contestant who received the most bottle top votes. A kid who played the accordion won that week.

Rock Springs and Green River listeners heard a much different radio sound sixty or so years ago than they do now. A lady would announce which mines would be working the next day, so coal miners knew when to come to work. Local talent performed weekly. Information shows, featuring people like the county agent, aired tips for gardening, irrigation and crop care.

Stations joined or were owned by national networks. While small town stations like KSL in Salt Lake aired network program-ming most of the day and well into the night. People relied on national commentators such as H.B. Kaltenbourn and Gabriel Heatter to bring national and world news.

Drama kept folks glued to their radios every evening. The Shadow, a crime-solver who "had the power to cloud men's minds" made himself invisible and caught another criminal. The Green Hornet had great sound effects. The squeaking door that opened the Inner Sanctum caused shivers from coast to coast.

Red Skelton, Jack Benny, Fred Allen and other comics ruled the evening airwaves. Each had a consistent cast that feuded, sang and insulted each other weekly. Rivalry boosted listener audience. It was a big deal when Benny and Allen visited each other because the best quips were often spontaneous. Audience reaction was important so most shows were live.

Network programming kept listeners entertained all day long. We marched around the breakfast table with Don McNeil. Snipes, jabs and insults of the Bickersons kept us giggling over our cereal.

Afternoons featured dramas sponsored by soap manufacturers. They sounded much like today's afternoon TV. The difference was that we could imagine what the characters looked like.

Major Bowes brought amateur singers, instrumentalists and dancers to national prominence. Studio audiences applauded wildly as tap dancers did contortions that we at home could only imagine. Guy Lombardo, the Dorseys and other big bands often introduced new talent on their shows to keep programs fresh.

By the 1950s, television's popularity drew away dramas, comedies and big name entertainers. Sunday afternoons were dramatic radio's last stand, but shows like "True Detective Mysteries" didn't survive TV's weekend sports menu.

Radio's new path featured "disk jockeys" with tunes and patter designed for specific audiences. Wolfman Jack captivated kids on the West Coast. Allen Freed introduced rock and roll to Cleveland and the Midwest. Some regional stations played country music, others played "easy listening" or "middle of the road." Big city stations on each coast discovered that people wanted to listen to news, road conditions and weather while driving to work.

Local stations also found that people would listen to them in the daytime and watch TV at night. Wyoming kids waited until after dark to tune in KOMA in Oklahoma City. The 1520 sound (its AM frequency) blasted from open car windows dragging Main or around unlit tennis courts, any place kids hung out.

Radio became a Civil Defense tool about this time. Remember the little triangles at 640 and 1430 on AM? The theory was that a person could turn there to receive information. That lasted about as long as the 8-track tapes some cars featured. Eight-tracks are gone, but portable music via cassette and CD is here to stay.

Following popular music patterns, radio sounds evolved radically during the 1960s and 1970s. Beatles, Jimi Hendrix, Elvis and Perry Como vied for audience. Local stations featured local news, opportunities to trade goods and services and increased sports coverage. Politicians, promoters and fund raisers talked with hosts about community issues.

In 1976, Al Harris brought radio to Green River. KUGR started as a country station and locals could hear GRHS sports broadcasts. About this time, FM commercial stations began providing competition with their static-free, hi-fidelity performance. Sweetwater County now has 2 AM and 3 FM stations, with more on the horizon. Most disk jockeys and their tunes come by satellite. A public broadcasting station is relayed from Laramie. Listeners can get radio from satellite dish, cable or Internet.

Fibber McGee and Molly, Baby Snooks and Duffy's Tavern are only fond memories of long long ago radio. Audience participation on late night talk shows has replaced live studio audiences. Television and computers (maybe they are almost the same now) satisfy a lot of entertainment appetite.

Where is radio going? On a recent trip to California, I watched cable television broadcast a live radio studio. Two radio announcers performed from the radio control room for six hours each day. I'm not suggesting that Bill and Dave or Steve and Al go live on cable. I just know that radio will continue to change. And I'll continue to listen.

❖

CPSIA information can be obtained
at www.ICGtesting.com
Printed in the USA
FSHW011019210120
66319FS